DYLAN THOMAS

On the Air with Dylan Thomas

The Broadcasts

EDITED BY RALPH MAUD

A NEW DIRECTIONS BOOK

HOUSTON PUBLIC LIBRARY

Acknowledgments: For help with the broadcasts to Jeff Towns, Dylan's Bookshop,
Swansea; John Jordan, BBC Written Archives; David J. Evans, BBC Radio Reference
Library; Masha Karp, BBC Russian Division; the late Aneirin Talfan Davies, BBC
Wales; the late Douglas Cleverdon, BBC London.
The editor is grateful for a research grant from the Social Sciences and Humanities
Research Council of Canada, and for continuing support from Simon Fraser University.
Permission to publish manuscripts in its collection has been gratefully received from the
Harry Ransom Humanities Research Library, Texas.

Manufactured in the United States of America
New Directions books are printed on acid-free paper
First published clothbound by New Directions in 1992
Published simultaneously in Canada by Penguin Books Canada Limited

Library of Congress Cataloging-in-Publication Data

Thomas, Dylan, 1914–1953.
    On the air with Dylan Thomas : the broadcasts / Dylan Thomas ;
    edited by Ralph Maud.
        p.   cm.
    Includes bibliographical references.
    ISBN 0-8112-1209-2 (alk. paper)
    1. Radio scripts.   2. Poetry.   3. Wales—Civilization.   I. Maud,
Ralph.   II. Title.
PR6039.H52A6   1992   91-39495
821'.912—dc20   CIP

New Directions Books are published for James Laughlin
by New Directions Publishing Corporation
80 Eighth Avenue, New York 10011

Contents

Introduction   v

 1 Reminiscences of Childhood (1943)   1
 2 Quite Early One Morning (1944)   9
 3 Reminiscences of Childhood (1945)   15
 4 Memories of Christmas (1945)   21
 5 Welsh Poetry (1946)   29
 6 On Reading Poetry Aloud (1946)   51
 7 Poets on Poetry (1946)   55
 8 Poems of Wonder (1946)   63
 9 The Londoner (1946)   75
10 Wilfred Owen (1946)   93
11 Margate – Past and Present (1946)   103
12 How to Begin a Story (1946)   121
13 What Has Happened to English Poetry? (1946)   127
14 Holiday Memory (1946)   137
15 Walter de la Mare as a Prose Writer (1946)   145
16 The Crumbs of One Man's Year (1946)   151
17 Sir Philip Sidney (1947)   159
18 The Poet and his Critic (1947)   169
19 Return Journey (1947)   177
20 A Dearth of Comic Writers (1948)   191
21 The English Festival of Spoken Poetry (1948)   197
22 Living in Wales (1949)   201
23 Edward Thomas (1949)   207

24 On Reading One's Own Poems (1949)   213
25 Swansea and the Arts (1949)   217
26 Three Poems (1950)   223
27 Poetic Licence (1950)   227
28 Persian Oil (1951)   241
29 The Festival Exhibition (1951)   245
30 Edgar Lee Masters (1952)   253
31 Home Town – Swansea (1953)   259
32 The International Eisteddfod (1953)   267
33 A Visit to America (1953)   273
34 Laugharne (1953)   279

BBC *Engagements Calendar*   283
Works Cited   307

Publisher's Note

The script for Dylan Thomas's *Under Milk Wood*, the last piece he completed for the BBC, was delivered in October 1953 and broadcast posthumously in January 1954. For reasons of length it is not included in this volume. It is available in a separate edition published by New Directions.

Introduction

It is a measure of how important radio was to the ordinary households of Britain – happily cohesive in the thirties, and vitally so in the war years – that a poetry competition launched on the air on 30 December 1932 could have elicited 11,000 entries by the end of February 1933. A young listener, Dylan Thomas of Swansea, aged nineteen, sent in 'The Romantic Isle'. We know the poem only from the title printed in the *Radio Times* under programmes for 28 June 1933; it was one of the thirty successful poems chosen for broadcasting. The chief adjudicator of the competition was Walter de la Mare; thirteen years later Thomas took the opportunity to devote a radio talk (script 15) to the man who gave him this first nod of recognition.

It was apparently Wynford Vaughan Thomas who got the BBC representative at Swansea studios, Tom Pickering, to give Dylan Thomas his first contract: fifteen minutes of poetry. 'Life and the Modern Poet', 4 guineas, signed 26 March 1937. However, in a very real sense Thomas was already an experienced broadcaster, having had many years with the 'Warmley Broadcasting Corporation'. The 'WBC' relayed programmes from the upstairs sitting room of the Jones' house, 'Warmley'. Daniel Jones tells about it in *My Friend Dylan Thomas* (pp. 32–3):

> Two hidden wires led downstairs to the radiogram pick-up in the sitting-room and the 'transmission' came, of course, from the radiogram loud-speaker. The station signal was a metronome; this allowed us to leave the studio empty while adjusting the reception... Disputes about participation were best resolved by the designing of complicated mis-

cellaneous programmes, consisting of verse-reading, music, drama, and talks. Actors and audience would rush wildly up or downstairs in the time it took one of us to announce the next item in a calm, level voice.

Dylan, Jones tells us, would try out different ways of 'putting over' a poem, and undergo criticism from the 'listeners'.

With no essential difference in technique between the WBC studio and a BBC studio, it would not be too much to say that Dylan served his broadcasting apprenticeship at Warmley.

In fact, Thomas's first BBC broadcast turned out to be as hectic as a typical Warmley production. The story told by Constantine FitzGibbon in *The Life of Dylan Thomas* (p. 115) is that John Pudney, the poet, who was working for the BBC at the time, 'found Dylan in a somewhat distraught state in a public house in London only an hour or so before he was due to broadcast from Swansea. Pudney most competently took Dylan to Broadcasting House, arranged that the cables be rearranged, and the broadcast, Dylan's first, went out on time.' Dylan's father, in Swansea, told A. E. Trick that he expected to hear the announcer say, 'Owing to a sudden indisposition, Mr. Dylan Thomas is unable to give a reading of his poems and in its place we shall broadcast some music by Debussy.' According to his account, published in *Texas Quarterly* (Summer 1967), Trick dashed home and told his wife to switch on the radio.

Whilst listening to the news bulletin we conjectured on what would really happen at the crucial moment. Suddenly Dylan's glorious voice boomed out of the loudspeaker. It was an unforgettable experience – hearing him on the radio that first time. The living-room was filled with the presence of Dylan.

Roy Campbell, the South African poet, who as a disabled ex-serviceman got a producer's job at the BBC, tells of a later narrow escape:

Dylan was the best all round reader of verse that I ever produced, though John Lawrie ran him close, and an Irishman called Hutchinson. Dylan only had one weakness – he could not read correct poets like Pope or Dryden. He was best at the 'wild and woolly' poets. I used to keep him on beer all day till he had done his night's work and then take him down to the Duty room where the charming Miss Backhouse or Miss Tofield would pour us both a treble whiskey as a reward for our labors. It was with Blake and Manley Hopkins that Dylan became almost Superman: but we had bad luck with Dryden. Dylan had got at the whiskey first and he started behaving like a prima donna. He insisted on having an announcer instead of beginning the program right away as we used to on the Third Program. There were only two minutes to go and I rushed back to the studio and found Dylan snoring in front of the mike with only twenty seconds left. He was slumped back in his chair, with an almost seraphic expression of blissful peace. I shook him awake, and, to his horror and consternation, began announcing him in my South African accent, but trying to talk like an English announcer, with my tonsils, in an 'Oxford accent'. Dylan nearly jumped out of his skin with fright and horror: and was almost sober when he got the green light, though he did bungle the title as *Ode on Shaint Sheshilia's Day*; but after that his voice cleared up and I began to breathe again. When he had finished reading the *Ode* I got another fright: he began to beckon me wildly with his arms and point to the page before him. I got the engineer to switch off the mike and slipped into the studio again. Dylan had forgotten how to pronounce 'Religio Laici'. I told him and slipped out. He had about three shots at it, bungled it, gave it up; and then went on reading. The next day I was hauled up in front of George Barnes, but he was a good boss and had a sense of humor. I promised to keep an eye on Dylan: Dylan promised me to keep an eye on himself – and he kept his word. (*Poetry* November 1955 pp. 112–13)

Campbell adds that 'his performance was always flawless from then on.' And this testimony is echoed by other producers who worked with Thomas over a long period; John Arlott, for instance, who, well-known as a cricket commentator, also produced verse anthologies to be beamed weekly to India during 1945–50. In writing of Thomas as a broadcaster in *Adelphi* (February 1954), Arlott spoke of 'his very real integrity which made him a perfect touchstone for a producer':

he took production like a professional actor and, when he stepped up to the microphone to read, made a happily extravagant figure. Round, with the roundness of a Tintoretto urchin-cherub, and in a large, loose tweed jacket, he would stand, feet apart and head thrown back, a dead cigarette frequently adhering wispily to his lower lip, curls a little tousled and eyes half-closed, barely reading the poetry by eye, but rather understanding his way through it, one arm beating out a sympathetic double rhythm as he read. His voice would be sometimes almost naïvely young and

clearly tenor, while, at others, a dynamo throbbing seemed to drive him
to an intense rolling depth.

Asked to sum up his impressions for the BBC programme, 'The Dylan
Thomas File' in 1973, Arlott attested: 'In all the time I worked with
him he never let me down in any way at all. I can only say that he
worked for some five years for me, and I believe did some two thirds
of all his broadcasts for me. He was never late; he was never drunk;
and he never did a bad job.' Aneirin Talfan Davies, on reading the
above comment, wrote in a personal communication: 'I can say the
same as Arlott in affirming that Dylan never let me down. He never
appeared drunk at the studio, and never botched a job.' Another voice,
from someone who had almost as much experience with Thomas on
the air as the previous two producers, is Douglas Cleverdon's statement
in *The Growth of Milk Wood* p. 14:

> I think it is worth putting on record that during B.B.C. rehearsals his
> standards were thoroughly professional. He had a wonderful ear for
> rhythms and inflexions and accents, and could apprehend immediately
> the subtlest points of interpretation. He was, moreover, sober, hard-
> working, and punctilious. So conscientious was he that I have known
> him leave a pub at lunch-time earlier than was necessary in order to
> return to the studio and con his script before the afternoon rehearsal.

Thomas participated in about forty programmes for John Arlott,
about fifteen each with Roy Campbell, Aneirin Talfan Davies, and
Douglas Cleverdon. He made eight appearances as reader for Patric
Dickinson, and fifteen miscellaneous productions for R. D. Smith, and
did eight dramatic roles for Louis MacNeice. Add to these another
twenty-eight broadcasts of various sorts, and one gets an approximate
total of 145 separate engagements, an average of more than one a
month over the ten-year period 1943–53. The reason one stresses the
sum total of Thomas's commitment to BBC work is to rectify, if need
be, his reputation as a wastrel. He was in fact a professional radio
broadcaster, whose services as a performer and scriptwriter were
sought and appreciated.

There was even at one point some talk of Thomas joining the BBC
as a staff employee. When Louis MacNeice was planning to be away
in Athens for the British Council in 1950, he suggested Thomas take
over his post (*Letters* p. 737). Nothing of the sort happened, and

Thomas went to the United States. When he returned he made an appointment with Harmon Grisewood, Controller of the Third Programme, for 16 August 1950 to request regular employment. A Grisewood memo suggests that 'he might be worth putting on a list of possibles to cover the Festival of Britain'; but in the end it was decided 'not to proceed'. Thomas's 'Festival Exhibition' talk (script 29) was commissioned through Aneirin Talfan Davies in Wales. A Third Programme internal memo of 10 December 1951 put a stop to anything but contractual piece work, payment on results.

Thomas had not shown himself to be adaptable to the desirable BBC personality profile of a consistent worker. His first scripts are not extant, which – for the sake of the balance of the present volume, if nothing else – is a blessing. They were written for translation into Portuguese for transmission to Brazil on the Latin America Service. The first was on a little known soldier and patron of the Brazilian army, Duque de Caxias, broadcast 26 August 1940. The second script, 'Cristobal Colon', had to be rewritten in the studio, the BBC said, so Thomas had only a reduced fee. The third script was called 'March of the Czech Legion across Russia in the last war'. A letter of 8 January 1941 to John Davenport, who appears to have got him these jobs, gives us a glimpse of it: 'War. The shadow of the eagle is cast on the grazing lands, the meadows of Belgium are green no longer, and the pastures are barbed with bayonets. War. War.' It was, Thomas says, written for five narrators and a chorus of patriots crying 'Siberia', 'Freedom of Man', 'Strengthen us for the approaching hour' (*Letters* p. 472). Thomas was not exhibiting quite the right attitude. He got the script in three weeks late, and asked the producer: 'Could I have a script to do without battles, d'you think? Or perhaps only 20 or 30?' (*Letters* p. 467). On 22 May 1941 the Czech script was finally declared 'not suitable'.

Not a very auspicious beginning. But, as Thomas had already explained to T. Rowland Hughes of BBC Cardiff in a letter of 3 November 1938: 'I don't think I'd be able to do one of those long dramatic programmes in verse; I take such a long time writing anything and the result, dramatically, is too often like a man shouting under the sea' (*Letters* p. 337). Suspenseful drama was not Thomas's forte, and the two play scripts that survive to be included in this volume (scripts 9 and 11) are not of the calibre to make one long for more. Thomas found his genre in the personal reminiscence; and *Under Milk Wood* should probably be considered the last in a line which began with 'Reminiscences of Childhood' in 1943 (script 1). There was immediate recognition that Thomas had hit the right note: the talk was printed in *The Listener* (25 February 1943), and a repeat was asked for. Following Aneirin Talfan Davies's lead in *Quite Early One Morning*, we have also included the revised 'Reminiscences of Childhood' (1945, script 3) because its tightness needs to be seen and appreciated as much as the first version's impulsiveness. Meanwhile, Thomas had done another in the same genre, 'Quite Early One Morning' (1944, script 2), to be followed in the same mode by 'Memories of Christmas' (1945, script 4), 'Holiday Memory' (1946, script 14), and 'The Crumbs of One Man's Year' (1946, script 16). 'Return Journey' (1947, script 19) used very well the ability of radio to set scenes quickly and objectify the personal material. 'Living in Wales' (1949, script 22), the author looking at himself with wryness, could perhaps be considered the last in this highly successful genre, though all of Thomas's later journalistic scripts have some combination of nostalgic world-weariness and naïve eagerness: 'Persian Oil' (1951, script 28), 'The Festival Exhibition' (1951, script 29), 'The International Eisteddfod' (1953, script 32), 'A Visit to America' (1953, script 33) and 'Laugharne' (1953, script 34).

When one can list a run like the above, it makes Thomas's failures seem fairly inconsequential. In October 1945 he agreed to do a script on Augustus John, but couldn't, and Michael Ayrton came in at short notice to write it. He said he would make up for it with a script to be called 'Nationalism in Poetry', but there is no evidence that he did. His two big failures, adaptations of *Peer Gynt* and Wycherley's *Plain Dealer*, are quite understandable. Not so understandable is why he thought he could get them done in the time proposed. Writing to his agent David Higham on 9 July 1949, Thomas realized he had overextended himself, but made some telling points:

The Boat House Laugharne Carmarthenshire

Dear David,
    Peer Gynt.
    I was told of no dead-line date.

I have received, from Miss Ramsden, a literal translation of only *two* of *five* acts. Am I to learn Norwegian & translate the other three acts for myself?

And, most important of all, I should like to bring this to the attention of the B.B.C.:

Louis MacNeice is translating a work of similar stature to Peer Gynt: Goethe's Faust. For this, the B.B.C. has allowed him one whole year, during which time no other work is expected from him. On top of a special fee, he is, for that year, paid his usual B.B.C. salary, which means that he is not obliged, for that year, to do any other work.

I, on the other hand, am expected to produce a five act play in a few months, for a fee not sufficiently large to allow me to devote *all* my time to this work. Far from it. And now the B.B.C. is cutting up rough at a time when not *half* of the literal translation has been given me.

I bring in MacNeice's case only because I think that the BBC is treating him fairly and can expect a thorough & painstaking job. Peer Gynt is just as difficult to work upon as is Goethe's Faust. Both are enormous plays. Why should one have to be scamped through insufficient money & time?

Perhaps I should have insisted, earlier, on a long & elastic period of time in which to do this work. But certainly I have to insist now. I cannot begin to work upon the play until the whole literal translation is in my hands. And then, by the very magnitude of the job, it is bound to take a long time.

Also: MacNeice is translating Faust in the only way possible for a non-German scholar. He is going through the text, line by line, word by word, with the German expert who is supplying the literal translation. Only in this way can he appreciate the texture of the German; & do justice to its word-music.

Maybe it is not in order for me to parallel MacNeice's case with mine. But I am certain that the way he is working upon Faust, & the time he is allowed for that work, & the money he is paid, should also be the way in which I shd work upon this important & complex play.

If the BBC decide to cancel my contract, then they must. And somehow we must pay them back the £150 I have been advanced. But if they think that someone else can trot out a translation in the very short [?space] of time they have allowed me, then they must, of necessity, be content with an inferior job.

Perhaps you can convey to them some of these – to me – most justifiable points?

And forgive me if I am, for once, riding a high horse.

It seems that Higham managed an elasticity which stretched these projects out, with occasional rumblings from the BBC about the advances that had been paid, until Thomas was beyond all deadlines. But this meant that in the last three years of his life the BBC held back payment until goods were delivered; 'Three Poems' (1950, script 26) and 'Edgar Lee Masters' (1952, script 30) were two deliberately concocted short projects by which Douglas Cleverdon helped Thomas earn a little money while *Under Milk Wood* was being written without benefit of an advance, with only an agreement for five guineas for every thousand words finished.

The envy of Louis MacNeice that Thomas expressed to his agent did not mar their working relations, which extended from 'The Careerist' (23 October 1946) to 'The Golden Ass' (31 December 1951). 'As a producer', MacNeice has attested, in *Ingot* (December 1954),

> I realised that he was a god-send to radio. His famous 'organ voice' was already well known in straightforward readings of verse, but the same voice combined with his sense of character, could be used for all sorts of strange purposes. I cast him (and was never disappointed) in a variety of dramatic parts, including that of a funereal but benevolent raven in a dramatised fairy story. What was more surprising was that he was capable, when necessary, of *underplaying* – but the need for this had to be made clear to him. He took his radio acting very seriously and between rehearsals would always keep asking if he were giving satisfaction. He was a joy to have around in the studio, causing a certain amount of anxiety to the studio managers, who could never be sure that he would speak into the right microphone, and a great deal of delight to the rest of the cast who particularly admired the queer little dance steps that he always performed (it seems quite unconsciously) while broadcasting.

We should not forget that Thomas in his youth appeared on the local stage many times, often taking the centre of it as the main lead. His first entry into Broadcasting House was to act for Francis Dillon in wartime propaganda plays, 'Civilian's War' (19 September 1941) and 'The British Tommy' (29 November 1942). Douglas Cleverdon cast him as a British Tommy in David Jones's *In Parenthesis*, in the first production of November 1942 (which was cancelled), and then in the Third Programme on 19 November 1946. This was the occasion Richard Burton described in vivid terms in *Book Week*, 24 October 1965:

Dylan as an actor and as an explosive dynamic performing force was a dangerous rival for other actors, as I know, for I worked with him a few times or several, and once for instance a director said to him, we were rehearsing a radio play at the time, Dylan will you take the words "Mam! Mam!" and scream them for me; you understand that you are dying in No Mans Land, and when you hear the Royal Welsh sing, I will give you a cue light and then scream for me woodjew there's a good chap. And the Royal Welsh did sing in this rehearsal, it was a record of course, and they sang of what you could see from the hills above Jerusalem, and was in the minor key and sad as the devil or death, and the green light flickered and Dylan short, bandy, prime, obese, and famous among the bars screamed as I have never heard, but sometimes imagined a scream, and we were all appalled, our pencils silent above the crossword puzzles, and invisible centuries-gone atavistic hair rose on our backs. And there was a funny silence and Dylan said that he'd bet I couldn't do that scream like that with a cigarette in my mouth and I shook off the centuries, stopped staring, smiled a little, noted that he had indeed monumentally screamed with a cigarette in his mouth and went stunned back to my crossword.

Thomas's range as a radio performer was wide, from the Light Programme's 'Rogues and Vagabonds' for R. D. Smith, three times in May 1946, to John Milton for Douglas Cleverdon, 'Comus' on 30 September 1946 and again on 29 September 1947, and the part of Satan in *Paradise Lost*, October–December 1947. But after a certain point Thomas, perforce, stepped over the line from actor to radio personality. Acting himself for three months in America, from March to May 1950, contributed to this, but already in 1946 the process had begun with his appearance on 'The World Goes By' (script 6 'On Reading Poetry Aloud'), a magazine programme 'introducing people of popular interest' – Thomas had given a poetry reading before Royalty the week before. He came to be considered a fit sparring partner for James Stephens in 'Books and Writers', 18 June 1946 (script 7), and for Edward Shanks in 'Freedom Forum', 11 October 1946 (script 13), and was the second poet chosen, after Edith Sitwell, to be the focus of attention in 'The Poet and His Critic' series (script 18). Perhaps in terms of that wider radio audience, the households of Britain, a greater testimony of Thomas's having 'arrived' would be his role as 'word expert' once in 'Say the Word', 10 November 1951, and master of ceremonies twice for 'Country Magazine', 8 February 1948 and 13 June 1948. As impresario in 'Swansea and the Arts', 24 October 1949 (script 25), and the television production 'Home Town – Swansea', 9 April 1953 (script 31), he was, amongst his local friends, something of a big fish in a small pond, for he had already, for instance, chaired a round-table discussion in London with poets of international reputation, Roy Campbell, George Barker, and W. R. Rodgers (script 27 'Poetic Licence'), and had travelled as far as Tehran to research a script (script 28 'Persian Oil'). Even if no radio play to match *Under Milk Wood* appeared to be in the offing, and Thomas might never have finished the *Peer Gynt* adaptation or anything like it, we have every reason to feel deprived by his untimely death of further interesting programmes like an impromptu discussion of 'bad poetry' with poet friends after lunch, or reports from afar like the assignment in Iran, where he went, as he put it, 'to pour water on troubled oil', and brought back a piece not lacking in serious social commentary.

Ralph Maud

1
Reminiscences of Childhood

Aneirin Talfan Davies, interviewed for the 'Dylan Thomas File' broadcast in 1973, described the circumstances which led to this first of Thomas's talks:

> I came close to Dylan Thomas during the war years ... At that time I was a new talks producer looking for new stuff, and I said to myself, 'If this man can write poetry, he could certainly write great prose as well.' I think I was the first to suggest that he should write a talk about Swansea, a town he loved very much indeed. And when I received the script I was really excited; it was a marvellous script. And then when I sent it through to London, a very uppity kind of memo, from a higher official in the Talks Department, rapped me over the knuckles as a very junior talks producer, really going to town and telling me that the first sentence, which is a long sentence, was unreadable. It was only later, I think, that London accepted the talk and put it out.

Thomas recorded the talk on 7 January 1943, for transmission in most of the Home Services 15 February 1943. Thomas's fee was seven guineas. The talk was printed in *The Listener* (25 February 1943).

Vernon Watkins in the *Times Literary Supplement* (19 November 1954) supplied the information that Thomas originally intended to use the title, 'Nostalgia for an Ugly Town', and added:

> The last sentence of the talk, 'The fine, live people, the spirit of Wales itself,' did not belong to the original script, but was diplomatically added, there being an unwritten rule that all talks on the Welsh Service should end with the spirit of Wales.

Aneirin Talfan Davies in a letter to the *TLS* (17 December 1954) disputed the accuracy of this assertion.

The present text is from the extant BBC script.

Reminiscences of Childhood

(*First Version*)

I was born in a large Welsh industrial town at the beginning of the Great War: an ugly, lovely town (or so it was, and is, to me), crawling, sprawling, slummed, unplanned, jerry-villa'd, and smug-suburbed by the side of a long and splendid-curving shore where truant boys and sandfield boys and old anonymous men, in the tatters and hangovers of a hundred charity suits, beachcombed, idled, and paddled, watched the dock-bound boats, threw stones into the sea for the barking, outcast dogs, and, on Saturday summer afternoons, listened to the militant music of salvation and hell-fire preached from a soap-box.

This sea-town was my world; outside, a *strange* Wales, coal-pitted, mountained, river-run, full, so far as I knew, of choirs and sheep and story-book tall hats, moved about its business which was none of mine; beyond that unknown Wales lay England, which was London, and a country called 'The Front' from which many of our neighbours never came back. At the beginning, the only 'front' I knew was the little lobby before our front door; I could not understand how so many people never returned from there; but later I grew to know more, though still without understanding, and carried a wooden rifle in Cwmdonkin Park and shot down the invisible, unknown enemy like a flock of wild birds. And the park itself was a world within the world of the sea-town; quite near where I lived, so near that on summer evenings I could listen, in my bed, to the voices of other children playing ball on the sloping, paper-littered bank; the Park was full of terrors and treasures. The face of one old man who sat, summer and winter, on the same bench looking over the swanned reservoir, I can see more clearly, I think, than the city-street faces I saw an *hour* ago:

3

and years later I wrote a poem about, and for, this never, by me, to-be-forgotten 'Hunchback in the Park'.

> The hunchback in the park,
> A solitary mister
> Propped between trees and water
> From the opening of the garden lock
> That lets the trees and water enter
> Until the Sunday-sombre bell at dark,
>
> Eating bread from a newspaper,
> Drinking water from the chained cup
> That the children filled with gravel
> In the fountain basin where I sailed my ship,
> Slept at night in a dog-kennel
> But nobody chained him up.
>
> Like the park birds he came early,
> Like the water he sat down,
> And Mister, they called, Hey Mister,
> The truant boys from the town
> Running when he had heard them clearly
> On out of sound,
>
> Past lake and rockery,
> Laughing when he shook his paper,
> Through the loud zoo of the willow groves,
> Hunchbacked in mockery
> Dodging the park-keeper
> With his stick that picked up leaves.
>
> And the old dog sleeper,
> Alone between nurses and swans
> While the boys among willows
> Made the tigers jump out of their eyes
> To roar on the rockery stones
> And the groves were blue with sailors,
>
> Made all day until bell-time
> A woman's figure without fault
> Straight as a young elm,

4

> Straight and tall from his crooked bones
> That she might stand in the night
> After the locks and the chains
>
> All night in the unmade park
> After the railings and shrubberies,
> The birds, the grass, the trees and the lake,
> And the wild boys innocent as strawberries,
> Had followed the hunchback
> To his kennel in the dark.

And that Park grew up with me; that small, interior world widened as I learned its names and its boundaries; as I discovered new refuges and ambushes in its miniature woods and jungles, hidden homes and lairs for the multitudes of the young, for cowboys and Indians and, most sinister of all, for the far-off race of the Mormons, a people who every night rode on nightmares through my bedroom. In that small, iron-railed universe of rockery, gravel-path, playbank, bowling-green, bandstand, reservoir, chrysanthemum garden, where an ancient keeper known as Smokey was the tyrannous and whiskered snake in the Grass one must Keep Off, I endured, with pleasure, the first agonies of unrequited love, the first slow boiling in the belly of a bad poem, the strutting and raven-locked self-dramatization of what, at the time, seemed *incurable* adolescence. I wrote then, in a poem never to be published:

> See, on gravel paths under the harpstrung trees,
> Feeling the summer wind, hearing the swans,
> Leaning from windows over a length of lawns,
> On tumbling hills admiring the sea,
> I am alone, alone complain to the stars.
> Who are his friends? The wind is his friend,
> The glow-worm lights his darkness, and
> The snail tells of coming rain.

But before that, several years even before those lines, that cry from a *very* happy heart waiting, like an egg, to be broken, I had written:

> Where could I ever listen for the sound of seas asleep,
> Or the cold and graceful song of a swan that dies and wakes,

5

> Where could I ever hear the cypress speak in its sleep,
> And cling to a manhood of flowers, and sing the unap-
> proachable lakes?

I am afraid the answer was, the Park. (I had 'the swan' on the brain in those days; luckily, there were very few rhymes for 'parrot'.) The answer was, the Park; a bit of bush and flowerbed and lawn in a snug, smug, trim, middling-prosperous suburb of my utterly confining outer world, that splendidly ugly sea-town where, with my friends, I used to dawdle on half-holidays along the bent and Devon-facing seashore, hoping for corpses or gold watches or the skull of a sheep or a message in a bottle to be washed up in the wreck; or where we used to wander, whistling and being rude to strangers, through the packed streets, stale as station sandwiches, around the impressive gas-works and the slaughter-house, past the blackened monuments of civic pride and the museum, which should have been *in* a museum; where we scratched at a kind of cricket on the bald and cindery surface of the Recreation-ground, or winked at unapproachably old girls of fifteen or sixteen on the Promenade opposite; where we took a tram that shook like an iron jelly down from our neat homes to the gaunt pier, there to clamber *under* the pier, hanging perilously on its skeleton-legs; or to run along to the end where patient men with the seaward eyes of the dockside unemployed, capped and mufflered, dangling from their mouths pipes that had long gone out, angled over the edge for unpleasant-tasting fish. Never *was* there such a town as ours, I thought, as we fought on the sandhills with the boys that our mothers called 'common', or dared each other up the scaffolding of half-built houses, soon to be called Laburnums or the Beeches, near the residential districts where the solider business families 'dined' at half past seven and never drew the curtains. Never *was* there such a town (I thought) for the smell of fish and chips on Saturday nights; for the Saturday afternoon cinema matinées where we shouted and hissed our threepences away; for the crowds in the streets, with leeks in their pockets, on International Nights, for the singing that gushed from the smoky doorways of the pubs in the quarters we never should have visited; for the Park, the Park, the inexhaustibly ridiculous and mysterious, the bushy Red-Indian-hiding Park, where the hunchback sat alone, images of perfection in his head, and 'the groves were blue with sailors'.

6

The recollections of childhood have no order; of all those every-coloured and shifting scented shoals that move below the surface of the moment of recollection, one, two, indiscriminately, suddenly, dart up out of their revolving waters into the present air: immortal flying-fish.

So I remember that never was there such a dame-school as ours: so firm and kind and smelling of galoshes, with the sweet and fumbled music of the piano-lessons drifting down from upstairs to the lonely schoolroom where only the sometimes tearful wicked sat over undone sums or to repent a little crime, the pulling of a girl's hair during geography, the sly shin-kick under the table during prayers. Behind the school was a narrow lane where the oldest and boldest threw pebbles at windows, scuffled and boasted, lied about their relations –

'My father's got a chauffeur.'

'What's he want a chauffeur for, he hasn't got a car.'

'My father's the richest man in Swansea.'

'My father's the richest man in Wales.'

'My father's the richest man in the world' –

and smoked the butt-ends of cigarettes, turned green, went home, and had little appetite for tea.

The lane was the place to tell your secrets; if you did not have any, you invented them; I had few. Occasionally, now, I dream that I am turning, after school, into the lane of confidences where I say to the children of my class: 'At last I have a secret.'

'What is it? What is it?'

'I can fly!'

And when they do not believe me, I flap my arms like a large, stout bird and slowly leave the ground, only a few inches at first, then gaining air until I fly, like Dracula in a schoolboy cap, level with the windows of the school, peering in until the mistress at the piano screams, and the metronome falls with a clout to the ground, stops, and there is no more Time; and I fly over the trees and chimneys of my town, over the dockyards, skimming the masts and funnels; over Inkerman Street and Sebastopol Street and the street of the man-capped women hurrying to the Jug and Bottle with a fish-frail full of empties; over the trees of the eternal Park, where a brass band shakes the leaves and sends them showering down on to the nurses and the children, the cripples and the out-of-work. This is only a dream. The ugly, lovely, at least to me, town is alive, exciting and real though war has made a hideous hole in it. I do not need to remember a dream. The reality is there. The fine, live people, the spirit of Wales itself.

2
Quite Early One Morning

Thomas recorded this imaginative description of New Quay on 14 December 1944 when he was a resident of that Cardiganshire seaside village. G. R. Barnes, Director of Talks in London, wrote a memo to the producer Aneirin Talfan Davies at BBC Wales, then situated in Carmarthen:

> Neither of us thought that Dylan Thomas did justice to his script until he came to the excellent character speech of the last page. I should have thought that he was wrong to use that breathless poetic voice, for the words don't seem to us to carry it... The wit would have been much better appreciated if it had been read caustically or at least dryly.

When it was finally put on the air 31 August 1945, Martin Armstrong, the independent reviewer of 'The Spoken Word' in *The Listener* wrote in the issue of 6 September 1945:

> It produced a delightful picture of a small seaside town, a beautiful, richly imaginative, humorous piece of work to which the poet did full justice by his excellent reading.

For the present text, the BBC script has been checked against the extant recording, done for Aneirin Talfan Davies on 2 April 1953 and broadcast 17 June 1953.

Quite Early One Morning

Quite early one morning in the winter in Wales, by the sea that was lying down still and green as grass after a night of tar-black howling and rolling, I went out of the house, where I had come to stay for a cold unseasonable holiday, to see if it was raining still, if the outhouse had been blown away, potatoes, shears, rat-killer, shrimp-nets, and tins of rusty nails aloft on the wind, and if all the cliffs were left. It had been such a ferocious night that someone in a smoky ship-pictured bar had said he could feel his tombstone shaking even though he was not dead, or at least was moving; but the morning shone as clear and calm as one always imagines tomorrow will shine.

The sun lit the sea-town, not as a whole, from topmost down-reproving zinc-roofed chapel to empty-but-for-rats-and-whispers grey warehouse on the harbour, but in separate bright pieces. There, the quay shouldering out, nobody on it now but the gulls and the capstans like small men in tubular trousers. Here, the roof of the police-station, black as a helmet, dry as a summons, sober as Sunday. There, the splashed church, with a cloud in the shape of a bell poised above it, ready to drift and ring. Here the chimneys of the pink-washed pub, the pub that was waiting for Saturday night as an over-jolly girl waits for sailors.

The town was not yet awake. The milkman lay still lost in the clangour and music of his Welsh-spoken dreams, the wish-fulfilled tenor voices more powerful than Caruso's, sweeter than Ben Davies's, thrilling past Cloth Hall and Manchester House up to the frosty hills. The town was not yet awake. Babies in upper bedrooms of salt-white houses dangling over water, or of bow-windowed villas squatting prim

10

in neatly treed but unsteady hill streets, worried the light with their half in sleep cries. Miscellaneous retired sea captains emerged for a second from deeper waves than ever tossed their boats, then drowned again, going down down into a perhaps Mediterranean-blue cabin of sleep, rocked to the sea-beat of their ears. Landladies, shawled and bloused and aproned with sleep in the curtained, bombazine-black of their once spare rooms, remembered their loves, their bills, their visitors, dead, decamped, or buried in English deserts until the trumpet of next expensive August roused them again to the world of holiday rain, dismal cliff and sand seen through the weeping windows of front parlours, tasselled table-cloths, stuffed pheasants, ferns in pots, fading photographs of the bearded and censorious dead, autograph albums with a lock of limp and colourless beribboned hair lolling out between the thick black boards.

The town was not yet awake. Birds sang in eaves, bushes, trees, on telegraph wires, rails, fences, spars, and wet masts, not for love or joy, but to keep other birds away. The landlords in feathers disputed the right of even the flying light to descend and perch.

The town was not yet awake, and I walked through the streets like a stranger come out of the sea, shrugging off weed and wave and darkness with each step, or like an inquisitive shadow, determined to miss nothing – not the preliminary tremor in the throat of the dawn-saying cock or the first whirring nudge of arranged time in the belly of the alarm clock on the trinketed chest of drawers under the knitted text and the done-by-hand watercolours of Porthcawl or Trinidad.

I walked past the small sea-spying windows, behind whose trim curtains lay mild-mannered men and women not yet awake and, for all I could know, terrible and violent in their dreams. In the head of Miss Hughes, 'The Cosy', clashed the cymbals of an Eastern court. Eunuchs struck gongs the size of Bethesda Chapel. Sultans with voices fiercer than visiting preachers demanded a most un-Welsh dance. Everywhere there glowed and rayed the colours of the small, slate-grey woman's dreams, purple, magenta, ruby, sapphire, emerald, vermilion, honey. But I could not believe it. She knitted in her tidy sleep-world a beige woollen shroud with 'Thou Shalt Not' on the bosom.

I could not imagine Cadwallader Davies the grocer in his near-to-waking dream, riding on horse-back, two-gunned and Cody-bold, through the cactus prairies. He added, he subtracted, he receipted, he filed a prodigious account with a candle dipped in dried egg.

What big seas of dreams ran in the Captain's sleep? Over what blue-whaled waves did he sail through a rainbow hail of flying-fishes to the music of Circe's swinish island? Do not let him be dreaming of dividends and bottled beer and onions.

Someone was snoring in one house. I counted ten savage and indignant grunts and groans, like those of a pig in a model and mudless farm, which ended with a window rattler, a wash-basin shaker, a trembler of tooth glasses, a waker of dormice. It thundered with me to the chapel railings, then brassily vanished.

The chapel stood grim and grey, telling the day there was to be no nonsense. The chapel was not asleep, it never cat-napped nor nodded nor closed its long cold eye. I left it telling the morning off and the sea-gull hung rebuked above it.

And climbing down again and up out of the town I heard the cocks crow from hidden farmyards, from old roosts above waves where fabulous sea-birds might sit and cry: 'Neptune!' And a far-away clock struck from another church in another village in another universe, though the wind blew the time away. And I walked in the timeless morning past a row of white cottages almost expecting that an ancient man with a great beard and an hour-glass and a scythe under his night-dressed arm might lean from the window and ask *me* the time. I would have told him: 'Arise old counter of the heartbeats of albatrosses, and wake the cavernous sleepers of the town to a dazzling new morning.' I would have told him: 'You unbelievable Father of Eva and Dai Adam, come out, old chicken, and stir up the winter morning with your spoon of a scythe.' I would have told him – I would have scampered like a scalded ghost over the cliffs and down to the bilingual sea.

Who lived in these cottages? I was a stranger to the sea town, fresh or stale from the city where I worked for my bread and butter wishing it were laver-bread and country salty butter yolk-yellow. Fishermen certainly; no painters but of boats; no man-dressed women with shooting-sticks and sketch-books and voices like macaws to paint the reluctant heads of critical and sturdy natives who posed by the pint against the chapel-dark sea which would be made more blue than the bay of Naples, though shallower.

12

I walked on to the cliff path again, the town behind and below waking up now so very slowly; I stopped and turned and looked. Smoke from one chimney – the cobbler's, I thought, but from that distance it may have been the chimney of the retired male nurse who had come to live in Wales after many years' successful wrestling with the mad rich of Southern England. (He was not liked. He measured you for a strait-jacket carefully with his eye; he saw you bounce from rubber walls like a sorbo ball. No behaviour surprised him. Many people of the town found it hard to resist leering at him suddenly around the corner, or convulsively dancing, or pointing with laughter and devilish good humour at invisible dog-fights merely to prove to him that they were normal.)

Smoke from another chimney now. They were burning their last night's dreams. Up from a chimney came a long-haired wraith like an old politician. Someone had been dreaming of the Liberal Party. But no, the smoky figure wove, attenuated, into a refined and precise grey comma. Someone had been dreaming of reading Charles Morgan. Oh! the town was waking now and I heard distinctly, insistent over the slow-speaking sea, the voices of the town blown up to me. And some of the voices said:

> I am Miss May Hughes 'The Cosy', a lonely lady,
> Waiting in her house by the nasty sea,
> Waiting for her husband and pretty baby
> To come home at last from wherever they may be.

> I am Captain Tiny Evans, my ship was the 'Kidwelly'
> And Mrs Tiny Evans has been dead for many a year.
> 'Poor Captain Tiny all alone', the neighbours whisper,
> But I like it all alone, and I hated her.

> Clara Tawe Jenkins, 'Madam' they call me,
> An old contralto with her dressing-gown on,
> And I sit at the window and I sing to the sea,
> For the sea does not notice that my voice has gone.

> Parchedig Thomas Evans making morning tea,
> Very weak tea, too, you mustn't waste a leaf.
> Every morning making tea in my house by the sea
> I am troubled by one thing only, and that, belief.

13

Open the curtains, light the fire, what are servants for?
I am Mrs Ogmore-Pritchard and I want another snooze.
Dust the china, feed the canary, sweep the drawing-room floor;
And before you let the sun in, mind he wipes his shoes.

I am only Mr Griffiths, very short-sighted, B.A., Aber.
As soon as I finish my egg I must shuffle off to school.
O patron saint of teachers, teach me to keep order,
And forget those words on the blackboard – 'Griffiths Bat is a fool.'

Do you hear that whistling? – It's me, I am Phoebe,
The maid at the King's Head, and I am whistling like a bird.
Someone spilt a tin of pepper in the tea.
There's twenty for breakfast and I'm not going to say a word.

I can see the Atlantic from my bed where I always lie,
Night and day, night and day, eating my bread and slops.
The quiet cripple staring at the sea and the sky.
I shall lie here till the sky goes out and the sea stops.

Thus some of the voices of a cliff-perched town at the far end of
Wales moved out of sleep and darkness into the new-born, ancient
and ageless morning, moved and were lost.

3
Reminiscences of Childhood

The Welsh Region Children's Hour commissioned Thomas to repeat 'Reminiscences of Childhood'. He rewrote it substantially for that occasion. The new version was recorded 23 February 1945 for broadcasting 21 March 1945. The fee was five guineas.

Aneirin Talfan Davies asked Thomas to read the piece for a new recording on 13 March 1953 in Swansea. The present text follows this recording, as broadcast in the Welsh Region Home Service on 6 May 1953.

Reminiscences of Childhood

I like very much people telling me about their childhood, but they'll have to be quick or else I'll be telling them about mine.

I was born in a large Welsh town at the beginning of the Great War, an ugly, lovely town – or so it was and is to me – crawling, sprawling, by a long and splendid curving shore, where truant boys and Sandfield boys and old men from nowhere beachcombed, idled, and paddled, watched the dock-bound ships or the ships steaming away into wonder and India, magic and China, countries bright with oranges and loud with lions, threw stones into the sea for the barking outcast dogs, made castles and forts and harbours and race-tracks in the sand, and on Saturday summer afternoons listened to the brass band, watched the Punch and Judy, or hung about on the fringes of the crowd to hear the fierce religious speakers who shouted at the sea as though it were wicked and wrong to roll in and out like that, white-horsed and full of fishes.

One man, I remember, used to take off his hat and set fire to his hair every now and then, but I do not remember what it proved, if it proved anything at all, except that he was a very interesting man.

This sea-town was my world; outside a strange Wales, coal-pitted, mountained, river-run, full, so far as I knew, of choirs and football teams and sheep and story-book-tall black hats and red flannel petticoats, moved about its business which was none of mine.

Beyond that unknown Wales with its wild names like peals of bells in the darkness, and its mountain men clothed in the skins of animals perhaps, and always singing, lay England which was London and the country called the Front, from which many of our neighbours never

16

came back. It was a country to which only young men travelled.

At the beginning the only front I knew was the little lobby before our front door. I could not understand how so many people never returned from there, but later I grew to know more, though still without understanding, and carried a wooden rifle in the park and shot down the invisible unknown enemy like a flock of wild birds. And the park itself was a world within the world of the sea-town. Quite near where I lived, so near that on summer evenings I could listen in my bed to the voices of older children playing ball on the sloping paper-littered bank, the park was full of terrors and treasures. Though it was only a little park, it held within its borders of old tall trees, notched with our names and shabby from our climbing, as many secret places, caverns and forests, prairies and deserts, as a country somewhere at the end of the sea.

And though we would explore it one day, armed and desperate, from end to end, from the robbers' den to the pirates' cabin, the highwayman's inn to the cattle ranch, or the hidden room in the undergrowth where we held beetle races and lit the wood fires and roasted potatoes and talked about Africa and the makes of motor-cars, yet still the next day it remained as unexplored as the Poles, a country just born and always changing.

There were many secret societies but you could belong only to one, and in blood or red ink, and a rusty pocket-knife, with, of course, an instrument to remove stones from horses' feet, you signed your name at the foot of a terrible document, swore death to all the other societies, crossed your heart that you would divulge no secret and that, if you did, you would consent to torture by slow fire, and undertook to carry out by yourself a feat of either daring or endurance. You could take your choice: would you climb to the top of the tallest and most dangerous tree, and from there hurl stones and insults at grown-up passers-by, especially postmen, or any other men in uniform? Or would you ring every doorbell in the terrace, not forgetting the doorbell of the man with the red face who kept dogs and ran fast? Or would you swim in the reservoir, which was forbidden and had angry swans? Or would you eat a whole old jam jar full of mud? There were many more alternatives. I chose one of endurance, and for half an hour, it may have been longer or shorter, held up off the ground a very heavy broken pram we had found in a bush. I thought my back would break

17

and the half hour felt like a day, but I preferred it to braving the red face and the dogs, or to swallowing tadpoles.

We knew every inhabitant of the park, every regular visitor, every nursemaid, every gardener, every old man. We knew the hour when the alarming retired policeman came in to look at the dahlias and the hour when the old lady arrived in the bath-chair with six pekinese, and a pale girl to read aloud to her. (I think she read the newspaper, but we always said she read the *Wizard*.) The face of the old man who sat summer and winter on the bench looking over the reservoir, I can see clearly now, and I wrote a poem long long after I'd left the park and the sea-town called 'The Hunchback in the Park'.

[Reads 'The Hunchback in the Park'.]

And that park grew up with me; that small world widened as I learned its secrets and boundaries, as I discovered new refuges and ambushes in its woods and jungles, hidden homes and lairs for the multitudes of imagination, for cowboys and Indians, and the tall terrible half-people who rode on nightmares through my bedroom. But it was not the only world – that world of rockery, gravel path, playbank, bowling-green, bandstand, reservoir, dahlia garden, where an ancient keeper, known as Smokey, was the whiskered snake in the grass one must keep off. There was another world where with my friends I used to dawdle on half holidays along the bent and Devon-facing seashore, hoping for gold watches or the skull of a sheep or a message in a bottle to be washed up by the tide; and another where we used to wander whistling through the packed streets, stale as station sandwiches, round the impressive gas-works and the slaughter-house, past the blackened monuments and the museum that should have been in a museum. Or we scratched at a kind of cricket on the bald and cindery surface of the recreation ground, or we took a tram that shook like an iron jelly down to the gaunt pier, there to clamber under the pier, hanging perilously on to its skeleton legs or to run along to the end where patient men with the seaward eyes of the dockside unemployed, capped and mufflered, dangling from their mouths pipes that had long gone out, angled over the edge for unpleasant tasting fish.

Never was there such a town as ours, I thought, as we fought on

18

the sand-hills with rough boys or dared each other to climb up the scaffolding of half-built houses soon to be called Laburnum or The Beeches. Never was there such a town, I thought, for the smell of fish and chips on Saturday evenings, for the Saturday afternoon cinema matinées where we shouted and hissed our threepences away, for the crowds in the streets with leeks in their hats on international nights, for the park, the inexhaustible and mysterious, bushy Red-Indian hiding park. The memories of childhood have no order, and so I remember that never was there such a dame school as ours, so firm and kind and smelling of galoshes, with the sweet and fumbled music of the piano lessons drifting down from upstairs to the lonely schoolroom, where only the sometimes tearful wicked sat over undone sums, or to repent a little crime – the pulling of a girl's hair during geography, the sly shin-kick under the table during English literature. Behind the school was a narrow lane where only the oldest and boldest threw pebbles at windows, scuffled and boasted, fibbed about their relations:

'My father's got a chauffeur.'

'What's he want a chauffeur for, he hasn't got a car.'

'My father's the richest man in the town.'

'My father's the richest man in Wales.'

'My father owns the world.'

And swopped gob-stoppers for slings, old knives for marbles, kite-string for foreign stamps.

The lane was always the place to tell your secrets; if you did not have any you invented them. Occasionally now I dream that I am turning out of school into the lane of confidences when I say to the boys of my class, 'At last, I have a real secret.'

'What is it? What is it?'

'I can fly.'

And when they do not believe me, I flap my arms and slowly leave the ground, only a few inches at first, then gaining air until I fly waving my cap level with the upper windows of the school, peering in until the mistress at the piano screams and the metronome falls to the ground and stops, and there is no more time.

And I fly over the trees and chimneys of my town, over the dockyards, skimming the masts and funnels, over Inkerman Street, Sebastopol Street, over the trees of the everlasting park, where a brass band shakes the leaves and sends them showering down on to the

19

nurses and the children, the cripples and the idlers, and the gardeners, and the shouting boys, over the yellow seashore and the stone-chasing dogs and the old men and the singing sea.

The memories of childhood have no order, and no end.

4
Memories of Christmas

'Thank you for wanting me to do something else for the Children's Hour', Thomas wrote on 4 August 1945, in reply to an invitation from Lorraine Jameson of the BBC in Cardiff, following the second 'Reminiscences of Childhood' broadcast. 'I think "Memories of Christmas" a perfectly good title to hang something on, and I'll get down to it soon' (*Letters* p. 562). He forwarded the script on 25 September 1945, and his reading of it was recorded on 6 December 1945 in London, where he was living at the time. It was transmitted in the BBC Wales Children's Hour 16 December 1945; his fee was twelve guineas.

The perennially popular 'A Child's Christmas in Wales' is an amalgam of 'Memories of Christmas' and 'Conversation about Christmas', a piece Thomas did for *Picture Post* in December 1947. *Harper's Bazaar* (December 1950) first published the combined story, and Thomas read it for Caedmon Records in New York 22 February 1952. No recording of the original 'Memories of Christmas' seems to have been retained. The present text is the 1945 script typed at the BBC from Thomas's submitted manuscript.

21

Memories of Christmas

One Christmas was so much like another, in those years around the sea-town corner now and out of all sound except the distant speaking of the voices I sometimes hear a moment before sleep, that I can never remember whether it snowed for six days and six nights when I was twelve or whether it snowed for twelve days and twelve nights when I was six; or whether the ice broke and the skating grocer vanished like a snowman through a white trapdoor on that same Christmas day that the mincepies finished Uncle Arnold and we tobogganed down the seaward hill, all the afternoon, on the best tea-tray, and Mrs Griffiths complained, and we threw a snowball at her niece, and my hands burned so, with the heat and the cold, when I held them in front of the fire, that I cried for twenty minutes and then had some jelly.

All the Christmases roll down the hill towards the Welsh-speaking sea, like a snowball growing whiter and bigger and rounder, like a cold and headlong moon bundling down the sky that was our street; and they stop at the rim of the ice-edged, fish-freezing waves, and I plunge my hands in the snow and bring out whatever I can find: holly or robins or pudding, squabbles and carols and oranges and tin whistles, and the fire in the front room, and bang go the crackers, and holy holy holy ring the bells, and the glass bells shaking on the tree, and Mother Goose, and Struwwelpeter – oh! the baby-burning flames and the clacking scissorman! – Billy Bunter and Black Beauty, Little Women and boys who have three helpings, Alice and Mrs Potter's badgers, penknives, teddy-bears – named after a Mr Theodore Bear, their inventor, or father, who died recently in the United States –

22

mouthorgans, tin-soldiers, and blancmange, and Auntie Bessie playing 'Pop Goes the Weasel' and 'Nuts in May' and 'Oranges and Lemons' on the untuned piano in the parlour all through the thimblehiding musical chairing blindmanbuffing party at the end of the never-to-be-forgotten day at the end of the unremembered year.

In goes my hand into that wool-white bell-tongued ball of holidays resting at the margin of the carolsinging sea, and out comes Mrs Prothero and the firemen.

It was on the afternoon of the day of Christmas Eve, and I was in Mrs Prothero's garden, waiting for cats, with her son Jim. It was snowing. It was always snowing at Christmas; December, in my memory, is white as Lapland, though there were no reindeers. But there were cats. Patient, cold, and callous, our hands wrapped in socks, we waited to snowball the cats. Sleek and long as jaguars and terrible-whiskered, spitting and snarling they would slink and sidle over the white backgarden walls, and the lynxeyed hunters, Jim and I, fur-capped and moccasined trappers from Hudson's Bay off Eversley Road, would hurl our deadly snowballs at the green of their eyes. The wise cats never appeared. We were so still, Eskimo-footed arctic marksmen in the muffling silence of the eternal snows – eternal, ever since Wednesday – that we never heard Mrs Prothero's first cry from her igloo at the bottom of the garden. Or, if we heard it at all, it was, to us, like the far-off challenge of our enemy and prey, the neighbour's Polar Cat. But soon the voice grew louder. 'Fire!' cried Mrs Prothero, and she beat the dinner-gong. And we ran down the garden, with the snowballs in our arms, towards the house, and smoke, indeed, was pouring out of the dining-room, and the gong was bombilating, and Mrs Prothero was announcing ruin like a towncrier in Pompeii. This was better than all the cats in Wales standing on the wall in a row. We bounded into the house, laden with snowballs, and stopped at the open door of the smokefilled room. Something was burning all right; perhaps it was Mr Prothero, who always slept there after mid-day dinner with a newspaper over his face; but he was standing in the middle of the room, saying 'A fine Christmas!', and smacking at the smoke with a slipper. 'Call the firebrigade', cried Mrs Prothero as she beat the gong. 'They won't be there,' said Mr Prothero, 'it's Christmas.' There was no fire to be seen, only clouds of smoke and Mr Prothero standing in the middle of them, waving his slipper as though he were conducting. 'Do something,' he said. And we threw all our snowballs into the smoke – I think we missed Mr Prothero – and ran out of the house to the telephone box. 'Let's call the police as well', Jim said. 'And the ambulance.' 'And Ernie Jenkins, he likes fires.' But we only called the firebrigade, and soon the fire-engine came and three tall men in helmets brought a hose into the house and Mr Prothero got out just in time before they turned it on. Nobody could have had a noisier Christmas Eve. And when the firemen turned off the hose and were standing in the wet and smoky room, Jim's aunt, Miss Prothero, came downstairs and peered in at them. Jim and I waited, very quietly, to hear what she would say to them. She said the right thing, always. She looked at the three tall firemen in their shining helmets, standing among the smoke and cinders and dissolving snowballs, and she said: 'Would you like something to read?'

Now out of that bright white snowball of Christmases gone comes the stocking, the Stocking of stockings, that hung at the foot of the bed with the arm of a golliwog dangling over the top and small bells ringing in the toes. There was a company, gallant and scarlet but never nice to taste though I always tried when very young, of belted and busbied and musketed lead soldiers so soon to lose their heads and legs in the wars on the kitchen table after the tea-things, the mincepies and the cakes that I helped to make by stoning the raisins and eating them, had been cleared away; and a bag of moist and many coloured jellybabies and a folded flag and a false nose and a tramconductor's cap and a machine that punched tickets and rang a bell; never a catapult; once, by mistake that no one could explain, a little hatchet; and a rubber buffalo, or it may have been a horse, with a yellow head and haphazard legs; and a celluloid duck that made, when you pressed it, a most unducklike noise, a mewing moo that an ambitious cat might make who wishes to be a cow; and a paintingbook in which I could make the grass, the trees, the sea, and the animals any colours I pleased: and still the dazzling sky-blue sheep are grazing in the red field under a flight of rainbow-beaked and pea-green birds.

Christmas morning was always over before you could say Jack Frost. And look! suddenly the pudding was burning! Bang the gong and call the fire-brigade and the bookloving firemen! Someone found the silver threepenny bit with a currant on it; and the someone was always Uncle Arnold. The motto in my cracker read:

Let's all have fun this Christmas Day,
Let's play and sing and shout hooray!

and the grown-ups turned their eyes towards the ceiling, and Auntie Bessie, who had already been frightened, twice, by a clockwork mouse, whimpered at the sideboard and had some elderberry wine. And someone put a glass bowl full of nuts on the littered table, and my Uncle said, as he said once every year, 'I've got a shoe-nut here. Fetch me a shoe-horn to open it, boy.' And dinner was ended.

And I remember that on the afternoon of Christmas Day, when the others sat round the fire and told each other that this was nothing, no, nothing, to the great snowbound and turkeyproud yulelog-crackling holly-berry-bedizened and kissing-under-the-mistletoe Christmas when *they* were children, I would go out, schoolcapped and gloved and mufflered, with my bright new boots squeaking, into the white world, on to the seaward hill, to call on Jim and Dan and Jack and to walk with them through the silent snowscape of our town.

We went padding through the streets, leaving huge deep footprints in the snow, on the hidden pavements. 'I bet people'll think there's been hippoes.' 'What would you do if you saw a hippo coming down Terrace Road?' 'I'd go like this, bang! I'd throw him over the railings and roll him down the hill and then I'd tickle him under the ear and he'd wag his tail ...' 'What would you do if you saw *two* hippos ...?' Iron-flanked and bellowing he-hippoes clanked and blundered and battered through the scudding snow towards us as we passed by Mr Daniel's house. 'Let's post Mr Daniel a snowball through his letterbox.' 'Let's write things in the snow.' 'Let's write Mr Daniel looks like a spaniel all over his lawn.' 'Look,' Jack said, 'I'm eating snow-pie.' 'What's it taste like?' 'Like snow-pie,' Jack said.

Or we walked on the white shore. 'Can the fishes see it's snowing?' 'They think it's the sky falling down.' The silent one-clouded heavens drifted on to the sea. 'All the old dogs have gone.' Dogs of a hundred mingled makes yapped in the summer at the sea-rim and yelped at the trespassing mountains of the waves. 'I bet St Bernards would like it now.' And we were snowblind travellers lost on the North hills, and the great dewlapped dogs, with brandy-flasks round their necks, ambled and shambled up to us, baying 'Excelsior'.

We returned home through the desolate poor sea-facing streets

25

where only a few children fumbled with bare red fingers in the thick wheelrutted snow and catcalled after us, their voices fading away, as we trudged uphill, into the cries of the dock-birds and the hooters of ships out in the white and whirling bay.

Bring out the tall tales now that we told by the fire as we roasted chestnuts and the gaslight bubbled low. Ghosts with their heads under their arms trailed their chains and said whooo like owls in the long nights when I dared not look over my shoulder; wild beasts lurked in the cubbyhole under the stairs where the gas-meter ticked. 'Once upon a time,' Jim said, 'there were three boys, just like us, who got lost in the dark in the snow, near Bethesda Chapel, and this is what happened to them ...' It was the most dreadful happening I had ever heard.

And I remember that we went singing carols once, a night or two before Christmas Eve, when there wasn't the shaving of a moon to light the secret, white-flying streets. At the end of a long road was a drive that led to a large house, and we stumbled up the darkness of the drive that night, each one of us afraid, each one holding a stone in his hand in case, and all of us too brave to say a word. The wind made through the drive-trees noises as of old and unpleasant and maybe webfooted men wheezing in caves. We reached the black bulk of the house. 'What shall we give them?' Dan whispered. 'Hark the Herald?' 'Christmas Comes But Once A Year?' 'No,' Jack said, 'we'll sing Good King Wenceslas. I'll count three.' One, two, three, and we began to sing, our voices high and seemingly distant in the snow-felted darkness round the house that was occupied by nobody we knew. We stood close together, near the dark door.

> Good King Wenceslas looked out
> On the Feast of Stephen ...

And then a small, dry voice, like the voice of someone who has not spoken for a long time, suddenly joined our singing: a small, dry voice from the other side of the door: a small, dry voice through the keyhole.

And when we stopped running we were outside *our* house; the front room was lovely and bright; the gramophone was playing; we saw the red and white balloons hanging from the gasmantle; uncles and aunts sat by the fire; I thought I smelt our supper being fried in the kitchen. Everything was good again, and Christmas shone through all the familiar town.

'Perhaps it was a ghost,' Jim said, 'Perhaps it was trolls,' Dan said, who was always reading. 'Let's go in and see if there's any jelly left,' Jack said. And we did that.

5
Welsh Poetry

After being used by John Arlott as a reader in three 'Book of Verse' programmes, Thomas suggested he might do a script of his own. 'One idea that I had was to be asked to broadcast a short series of readings from the work of Welsh poets, or poets of Welsh ancestry, who wrote or write in English: from Vaughan to Edward Thomas, Wilfred Owen, W. H. Davies, and the younger men, contributors to the periodical *Wales*' – this, anyway, is how Thomas had put it to T. Rowland Hughes of the BBC Welsh Region in October 1938 (*Letters* p. 336). The idea was not at that time proceeded with. Eight years later John Arlott gave him the chance to do such an anthology. Thomas wrote the script in the first two weeks of December 1945 to meet a deadline of 15 December 1945. He recorded the programme as narrator, with Alan Price as reader of the verse, on 2 January 1946, for transmission in the BBC Eastern Service 5 January 1946, 'Book of Verse 65'. His fee was twenty guineas.

The surviving BBC script shows evidence of much editing in rehearsal, mainly deletion of chosen poems. The present text is the full script as Thomas presented it to the BBC typist. The holograph manuscript at Texas indicates that Thomas was originally intending to include Vernon Watkins, with the following paragraph:

Vernon Watkins, the last but one of the poets we shall hear today, has acknowledged his deep devotion to the poetry of W. B. Yeats. He is also a skilled translator from Heine, Holderlin, Verlaine, Paul Valery, and many other 19th and 20th century German and French poets. I believe him to be among the most technically accomplished poets writing in this country today. He is often obscure, but never wilfully; his symbolism,

29

for he is rarely a poet who works through images towards his ultimate meaning, is strange but never private. An acquaintanceship with the later work of Yeats undoubtedly helps one to understand, with the ears of the mind, this delicate, unsensational, subtle music. I would like you to hear: –

There is no title of a Watkins poem given; and the whole paragraph was crossed through by Thomas before he submitted the script.

John Arlott apparently insisted that Thomas himself be included, and added the comment that ends the programme. He also wrote of this occasion in *Adelphi* (February 1954):

When an extract from a poem by Sir Lewis Morris was included in a programme, Dylan doubted that he ought to attempt to read it, and thought it might be better 'thrown away' by a lighter reader. He agreed to try it, however, and on first reading, fell into a fairly strong Welsh accent which lifted the poem higher than we had thought possible, for Morris, also a Welshman, had written it in a pattern of Welsh speech-rhythms not apparent to the reading eye.

Welsh Poetry

ANNOUNCER *'live'*:   This is London Calling in the Eastern Service of
the BBC. We present this evening the sixty-fifth programme in the
series 'Book of Verse'. These programmes, based in general on the
poems being studied at Universities in India, are produced by John
Arlott.

[SIGNATURE TUNE]

ANNOUNCER: 'Book of Verse' – Welsh Poetry.

[MUSIC]

DYLAN THOMAS: This is not a programme of Welsh poetry, because
Welsh poetry is written in the Welsh language, which few of us,
including myself, can understand. The position – if poets must have
positions, other than upright – of the poet born in Wales or of Welsh
parentage and writing his poems in English is, today, made by many
people unnecessarily, and trivially, difficult. There is a number of
young Welshmen writing poems in English who, insisting passionately that they are Welshmen, should, by rights, be writing in Welsh,
but who, unable to write in Welsh or reluctant to do so because of
the uncommercial nature of the language, often give the impression
that their writing in English is only a condescension to the influence
and ubiquity of a tyrannous foreign tongue. I do not belong to that
number. This is not a programme of Welsh poetry, nor of Anglo-
Welsh poetry: the last is an ambiguous compromise. I am going to
introduce, with as little explanation and criticism as possible, poems
written in English by poets who are either Welsh by birth or who

31

have very strong Welsh associations. I want you to hear some of the poems in English that a small, and distinguished, number of Welshmen have written – mostly in the forty-five years of this century. I would prefer to call this an anthology, with comments, rather than a brief lecture with quotations. Really, this *has* to be an anthology, because, as far as I can read and understand, there is no logical thread running through the centuries of traditional poetry-in-English which can be said to possess a particularly Welsh charac-. teristic. There are not more than half a dozen Welsh poets who wrote in English of any genuine importance between 1622, when Henry Vaughan was born, and 1944, when Alun Lewis died, though there are many able and charming writers. All I can say, and all that the readers here can illustrate, is that Welshmen have written, from time to time, exceedingly good poetry in English. I should like to think that that is because they were, and are, good poets rather than good Welshmen. It's the poetry, written in the language which is most natural to the poet, that counts, not his continent, country, island, race, class, or political persuasion.

We begin with Henry Vaughan (1622–95). Before him was a magnificent tradition of poetry in the Welsh language. Dafydd ap Gwilym, for instance, a contemporary of Chaucer, is thought, by most Celtic scholars, to be as good a poet. Vaughan, who belonged to a very ancient Welsh family and who was educated in England, must surely have known ap Gwilym's poems. But he certainly did not follow in the exuberant bardsmanship of that great court-poet but derived, in the first place, his style and matter from George Herbert. He wrote in a time when one poet *could* derive manner and content from another and yet be original. He read, too, and loved, the poetry of John Donne, but he loved it most as he saw it reflected, and transmuted, in the work of Herbert. The world, to Vaughan, was 'no less than a veil of the Eternal Spirit, whose presence may be felt in any, and the smallest, part'. Readers today may prefer him not as a mystical theologist but as a wonderful poet of pieces: a magician of intervals. They remember odd lines, rather than odder poems. They think, perhaps, of this, from a poem on the Grave:

READER: A nest of nights, a gloomy sphere,
                Where shadows thicken, and the Cloud
                Sits on the Sun's brow all the year,
                And nothing moves without a shroud.

DYLAN THOMAS: Or a single image:

READER: ... stars nod and sleep
                And through the dark air spin a fiery thread.

DYLAN THOMAS: Or, again, from the 'Day-Spring':

READER: Early, while yet the dark was gay,
                And gilt with stars more trim than day,
                Heaven's Lily and the Earth's chaste Rose,
                The green, immortal Branch arose,
                And in a solitary place
                Bowed to his father His blessed face.

DYLAN THOMAS: And, of the many superb opening lines:

READER: I saw Eternity the other night,
                Like a great ring of pure and endless light.

DYLAN THOMAS: But, I have chosen one whole poem, 'The Night', in which the figures of his authentic and intense vision move across a wild, and yet inevitably ordered, sacred landscape.

READER: Through that pure virgin shrine,
                That sacred veil drawn o'er Thy glorious noon,
                That men might look and live, as glow-worms shine,
                      And face the moon,
                Wise Nicodemus saw such light
                As made him know his God by night.

                    Most blest believer he!
                Who in that land of darkness and blind eyes
                Thy long-expected healing wings could see,

When Thou didst rise;
And, what can never more be done,
Did at midnight speak with the Sun!

O who will tell me, where
He found Thee at that dead and silent hour?
What hallowed solitary ground did bear
    So rare a flower;
Within whose sacred leaves did lie
The fulness of the Deity?

No mercy-seat of gold,
No dead and dusty cherub, nor carved stone,
But His own living works did my Lord hold
    And lodge alone;
Where trees and herbs did watch and peep
And wonder, while the Jews did sleep.

Dear Night! this world's defeat;
The stop to busy fools; care's check and curb;
The day of spirits; my soul's calm retreat
    Which none disturb!
Christ's progress, and His prayer-time;
The hours to which high Heaven doth chime.

God's silent, searching flight;
When my Lord's head is filled with dew, and all
His locks are wet with the clear drops of night;
    His still, soft call;
His knocking-time; the soul's dumb watch,
When spirits their fair kindred catch.

Were all my loud, evil days
Calm and unhaunted as is thy dark tent,
Whose peace but by some angel's wing or voice
    Is seldom rent;
Then I in heaven all the long year
Would keep, and never wander here.

But living where the sun
Doth all things wake, and where all mix and tire

Themselves and others, I consent and run
    To every mire;
And by this world's ill-guiding light,
Err more than I can do by night.

    There is in God, some say,
A deep, but dazzling darkness; as men here
Say it is late and dusky, because they
    See not all clear.
O for that Night! where I in Him
Might live invisible and dim!

DYLAN THOMAS: After Vaughan, there is no other considerable Welsh poet – I needn't, I hope, explain again what I mean, in this context, by Welsh poetry – until the 20th century. (Gerard Manley Hopkins, in the 19th century, was influenced by bardic forms and measures, but cannot, I'm afraid, be included in even the broadest survey of this kind.) Two hundred years, and more, pass before a Welshman comes into his own again: his own, which is the one individual world of each true poet, and the same. There were Welshmen, certainly, who rhymed in English – Richard Lhwydd, the poet of Snowdon, for example – who wrote verse, who sometimes wrote poetry. But there was none who wrote a *poem*. Poetry is the material out of which poems are made. There was John Dyer (1700–58), of Carmarthenshire, whose 'Grongar Hill', an irregular Pindaric ode, is still remembered, if only as a name, by those who read poetry for a degree and by those who live near Grongar Hill. Dyer also wrote a blank verse epic in four books, 'The Fleece', in which he discoursed of the tending of sheep, of shearing and weaving, and of trade in woollen manufactures. We must read it together one day. Then there was Sir Lewis Morris (1833–1907), also of Carmarthenshire, who wrote nearly a thousand poems, many of them long, lyrics, idylls, tragedies, odes of welcome to the Trades' Union Congress, Swansea, 1901, triolets in ladies' albums, elegies on the deaths of statesmen. The contemporary press compared his work with the *Odyssey* and *Faust*, with 'L'Allegro' and 'Il Penseroso'. He was lauded by Mr. Gladstone. From him you can draw the portrait of the worthiest, and most popular, type of Victorian professional poet. At his best, he could write well of the Wales he knew, as in

35

this prosy, but vivid, extract from 'The Physicians of Myddfai'.

READER: Far, far away in wild Wales, by the shore of the boundless
Atlantic,
Where the cloud-capt peaks of the North are dwarfed to
the hills of the South,
And through the long vale to the sea, the full-fed, devious
Towy
Turns and returns on itself, like the coils of a silvery snake,
A grey town sits up aloft on the bank of the clear, flowing
river,
As it has sat since the days when the Roman was first in
the land.
A town, with a high ruined castle and walls mantled over
with ivy,
With church towers square and strong and narrow
irregular streets,
And, frequent in street and lane, many-windowed high-
shouldered chapels,
Whence all the still Sabbath ascend loud preaching and
passionate prayer,
Such violent wrestling with sin, that the dogs on the
pavement deserted
Wake with a growl from their dreams at the sound of the
querulous voice,
And the gay youths, released from the counter and bound
for the seaside or hillside,
Start as they wake on their way echoes of undevout feet,
And here and there a rude square, with statues of popular
heroes,
A long quay with scarcely a ship, and a hoary bridge
spanning the stream,
The stream which struggles in June by the shallows where
children are swimming,
The furious flood which at Yule roars seaward, resistless
along,
Though the white steam ribbons float by it, forlorn it seems,
almost forsaken.

All the day long in the week the dumb streets are hushed
　　in repose,
But on market or fair days there comes a throng of Welsh-
　　speaking peasants
From many a lonely farm in the folds of the rain-beaten
　　hills,
And the long streets are filled with the high-pitched speech
　　of the chaffering Cymry,
With a steeple-crowned hat, here and there, and the red
　　cloaks which daunted the French.
Scarce in Keltic Brittany's self, or in homely Teutonic
　　Silesia,
So foreign a crowd may you see as in this far corner of
　　Wales.

DYLAN THOMAS:　Now we come into the 20th century. From Edward
Thomas, who was killed in France in 1917, to Alun Lewis, who
died in India in 1944, there sprang into life a whole new body of
poetry written by Welshmen. I do not think that there was, in
common between these poets, anything but a love of poetry and of
their own country. They did not, to any marked degree, derive
from the same poetical sources. Edward Thomas, for instance, was
devoted, through all his pitifully short and too often melancholy
life, to the most English work of Thomas Hardy, John Clare the
Northamptonshire peasant, and William Barnes the Dorset poet. He
loved always the rich brown stables and paddocks of the painter
George Morland and the loving landscapes of old Crome. He loved
the fields, the woods, the winding roads, he knew a thousand
country things: the diamonds of rain on the grassblades, the ghostly
white parsley flower, mouse and wren and robin, each year's first
violets, the missel-thrush that loves juniper, hawthorn berry, hazel-
tuft, newmown hay, the cuckoo crying over the untouched dew,
churches, graveyards, farms and byres, children, wild geese, horses
in the sun. In the words of Walter de la Mare, Edward Thomas was
a 'faithful and solitary lover of the lovely that is not beloved by most
of us, at much expense'. And when, indeed, he was killed in Flanders,
a mirror of England was shattered of so pure and true a crystal that

37

a clearer and tenderer reflection can be found no other where than in these poems. Here is a poem of his written in Wales: 'The Child on the Cliffs'.

READER: Mother, the root of this little yellow flower
Among the stones has the taste of quinine.
Things are strange to-day on the cliff. The sun shines
     so bright,
And the grasshopper works at his sewing-machine
So hard. Here's one on my hand, mother, look;
I lie so still. There's one on your book.

But I have something to tell more strange. So leave
Your book to the grasshopper, mother dear, –
Like a green knight in a dazzling market-place, –
And listen now. Can you hear what I hear
Far out? Now and then the foam there curls
And stretches a white arm out like a girl's.

Fishes and gulls ring no bells. There cannot be
A chapel or church between here and Devon,
With fishes or gulls ringing its bell, – hark! –
Somewhere under the sea or up in heaven.
'It's the bell, my son, out in the bay
On the buoy. It does sound sweet to-day.'

Sweeter I never heard, mother, no, not in all Wales.
I should like to be lying under that foam,
Dead, but able to hear the sound of the bell,
And certain that you would often come
And rest, listening happily.
I should be happy if that could be.

DYLAN THOMAS: And now an early poem, 'The Owl'.

READER: Downhill I came, hungry, and yet not starved;
Cold, yet had heat within me that was proof
Against the North wind; tired, yet so that rest
Had seemed the sweetest thing under a roof.

38

Then at the inn I had food, fire, and rest,
Knowing how hungry, cold, and tired was I.
All of the night was quite barred out except
An owl's cry, a most melancholy cry.

Shaken out long and clear upon the hill,
No merry note, nor cause of merriment,
But one telling me plain what I escaped
And others could not, that night, as in I went.

And salted was my food, and my repose,
Salted and sobered, too, by the bird's voice
Speaking for all who lay under the stars,
Soldiers and poor, unable to rejoice.

DYLAN THOMAS: Edward Thomas was twenty-five years old when 'a bullet stopped his song'. Writing poems at the same time as himself was another young man soon to be killed also and at the same age. This was Wilfred Owen (1893–1918), the greatest of the poets who wrote in, and of, the Great War, and one of the greatest poets of this century. Nothing further can be imagined from Thomas's grave and tender meditations than Owen's sometimes bitter but always noble, experimental and mature, sensuous and pitiful elegies on the great *undying* dead of the massacred world about him. His earliest poems show a completely uncritical admiration, and even idolatory, of Shelley and, in particular, of Keats. But out of this he fashioned as true and just and exact an instrument as any in our language to express the enormous suffering, and the unconquerable hope through death, that was to be his and the heritage of his comrades. 'To be able to write as I know how,' he said in a letter from the Front, 'study is necessary; a period of study, then of intercourse with kindred spirits, then of isolation.' It is a miracle how, in his short and warring life, in the dirt, the blood, the despair, the scarcely tolerable cold, the fire and gas and death of France, he contrived to achieve all his ambitions and to perfect his original technique. 'My subject,' he said, 'is War and the pity of War. The Poetry is in the pity'. He is the *pleader* of the sufferings of men; he writes *as* the articulate dead: murdered manhood is given a great and dark golden tongue. Here is his last poem: 'Strange Meeting'.

READER: It seemed that out of battle I escaped
         Down some profound dull tunnel, long since scooped
         Through granites which titanic wars had groined.
         Yet also there encumbered sleepers groaned,
         Too fast in thought or death to be bestirred.
         Then, as I probed them, one sprang up, and stared
         With piteous recognition in fixed eyes,
         Lifting distressful hands as if to bless.
         And by his smile, I know that sullen hall,
         By his dead smile I know we stood in Hell.
         With a thousand pains that vision's face was grained;
         Yet no blood reached there from the upper ground,
         And no guns thumped, or down the flues made moan.
         'Strange friend,' I said, 'here is no cause to mourn.'
         'None,' said the other, 'save the undone years,
         The hopelessness. Whatever hope is yours,
         Was my life also; I went hunting wild
         After the wildest beauty in the world,
         Which lies not calm in eyes, or braided hair,
         But mocks the steady running of the hour,
         And if it grieves, grieves richlier than here.
         For by my glee might many men have laughed,
         And of my weeping something had been left,
         Which must die now. I mean the truth untold,
         The pity of war, the pity war distilled.
         Now men will go content with what we spoiled.
         Or, discontent, boil bloody, and be spilled.
         They will be swift with swiftness of the tigress,
         None will break ranks, though nations trek from progress.
         Courage was mine, and I had mystery,
         Wisdom was mine, and I had mastery;
         To miss the march of this retreating world
         Into vain citadels that are not walled.
         Then, when much blood had clogged their chariot-
             wheels
         I would go up and wash them from sweet wells,
         Even with truths that lie too deep for taint.
         I would have poured my spirit without stint

But not through wounds; not on the cess of war.
Foreheads of men have bled where no wounds were.
I am the enemy you killed, my friend.
I knew you in this dark; for so you frowned
Yesterday through me as you jabbed and killed.
I parried; but my hands were loath and cold.
Let us sleep now ...'

DYLAN THOMAS: In 1917, the year before Owen's death, a Welshman published, from the Marshalsea Prison, his first book of poems, *The Souls' Destroyer*. W. H. Davies (1871–1940) was born in Monmouthshire and apprenticed, very early, to a picture-frame maker. He tramped through America as a hobo, crossed the Atlantic many times on cattle boats, and was a pedlar and street singer in England. Utterly poor and alone, educated by chance reading in the slums of great cities, he began, suddenly, to write verse which was in the direct tradition of Robert Herrick. From the very beginning to the end, during which he wrote voluminously, his poems were always fresh and simple and assured. There was inevitability in his slightest verses; unique observation in his tiniest reflections on the natural world. His most famous poems are about birds and clouds and animals, the journeying of the planets and the seasons, the adventure of the coming and going of simple night and day. But I have chosen two of his more unfamiliar poems, which will, perhaps, show him, to many, in a strange new light, but in a light no less scrupulously fair and loving than that in which his kingfishers, his robin-redbreasts, the little hunchbacks in the snow, all the inhabitants of his small and pure world move about their mysterious errands in the sky and on the earth he so much loved.

READER: The Inquest

I took my oath I would inquire,
Without affection, hate or wrath,
Into the death of Ada Wright –
So help me God! I took that oath.

When I went out to see the corpse,
The four months' babe that died so young,
I judged it was seven pounds in weight,
And little more than one foot long.

One eye, that had a yellow lid,
Was shut – so was the mouth, that smiled;
The left eye open, shining bright –
It seemed a knowing little child.

For as I looked at that one eye,
It seemed to laugh, and say with glee:
'What caused my death you'll never know –
Perhaps my mother murdered me'.

When I went into court again,
To hear the mother's evidence –
It was a love-child, she explained.
And smiled, for our intelligence.

'Now, Gentlemen of the Jury,' said
The coroner – 'this woman's child
By misadventure met its death.'
'Aye, aye,' said we. The mother smiled.

And I could see that child's one eye
Which seemed to laugh, and say with glee:
'What caused my death you'll never know –
Perhaps my mother murdered me.'

The Bust

When I went wandering far from home,
I left a woman in my room
To clean my hearth and floor, and dust
My shelves and pictures, books and bust.

When I came back a welcome glow
Burned in her eyes – her voice was low;
And everything was in its place,
As clean and bright as her own face.

But when I looked more closely there,
The dust was on my dark, bronze hair;
The nose and eyebrows too were white –
And yet the lips were clean and bright.

The years have gone, and so has she,
But still the truth remains with me –
How that hard mouth was once kept clean
By living lips that kissed unseen.

DYLAN THOMAS: Davies lived much of his life in poverty, and in
sickening surroundings. It never made him angry, at least not in
his poems. But out of the mining valleys of South Wales, there were
poets who were beginning to write in a spirit of passionate anger
against the inequality of social conditions. They wrote, not of the
truths and beauties of the natural world, but of the lies and uglinesses
of the unnatural system of society under which they worked – or,
more often during the nineteen-twenties and thirties, under which
they were not allowed to work. They spoke, in ragged and angry
rhythms, of the Wales *they* knew: the coaltips, the dole-queues, the
stubborn bankrupt villages, the children scrutting for coal on the
slagheaps, the colliers' shabby allotments, the cheapjack cinema,
the whippet-races, the disused quarries, the still pit-wheels, the
gaunt tinroofed chapels in the soot, the hewers squatting in the cut,
the pubs, the Woolworths, the deacons and the gyppos, silicosis,
little Moscow up beyond the hills, sag-roof factory and plumeless
stack, stone-grey street, scummed river, the capped and mufflered
knots of men outside the grim Employment Exchange and the Public
Library. Among these poets, Idris Davies is perhaps the only one
who has attempted to shape his violence into real poems, and he
often achieves a lyrical simplicity which in no way lessens the
intensity of his hatred of injustice. In some of his poems he can even
bring himself to write with a kind of sad and jaunty happiness about
his people and his country:

READER: He won't talk any more of the distant days
Of his childhood in the coalface and the tavern
And all his cronies who had left him behind

In the ragged little hut by the river;
He who had given so much of his sweat
In the days of his youth and his vigour,
Now falling like a wrinkled apple into a ditch
To rot away in the everlasting dust of death.
Tonight he shall sleep in a grave on the slope,
And no more will he prattle of the days of his youth.
Days of the Truck System and the Tory Sabbath,
And the Chartists and the starved-out strikers.
No more will he lean on the bridge in the summer
    morning
And make a god of Gladstone and a devil of Disraeli,
And go into raptures on the young Lloyd George
Who strode into London with a dazzling sword,
A bright St David from the stormy mountain.
All his long and luckless days are over,
And the broken old body in the plain deal coffin
Will be deaf to all the birds above the hill,
The larks that sing and sing in the cloudless sky
As the men move away in slow black clusters
Down on the road to the colliery town.

DYLAN THOMAS: And Idris Davies has written, too, in *Gwalia Deserta*,
one very simple and moving song:

READER: O what can you give me?
                Say the sad bells of Rhymney.

                Is there hope for the future?
                Cry the brown bells of Merthyr.

                Who made the mineowner?
                Say the black bells of Rhondda.

                And who robbed the miner?
                Cry the grim bells of Blaina.

                They will plunder willy-nilly,
                Say the bells of Caerphilly.

They have fangs, they have teeth!
Shout the loud bells of Neath.

To the south, things are sullen,
Say the pink bells of Brecon.

Even God is uneasy,
Say the moist bells of Swansea.

Put the vandals in court!
Cry the bells of Newport.

All would be well if – if – if –
Say the green bells of Cardiff.

Why so worried, sisters, why?
Sing the silver bells of Wye.

DYLAN THOMAS: Glyn Jones, now a schoolmaster, is one of the few young Welshmen writing English poetry today who has a deep knowledge of *Welsh* poetry itself, and he has tried, in several English poems, to use the very difficult ancient bardic forms. These forms rely on a great deal of assonance and alliteration and most complicated internal rhyming; and these effects in English have, in the hands of the few who have attempted to use them, succeeded only in warping, crabbing and obscuring the natural genius of the English language. But, when Glyn Jones is not experimenting in what must always be, to ears accustomed to English poetry, unavoidably awkward sound and syntax, he can write as surely as this. The poem, in which I think you will be able to detect, straight away, the influence of D. H. Lawrence, especially in the last stanza, is called 'Esyllt'.

READER: As he climbs down our hill, my kestrel rises,
Steering in silence up from five empty fields,
A smooth sun brushed brown across his shoulders,
Floating in wide circles, his warm wings stiff.
Their shadows cut; in new soft orange hunting boots
My lover crashes through the snapping bracken.

The still gorse-hissing hill burns, brags gold broom's
Outcropping quartz; each touched bush spills dew.
Strangely, last moment's parting was never sad,

45

But unreal, like my promised years; less felt
Than this intense white silver snail calligraphy
Scrawled here in the sun across these stones.

Why have I often wanted to cry out
More against his going when he has left my flesh
Only for the night? When he has gone out
Hot from my mother's kitchen, and my combs
Were on the table under the lamp, and the wind
Was banging the doors of the shed in the yard.

DYLAN THOMAS: And so, lastly, we come to Alun Lewis, who was
killed by accident, while serving in India, in 1944. Three of the very
finest – perhaps *the* very finest it will be found, in another and a
quieter day – of the poets who wrote in the two Great Wars of this
century were Edward Thomas, Wilfred Owen, and Alun Lewis.
Thomas and Owen were twenty-five years of age; Lewis, twenty-
eight. All three were Welshmen. I have no comment, of any national
reference, to add to that. Lewis was a healer and an illuminator,
humble before his own confessions, awed before the eternal confession of love by the despised and condemned inhabitants of the
world crumbling around him. He wrote:

READER: I have no more desire to express
The old relationships, of love fulfilled
Or stultified, capacity for pain,
Nor to say gracefully all that the poets have said
Of one or other of the old compulsions,
For now the times are gathered for confession.

DYLAN THOMAS: And, always humbly, never as a priest but as a
servant, he heard them. He knew, like Wilfred Owen, that, in war,
the poetry is in the pity. And, like Owen, he could never place himself
above pity but must give it tongue. Here is an extract from an
unfinished play in which Sacco, the comrade of Vanzetti, writes
from prison to his son:

READER: And for yourself, remember in the play
Of happiness you must not act alone.
The joy is in the sharing of the feast.
Also be like a man in how you greet
The suffering that makes your young face thin.
Be not perturbed if you are called to fight.
Only a fool thinks life was made his way,
A fool or the daughter of a wealthy house.

DYLAN THOMAS: Alun Lewis was young to have the courage of his faith to say this. Listen to these verses from 'Odi et Amo':

READER: Yet in this blood-soaked forest of disease
Where wolfish men lie scorched and black
And corpses sag against the trees
And love's dark roots writhe back

Like snakes into the scorching earth;
In this corrupted wood where none can hear
The love songs of Ophelia
And the laughter of Lear,

My soul cries out with love
Of all that walk and swim and fly.
From the mountains, from the sky,
Out of the depths of the sea
Love cries and cries in me.

And summer blossoms break above my head
With all the unbearable beauty of the dead.

DYLAN THOMAS: And this poem, 'Christmas Holiday':

READER: Big-uddered piebald cattle low
The shivering chestnut stallion dozes
The fat wife sighs in her chair
Her lap is filled with paper roses
The poacher sleeps in the goose-girl's arms
Incurious after so much eating
All human beings are replete.

But the cock upon the dunghill feels
God's needle quiver in his brain
And thrice he crows: and at the sound
The sober and the tipsy men
Jump out of bed with one accord
And start the war again.

The fat wife comfortably sleeping
Sighs and licks her lips and smiles

But the goose-girl is weeping.

DYLAN THOMAS: And, last of all, 'The Sentry':

READER: I have begun to die.
               For now at last I know
               That there is no escape
               From Night. Not any dream
               Nor breathless images of sleep
               Touch my bat's-eyes. I hang
               Leathery-arid from the hidden roof
               Of Night, and sleeplessly
               I watch within Sleep's province.
               I have left
               The lovely bodies of the boy and girl
               Deep in each other's placid arms;
               And I have left
               The beautiful lanes of sleep
               That barefoot lovers follow to this last
               Cold shore of thought I guard.
               I have begun to die
               And the guns' implacable silence
               Is my black interim, my youth and age,
               In the flower of fury, the folded poppy,
               Night.

JOHN ARLOTT: If I may take over the narration from Mr Thomas, at
   this point, it is because as the producer of the programme I could
   not believe that any collection of Welsh poetry would be complete
   without some of Dylan Thomas's own poetry. He is undoubtedly the

most important and the most distinctive of the young poets in England today. I ask him to read his own poems not out of politeness, but because I believe no one else can do them such fine justice. They need little explanation, except to say that they have welded the typical Welsh religious consciousness with a profound depth of visual and emotional recollection which carry them to a high pitch of excitement.

[Thomas read 'Poem in October'.]

6
On Reading Poetry Aloud

Thomas read three poems, Blake's 'The Tyger', D. H. Lawrence's 'Snake', and his own 'Fern Hill' at a Royal Command Performance at Wigmore Hall on 13 May 1946. Because of this he was invited to appear in a magazine programme called 'The World Goes By', produced by Ian Cox, 'introducing people of popular interest, famous or little known'. His small contribution (fee five guineas) was recorded on 16 May 1946 for transmission in the Home Service on 19 May 1946. The interviewer was David Lloyd James, and Thomas was interviewed after A. G. Street and other guests.

The present text is taken from the extant BBC script, and incorporates a few *ad lib* phrases added to the typescript in ink either in the studio or from a disc recording subsequently discarded. The title is supplied by the editor.

On Reading Poetry Aloud

DAVID LLOYD JAMES: Now last Tuesday there was an occasion in London that interested me very much. There was a public reading of poetry in which a number of our contemporary poets, as well as some professional readers or actors, took part. The programme was introduced by the Poet Laureate and in the audience were the Queen and the Princesses Elizabeth and Margaret Rose. The reader who impressed me most was Dylan Thomas. He'll be well known to you as a poet, but I don't think many of you will have heard him read. For that reason, then, I'm going to ask him to say what his feelings are about the reading of poetry.

DYLAN THOMAS: You called Street an 'arrant countryman'. I'm even worse – an 'arrant poet'.

I've bored my wife to death for years by saying (among other things that also have bored her to death) that when you listen to poetry you should always be given an idea of the 'shape' of the poem. That doesn't make much sense but I mean that, in the first place, the reader should be able to tell you by his reading where each line ends. Really what it comes down to is that all a reader of poems should do is to use *his* voice in the place of *your* eyes. Take the beginning of Tennyson's 'Maud':

> Come into the garden, Maud,
> 　For the black bat, night, has flown,
> Come into the garden, Maud,
> 　I am here at the gate alone;
> And the woodbine spices are wafted abroad
> 　And the musk of the rose is blown.

Now that's six lines of verse, and I'm being presumptuous in saying that I hope you realized how those six lines might look on the page. Is my voice being your eyes? All right, it's not, but think of the many other ways that a reader could read those direct (and obviously lyrical) lines aloud. You may, for instance, hear them read by one of those dreary, defeated, deflated, and almost dehydrated voices that are (to everybody except people who *like* poetry) quite fashionable:

[Recites the above stanza again.]

I've said already that I was being presumptuous; well, let me presume again. This time I'm going to presume that you hate what *I* hate, and I hate those professional actors who 'come slumming' into the reading of poetry. Think of the reader you dislike most: the kind of chap who thinks that a poet (and it's an extremely hard craft *being* a poet) writes a poem in a certain shape to be ranted by a shapeless actor. Here we have him – wind, fury, and undigested Shakespeare:

> O Mistress mine, where are you roaming?
> O, stay and hear! your true love's coming,
> That can sing both high and low.
> Trip no further, pretty sweeting;
> Journeys end in lovers meeting,
> Every wise man's son doth know.

Well, I hope that sounded as bombastically beastly to you as it felt to me.

DAVID LLOYD JAMES: Quite beastly enough. But seriously, Dylan, I would like you to read Blake's 'Tyger', which I thought you read superbly on Tuesday.

DYLAN THOMAS: Thank you, David. I'll do my presumptuous best. And slowly too (probably too slowly).

[Reads 'The Tyger'.]

ANNOUNCER: Dylan Thomas reading Blake's 'Tyger' brings us to the end of this week's 'World Goes By'. The other speakers were Louis Byles, Keith Caldwell and A. G. Street. They were introduced by David Lloyd James. The programme was recorded.

53

7
Poets on Poetry

Roy Campbell was the producer of a series for the Light Programme called 'Books and Writers', and on 4 June 1946 he got Dylan Thomas together with James Stephens and the chairman of the series Gerald Bullett for a 'script conference' on poetry in general. The discussion was recorded at that time, or enough was said to create a script which was then broadcast live on 18 June 1946; probably the latter, since the extant script does not seem like a spontaneous interaction, as Vernon Watkins said in the *Times Literary Supplement* (19 November 1954): 'No sympathetic contact was made between the two poets, and all that emerged from their embarrassing proximity was one irreconcilable monologue impinging upon another in a discordant friction.' Martin Armstrong in *The Listener* (27 June 1945) provides a concurring opinion:

> To the listener who has a leaning towards poetry and is humbly desirous of guidance, Dylan Thomas's esoteric attitude (with which I happen to agree) must have been wholly incomprehensible, while James Stephens's extreme critical whimsicalities, though the actual phrases were simple enough, must have left him all at sea. Why, he must have wondered, was his favourite passage from the poetry of Byron *not* poetry, and not only not poetry but not good prose either? Listening as my highbrow self, I was in turn approving, amused and exasperated. I also had the feeling that the lack of focus and direction in the discussion was due to the unlucky fact that the substance Thomas and the substance Stephens are unmixable. You know what happens when you pour sour milk into your tea. The result is nobody's cup of tea, indeed it isn't a cup of tea at all.

Poets on Poetry

GERALD BULLETT: Tonight we have with us James Stephens and Dylan Thomas. This is the third of our weekly series of discussions about books and writers, and those of you who listened will have heard James Stephens a fortnight ago. I told you then what I thought ought to be said about him, and he's been blushing ever since, so I won't repeat it. He's a poet and an Irishman. He's been writing poetry for something like forty years, and when he's not writing it he's speaking it or talking about it. Our second guest, Dylan Thomas, comes from Wales, though you'd never guess it – or would you? He leapt into fame some years before the war, and he's recognized – even by other poets, which is saying something – as the possessor of an exciting and highly original talent. These two are going to discuss poetry together, what it is, and how, and why. Or at least that's the idea. But when you get a Welshman and an Irishman together, both poets and both good talkers, you never know what'll happen.

Now of course poetry can't be defined: it can only be pointed at. But, just to start the ball rolling, let's begin with something easier. The relation, if any, between poetry and verse. The popular idea has always been that all verse is poetry and all poetry is verse – in fact that the two words are interchangeable?

DYLAN THOMAS: That of course is nonsense.

JAMES STEPHENS: Yet there's a modicum of truth in it. A very large part of the produced verse that we have is just prose, shaped and quickened and vivified. A good deal of rhetoric passes for poetry,

56

because it is written in verse form – 'Roll on thou deep and dark blue ocean, roll, a thousand fleets sail over thee, Man marks the earth with ruin: the something or other that thunder strike the walls of rock-bound cities, bidding nations quake and monarchs tremble in their own dug-outs,' and all the rest of it – it's just excellent prose, no secret about it, no music, just measure and vehemence. Or the Macaulay ballads, 'But with a noise like thunder fell every loosened beam, and like a dam the mighty wreck lay stretched athwart the stream,' and the rest of it. It's magnificent, said the Frenchman one time, but it isn't war. So, with a vast area of our printed verse – some of it is very good indeed, but it's prose, disguised in the casts-off of verse. Get a copy of the longer poems of the English. More than three-quarters of these are prose, and bad prose at that.

DYLAN THOMAS: 'Paradise Lost'? 'Ancient Mariner'? 'Don Juan', which is really all good *verse*? But anyway, we want to know what poetry is. All I know is that it is memorable words-in-cadence which move and excite me emotionally. And, once you've got the hang of it, it should always be better when read aloud than when read silently with the eyes. Always.

JAMES STEPHENS: Poetry does two things, according to Keats. It must astonish and delight. If it doesn't do both, it does neither.

GERALD BULLETT: It doesn't consist of fine sentiments or great thoughts. It's something existing in its own right, something made out of words, a new creation – and the magic of it has something to do, hasn't it, with elements that are inherent in human speech – measure and cadence and so on? I don't expect an answer, but I should like to ask whether the *lyrical* quality is or is not the very essence of poetry?

JAMES STEPHENS: The poet is a fellow who can take hold of a thought and make it *sing*. Anyone who can compose to the measure of some kind of a dance is a poet.

DYLAN THOMAS: I hope you're listening, Tin Pan Alley!

> O Soo
> I'm blue as blue
> baby

I love yoo
Maybe
Maybe
oo
love me ...

JAMES STEPHENS: Nevertheless, I repeat, anyone who can compose to the measure of some kind of dance is a poet. All who write epics, and elegies, and lyrics and epi-and-prothalamiums, the wise-guys who write songs for music-halls, verses for Christmas cards, and mottoes for crackers – all these are poets, unless, of course, you can point out that they are just disguising prose in verse. Some of them are good, some not so good, and some are no good, but they are all of that Mystery, they are of that Licence. They are poets, which those Macaulays and people are not. The bits of things they give cannot be given at all in prose, or in any other form than even the 'bad' poet has given it. Not even Shakespeare could tackle twinkle, twinkle little star: he could not rewrite it, or improve it, or do anything whatever to it except, perhaps, to deplore it. Lots of poetry is poetry, but is no good.

DYLAN THOMAS: I'm not going to argue with all that. Sometimes I just sits and thinks. I agree that music-hall songs can be good poetry – so can limericks, drawing- or tap-room – but I don't think cracker-mottoes etc. ever have been. I think, Stephens, you must be pulling my (comparatively) young leg. The younger generation used to be called, by their elders, flippant. Not any longer. It's we, now, who deprecate their flippancy. I feel rather like the little pedantically reproving girl addressing Matthew Arnold in Max Beerbohm's picture: 'Why, Uncle Matthew, oh why, will not you be always wholly serious?' I'm all for taking the *serious* nonsense out of one's appreciation of poetry; I hate, as much as you do, the hushed voice and hats-off attitude, but I don't like the double-bluffing approach either that pretends to think that 'I'm one of the ruins that Cromwell knocked about a bit' is better poetry than, say, the serious, unfashionable work of Cowper or Francis Thompson. It's just very different poetry.

GERALD BULLETT: As Chairman, I'm not supposed to have any

opinions on anything. But I feel bound to say at this point that I think it's very perverse – and very confusing for the ordinary listener – to call such things poetry at all – such things as 'I'm one of the ruins that Cromwell knocked about a bit', and the like. I'm not being snobbish about it either. I'm merely asking that words should be used in their common meaning. Auden, I remember, some years ago brought out an anthology in which

> I have no pain, dear mother, now,
> But Oh I am so dry,
> Connect me to a brewery
> And leave me here to die –

was put next to an exquisite lyric by Yeats – the idea being, I suppose, that both equally belonged to the category of poetry. That, I think, is nonsense. One may enjoy music-hall rhythms, now and again you get something very entertaining in that line, but why muddle the man in the street by pretending that they belong to the same category of art as Keats's 'Nightingale' and Milton's 'Paradise Lost'? Things aren't poetry just because we happen to like them. One may like ginger pop, but that's no reason for pretending it's the same thing as Sauterne or Montrachet. Poetry, I suggest, is something that happens when language is used with so high a degree of exactness as to express something otherwise inexpressible.

DYLAN THOMAS: Ultimately, the magic of poetry is indefinable. Almost anything one says about it is as true and important as anything else that anyone else has said. Some people react *physically* to the magic of poetry, to the moments, that is, of authentic revelation, of the communication, the *sharing*, at its highest level, of personal experience; they say they feel a twanging at their tear-ducts, or a prickling of the scalp, or a tickling of the spine, or tremors in what they hope is their heart. Others say that they have a kind of sort of a vague feeling somewhere that 'this is the real stuff.' Others claim that their 'purely æsthetic emotion' was induced by certain assonances and alliterations. And some are content merely to say, as they said of the first cinematographic picture, 'By God, it moves.' And so, of course, by God it does, for that is another name for the magic beyond definition.

59

JAMES STEPHENS: Let's get down to it. Yes, there's a transforming that takes place in poetry. It is transformed right away from prose. AE (George Russell) once said to me – Poetry is written on the Mount of Transfiguration. Fine poetry sometimes subsists on nothing. When Chaucer says, 'The barren isle standing in the sea' he is next door to saying nothing, but I want to keep that line for ever. Or Marvell, with his 'Annihilating all that's made to a green thought in a green shade.' When Blake says 'Ah Sunflower, weary of time,' I'm satisfied that he is where he wants to go. Or 'Speak silence with thy glimmering eyes, and wash the dusk with silver.' There is no sense in it, but who wants sense when he can get poetry instead? So, also 'Darkness falls from the air: queens have died young and fair: dust hath closed Helen's eyes.' Anyone can say, well, what about it? Why there's nothing about it, except that something or other, quite unnamed and unnameable, has been transformed and is here only by grace.

DYLAN THOMAS: In other words, the magic in a poem is always accidental. No poet would labour intensively upon the intricate craft of poetry unless he hoped that, suddenly, the accident of magic would occur. He *has* to agree with Chesterton that the miraculous thing about miracles is that they *do* sometimes happen. And the best poem is that whose worked-upon unmagical passages come closest, in texture and intensity, to those moments of magical accident.

GERALD BULLETT: Let's have a few more examples, shall we?

JAMES STEPHENS: When the Abbé Bremond wrote his famous book, *Pure Poetry*, he gave seven examples of pure poetry from the French, and all the other examples, millions of 'em, were from the English. 'And through the glass window shines the sun, how should I love, and I so young? The bailey beareth the bell away, the lily, the lily, the rose I lay.' The most exciting and incomprehensible verse in English. 'Is she kind as she is fair? For beauty lives with kindness.' 'By shallow rivers, to whose falls melodious birds sing madrigals.' 'Fair love, let us go play: apples be ripe in my garden' and in one line love is switched from Piccadilly Circus to the Garden of Eden. But there are so many, and every line of them original, and unique, and properly inexpressible.

DYLAN THOMAS: And there's this to be said too. Poetry, to a poet, is the most rewarding work in the world. A good poem is a contribution to reality. The world is never the same once a good poem has been added to it. A good poem helps to change the shape and significance of the universe, helps to extend everyone's knowledge of himself and the world around him.

GERALD BULLETT: And a man who is himself a poet, people like you, Dylan Thomas, and Stephens, have a double interest in poetry. They make it and they read it. They're at both ends at once, the giving end and the receiving end.

JAMES STEPHENS: Let me tell you a story, It's a true one, but good, for all that.

GERALD BULLETT: Go ahead.

JAMES STEPHENS: I called on Yeats one day: he was in a bad temper. He pointed to a pile of books and explained that he wasn't going to read them, or do anything about them. He waved his arms, 'People think,' he complained, 'that I love poetry, and that I must be very glad to get some. I don't love poetry,' he went on: 'Why should I? It's the hardest work in the world, the most exacting, and the least rewarding that any intelligent person can undertake. Moreover,' he went on, 'I'm not interested in the least in other men's verse, I've trouble enough with my own. It's like those love stories in novels: as if we all didn't get misery enough out of our own love-lunacies without having to weep and wail about the fictitious love-yowling of people that never existed. I can't conceive,' said Yeats, 'how any working poet can take the smallest interest in anyone else's verse, and besides, out of any hundred poets ninety nine and a half of them are no good, and the whole hundred of them despise, and even loathe, every other poet that lives.'

GERALD BULLETT: Just a minute, Dylan Thomas wants to cut in.

DYLAN THOMAS: I can only believe those were casual, throw-away remarks, little spurts of annoyance never intended to be remembered. Anyway, he contradicts himself in his essays and letters any number of times, and in his rather erratic *Oxford Book of Modern Verse.*

61

JAMES STEPHENS: Yeats was in a very bad temper: 'Besides,' he said, 'England, Ireland and Scotland hate poetry and hate poets, and they only buy the stuff as table-ornaments anyway. Do people buy your stuff, Stephens?' he enquired. 'Oh, yes,' I answered: 'the whole forty-two millions of 'em clubbed together and bought nine of my books last year. In fact,' I went on proudly, 'no year has passed in which I haven't made from seven and six to twelve bob: beat that if you can, W. B.! There was,' I continued reminiscently, 'one marvellous year in which I knocked fifteen shillings out of my fellow men.' These intimate truths put Yeats into a wonderfully good temper.

DYLAN THOMAS: I think there's an inverted snobbery – and a suggestion of bad logic – in being proud of the fact that one's poems sell very badly. *Of course*, nearly *every* poet wants his poems to be read by as many people as possible. Craftsmen don't put their products in the attic. And contempt for the public, which is composed of potential readers, is contempt for the profound usefulness of your own craft. Go on thinking that you don't *need* to be read, and you'll find that it may become quite true: no one *will* feel the need to read it, because it is written for yourself alone; and the public won't feel any impulse to gatecrash such a private party. Moreover, to take no notice of the work of your contemporaries is to disregard a whole *vital* part of the world you live in, and necessarily to devitalise your own work: to narrow its scope and possibilities: to be half dead as you write. What's more, a poet is –

GERALD BULLETT: I don't want to interrupt but we have about two minutes to go.

DYLAN THOMAS: What's more, a poet is a poet for such a very tiny bit of his life; for the rest, he is a human being, one of whose responsibilities is to know and feel, as much as he can, all that is moving around and within him, so that his poetry, when he comes to write it, can be his attempt at an expression of the summit of man's experience on this very peculiar and, in 1946, this apparently hell-bent earth.

8
Poems of Wonder

'Time for Verse' was a long-running series, edited by Patric Dickinson for the BBC Home Service. For No. 39, Thomas selected a half-hour of poetry on a theme of his own choice, 'Poems of Wonder', as the announcer's introduction entitled the anthology. Rehearsal and broadcast were on 14 July 1946. Thomas's fee was fifteen guineas.

Poems of Wonder

ANNOUNCER: Time for Verse: the poems tonight have been chosen by Dylan Thomas, and he calls it a selection of poems of wonder.

NARRATOR: Wonder is defined as the emotion that you feel when your expectation or your experience is surpassed; and as a feeling of excitement at the inexplicable. But wonder in poems can be more than that: it can be an expression of what you always knew or felt but could never express; and it can be an expression of what you never knew but always wanted to express. It can be a way of saying something so old you had forgotten it; or so new you could not be expected to remember it. It can be a revelation of an innocence you have outgrown; or of a wisdom you have not achieved.

A poem of wonder can be merely the poet's own statement of what is wonderful to him, and what is wonderful to him might be to you simply dull or simply dazzling; it can describe, at second hand, the wonder of another person; or, at wonderful first hand, another world. In this small, simple, spoken anthology are several kinds of wonder; and the poems themselves must try to define for you some of its many meanings. Here, from Thomas Traherne's 'Centuries of Meditations', is the wonder of a child looking for the first time at the world.

READER: The corn was orient and immortal wheat, which never should be reaped, nor was ever sown. I thought it had stood from everlasting to everlasting. The dust and stones of the street were as precious as gold: the gates were at first the end of the world. The green trees when I saw them first through one of the gates

64

transported and ravished me, their sweetness and unusual beauty made my heart to leap, and almost mad with ecstasy, they were such strange and wonderful things. The men! O what venerable and reverend creatures did the aged seem! Immortal cherubims! And young men glittering and sparkling angels, and maids strange seraphic pieces of life and beauty! Boys and girls tumbling in the street, and playing, were moving jewels. I knew not that they were born or should die; but all things abided eternally as they were in their proper places. Eternity was manifest in the Light of the Day, and something infinite behind everything appeared: which talked with my expectation and moved my desire. The city seemed to stand in Eden, or to be built in Heaven. The streets were mine, the temple was mine, the people were mine, their clothes and gold and silver were mine, as much as their sparkling eyes, fair skins and ruddy faces. The skies were mine, and so were the sun and moon and stars, and all the world was mine; and I the only spectator and enjoyer of it. I knew no churlish proprieties, nor bounds, nor divisions; but all proprieties and divisions were mine: all treasures and the possessors of them.

NARRATOR: Here, in the 'Nurse's Song' of William Blake is the wonderful happiness of children in the evening – playing before bedtime.

READER: When the voices of children are heard on the green,
            And laughing is heard on the hill,
            My heart is at rest within my breast
            And everything else is still.

            'Then come home, my children, the sun is gone down,
            And the dews of night arise;
            Come, come, leave off play, and let us away
            Till the morning appears in the skies.'

            'No, no, let us play, for it is yet day,
            And we cannot go to sleep;
            Besides, in the sky the little birds fly,
            And the hills are all covered with sheep.'

'Well, well, go and play, till the light fades away,
And then go home to bed.'
The little ones leaped and shouted and laugh'd
And all the hills echoed.

NARRATOR: The lines you will hear next are from Blake's prophetic book 'Milton'.

READER: Thou perceivest the Flowers put forth their precious odours;
And none can tell how from so small a centre comes such
    sweets,
Forgetting that within that centre Eternity expands
Its ever-during doors, that Og and Anak fiercely guard.
First, ere the morning breaks, joy opens in the flowery
    bosoms,
Joy even to tears, which the Sun rising dries; first the Wild
    Thyme
And Meadow-Sweet, downy and soft, waving among the
    reeds,
Light springing on the air, lead the sweet dance; they wake
The Honeysuckle sleeping on the Oak; the flaunting beauty
Revels along upon the wind; the White-thorn, lovely May,
Opens her many lovely eyes; listening the Rose still sleeps
None dare to wake her; soon she bursts her crimson-cur-
    tain'd bed
And comes forth in the majesty of Beauty. Every flower,
The Pink, the Jessamine, the Wallflower, the Carnation,
The Jonquil, the mild Lily opes her heavens; every Tree
And Flower and Herb soon fill the air with an innumerable
    dance,
Yet all in order sweet and lovely.

NARRATOR: And now a New Year Carol. Nobody knows when this was written. Walter de la Mare has said, 'It must be as old as the dewponds on the Downs.' Such a carol was wont to be sung by five or six men, with a fiddle or flute or clarionet.

READER: Here we bring new water
    from the well so clear,
For to worship God with,
    this happy New Year.
Sing levy dew, sing levy dew,
    the water and the wine;
The seven bright gold wires
    and the bugles that do shine.

Sing reign of Fair Maid,
    with gold upon her too, –
Open you the West Door,
    and turn the Old Year go.

Sing reign of Fair Maid,
    with gold upon her chin, –
Open you the East Door,
    and let the New Year in.
Sing levy dew, sing levy dew,
    the water and the wine;
The seven bright gold wires
    and the bugles they do shine.

NARRATOR: Next, Robert Bridges' poem, 'London Snow' – though not quite all of it.

READER: When men were all asleep the snow came flying,
    In large white flakes falling on the city brown,
    Stealthily and perpetually settling and loosely lying,
        Hushing the latest traffic of the drowsy town;
    Deadening, muffling, stifling its murmurs failing;
    Lazily and incessantly floating down and down:
        Silently sifting and veiling road, roof and railing;
    Hiding difference, making unevenness even,
    Into angles and crevices softly drifting and sailing.
        All night it fell, and when full inches seven
    It lay in the depth of its uncompacted lightness,
    The clouds blew off from a high and frosty heaven;
        And all woke earlier for the unaccustomed brightness
    Of the winter dawning, the strange unheavenly glare:

The eye marvelled – marvelled at the dazzling whiteness;
   The ear hearkened to the stillness of the solemn air;
No sound of wheel rumbling nor of foot falling,
And the busy morning cries came thin and spare.
   Then boys I heard, as they went to school, calling,
They gathered up the crystal manna to freeze
Their tongues with tasting, their hands with snowballing;
   Or rioted in a drift, plunging up to the knees;
Or peering up from under the white-mossed wonder,
'O look at the trees!' they cried, 'O look at the trees!'

NARRATOR: And that leads us to another snow-poem: Walter de la Mare's childhood poem – 'Winter'.

READER:
        Green Mistletoe!
        Oh, I remember now
        A dell of snow,
        Frost on the bough;
        None there but I:
        Snow, snow, and a wintry sky.

        None there but I,
        And footprints one by one,
        Zigzaggedly,
        Where I had run;
        Where shrill and powdery
        A robin sat in the tree.

        And he whistled sweet;
        And I in the crusted snow
        With snow-clubbed feet
        Jigged to and fro,
        Till, from the day,
        The rose-light ebbed away.

        And the robin flew
        Into the air, the air,
        The white mist through;
        And small and rare
        The night-frost fell
        Into the calm and misty dell.

And the dusk gathered low,
And the silver moon and stars
On the frozen snow
Drew taper bars,
Kindled winking fires
In the hooded briers.

And the sprawling Bear
Growled deep in the sky;
And Orion's hair
Streamed sparkling by:
But the North sighed low:
'Snow, snow, more snow!'

NARRATOR: Let us hear some Blake again. Here is 'Vala in Lower
Paradise' from the 'Four Zoas'.

READER: So saying, she arose and walked round her beautiful house;
And then from her white door she look'd to see her bleating
    lambs,
But her flocks were gone up from beneath the trees into
    the hills.

'I see the hand that leadeth me doth also lead my flocks.'
She went up to her flocks, and turned oft to see her shining
    house.
She stopp'd to drink of the clear spring, and eat the grapes
    and apples;
She bore the fruits in her lap; she gather'd flowers for her
    bosom.
She call'd to her flocks, saying: 'Follow me, O my flocks!'

They follow'd her to the silent valley beneath the spreading
    trees,
And on the river's margin she ungirdled her golden girdle;
She stood in the river and view'd herself within the wat'ry
    glass
And her bright hair was wet with the waters. She rose up
    from the river,

And as she rose her eyes were open'd to the world of waters;
She saw Tharmas sitting upon the rocks beside the wavy
sea.

NARRATOR: And now a poem by a distinguished living American,
John Crowe Ransom: 'Little Boy Blue'.

READER: He rubbed his eyes and wound the silver horn.
Then the continuum was cracked and torn
With tumbling imps of music being born.

The blowzy sheep lethargic on the ground
Suddenly burned where no fire could be found
And straight up stood their fleeces every pound.

The old bellwether rose and rang his bell,
The seven-days' lambs went skipping and skipped well,
And Baa Baa Baa, the flock careered pellmell.

The yellow cows that milked the savoury cud
Propped on the green grass or the yellow mud
Felt such a tingle in their lady blood,

They ran and tossed their hooves and horns of blue
And jumped the fence and gambolled kangaroo,
Divinely singing as they wandered Moo.

A plague on such a shepherd of the sheep
That careless boy with pretty cows to keep!
With such a burden I should never sleep.

But when his notes had run around the sky,
When they proceeded to grow faint and die,
He stuffed his horn with straw and put it by.

And when the legs were tired beneath the sheep
And there were spent and sleepy cows to keep,
He rubbed his eyes again and went to sleep.

NARRATOR: Nearly everybody who reads poetry has read Keats'
'Belle Dame Sans Merci' at one time or another. But I wonder
whether people read it much or listen to it, *now*:

70

I

Ah, what can ail thee, wretched wight,
  Alone and palely loitering;
The sedge is wither'd from the lake,
  And no birds sing.

II

Ah, what can ail thee, wretched wight,
  So haggard and so woe-begone?
The squirrel's granary is full,
  And the harvest's done.

III

I see a lilly on thy brow,
  With anguish moist and fever dew;
And on thy cheek a fading rose
  Fast withereth too.

IV

I met a lady in the meads
  Full beautiful, a faery's child;
Her hair was long, her foot was light,
  And her eyes were wild.

V

I set her on my pacing steed,
  And nothing else saw all day long;
For sideways would she lean, and sing
  A faery's song.

VI

I made a garland for her head,
  And bracelets too, and fragrant zone;
She look'd at me as she did love,
  And made sweet moan.

71

VII

She found me roots of relish sweet,
 And honey wild, and manna dew;
And sure in language strange she said,
 I love thee true.

VIII

She took me to her elfin grot,
 And there she gaz'd and sighed deep,
And there I shut her wild sad eyes –
 So kiss'd to sleep.

IX

And there we slumber'd on the moss,
 And there I dream'd, ah woe betide,
The latest dream I ever dream'd
 On the cold hill side.

X

I saw pale kings, and princes too,
 Pale warriors, death-pale were they all;
Who cry'd – 'La belle Dame sans merci
 Hath thee in thrall!'

XI

I saw their starv'd lips in the gloam
 With horrid warning gaped wide,
And I awoke, and found me here
 On the cold hill side.

XII

And this is why I sojourn here
 Alone and palely loitering,
Though the sedge is wither'd from the lake,
 And no birds sing.

NARRATOR: And lastly, one of the strangest fragments of poetry in
   the English language!

READER: The maidens came
          When I was in my mother's bower;
          I had all that I would.
             The bailey beareth the bell away;
             The lily, the rose, the rose I lay.
          The silver is white, red is the gold;
          The robes they lay in gold.
             The bailey beareth the bell away;
             The lily, the rose, the rose I lay.
          And through the glass windows shines the sun.
          How should I love, and I so young?
             The bailey beareth the bell away;
             The lily, the lily, the rose I lay.

9
The Londoner

In January 1945 Thomas proposed to a publisher a book about the streets of London, 'to take the life of the streets from twelve noon to twelve midnight' (*Letters* p. 537). Eighteen months later, the producer of the series 'This is London', R. D. Smith, gave him the chance to put the idea into a radio drama, a day in the life of a family in busy Shepherd's Bush, including many street scenes. Beginning and ending with the dreams of the characters in sleep, Thomas's 'The Londoner' is like a trial run for *Under Milk Wood*.

The play was rehearsed and recorded on 15 July 1946, and relayed on the African Service the same day, and in the General Overseas Service and North American Service in the four days following. Thomas received forty guineas for the script and seven guineas for reading the narrator's part. Laurence Gilliam, Head of Features, wrote to Thomas that 'The Londoner' was 'a most sensitive and successful piece of radio' (*Letters* p. 598).

The Londoner

ANNOUNCER: 'When a man is tired of London,' said Dr. Johnson, 'he is tired of life, for there is in London all that life can afford.' We present the last in our series, 'This is London'. 'The Londoner', written and narrated by Dylan Thomas and produced by R. D. Smith.

[BOW BELLS]

NARRATOR: A day in the life of Mr and Mrs Jackson, Ted and Lily, of number forty nine Montrose Street, Shepherds Bush, London, West 12.

QUESTIONER: Where is Shepherds Bush?

NARRATOR: It is a busy inner-suburban centre, on one of the main west roads out of London. It is part of the borough of Hammersmith. It is a difficult district to describe, because it is neither a part of the mass of central London nor is it an outer suburb with its own separate identity, it is, rather, a ...

QUESTIONER: And what is Montrose Street? What does it look like?

VOICE OF AN EXPERT: It is a grey-bricked street of one hundred houses. Built in 1890. Two bedrooms, a front room and a kitchen. Bathrooms were built into less than half of the houses in 1912. A scullery and a backyard. Rent 28 shillings. Too cold in the winter, too hot in the summer. Ugly, inconvenient, and infinitely depressing.

VOICE OF AN OLD RESIDENT: No, no. You got it all wrong. It's a nice, lively street. There's all the shops you want at one end, and there's pubs at both ends. Mightn't be much to look at, but there's always things going on, there's always something to see, buses and trams

76

and lorries and prams and kids and dogs and dogfights sometimes and ...

QUESTIONER: And who are Mr and Mrs Jackson, Ted and Lily? How old are they? What do they look like?

ALFRED: Ted works for a builder's firm, Sedgman and Parker. Him and me – I'm his mate, Alfred – we're demolishing air-raid shelters. He's about thirty five. He looks like ... well, he's about average height, he's got kind of darkish brown hair, it's not *really* dark though, and kind of ordinary brownish eyes as far as I can remember, he looks like ... well, he looks like Ted Jackson.

MRS COOLEY: Lily's what's known as a housewife. That's what you put on all the forms you got to sign before you can call your name your own and then you can't. Housewife! Slaving morn noon and night and never a word of gratitude. And all for *men*! She's about thirty two. She's fair. I suppose some men'd call her pretty but then of course I'm a woman and I live next door. Oh, she'd pass in a crowd ... she's very sweet, I will say that for her ...

QUESTIONER: Are there any children?

SCHOOLTEACHER: Two. They both attend the school of which I am head-teacher. Carole, aged 12. Len, aged 10.

NARRATOR: It's nearly half past six on a summer morning. Montrose Street is awake.

[NOISE OF CARS AND LORRIES]

NARRATOR: But most of the houses are still sleeping. In number 49, all is quiet. Lily Jackson is dreaming.

[MUSIC]

LILY: Ooh, what a beautiful dress ... like the one Ingrid Bergman was wearing in what-was-the-name ... And the music! Lovelier than oh-I-can't-remember, the one with the violin and the big sad eyes. Look, they're walking down the aisle, white as Christmas. There's lights all over the place like victory night. Oh, it's all changing. They're dancing in a kind of palace now ... Look, there's Mrs Cooley next door with a dustcap on ... They're singing ... I'm there too ... I'm dancing on the falling snow ... Where's Ted ... where's Ted?

77

[MUSIC]

NARRATOR: Ted Jackson is dreaming.

TED: 'All right then, come outside' ... 'Don't you go outside with Ted Jackson he's champion of the world' ... right left right left short-arm jab ... why am I lying here in the rain behind the barbed wire ... there's a single drop of blood on Lily's photo ... Right left right left right uppercut ... Mr Jackson, may I present you with this road-drill made out of pure gold in honour of ... There goes the bell for the millionth round ...

[ALARM CLOCK RINGS]

NARRATOR: Number forty nine Montrose Street is awake. Lily Jackson is in the kitchen.

[KITCHEN NOISES: NOISE OF FRYING]

LILY: ... ever such a funny dream, Ted ... oh dear, where's the teacaddy gone, I know I put it down ... here it is ... I was in a kind of church and then, you know what it's like when you're dreaming, it wasn't a church it was a kind of palace and Mrs Cooley next door was there in a dustcap and a bathing-costume ...

TED: That old barrage balloon ...

LILY: Go on, you know you'd like to have seen her ...

TED: I'd like to see Mrs Cooley floating in with a couple of real eggs and some fried liver and ...

LILY: Here's your tea ...

TED: ... and sausages that aren't made out of old newspaper and minced shaving brushes ... Pictures tonight?

LILY: If I can get Mrs Cooley to keep an eye on the house ...

TED: Mrs Cooley'll be living here soon ... Keep her moored in the backyard ...

LILY: ... and then I was dancing in the palace, in my dream I mean, and I said to Mrs Cooley 'Where's Ted?' and then before I knew where I was we were all in somewhere like Kew Gardens only I saw the 11 bus too ... Oh, I'm losing everything this morning. Wish we had a nice modern kitchen you could put your hand on anything.

[SCRAPING OF CHAIR]

LILY: Don't forget your sandwiches. 'Bye, darling ...

TED (*at door*):   Hope *my* bus don't go through Kew Gardens ...

NARRATOR: And he catches the workman's bus ... Who's the conductor this morning? Tom Fletcher? Charlie Preston?

[DOOR SLAMMING   TRAFFIC   BUS DRAWING UP]

TED: Morning, Charlie ...

CONDUCTOR: Morning, Ted ...

[BUS MOVING OFF   BUS NOISE BACKGROUND   MEN'S VOICES IN BUS]

WORKMAN: Black Boy closed again last night.

ALFRED: ... Get their supplies Wednesday ... Open seven to nine every night except Monday and Tuesday.

TED: You should open an information bureau, Alfred, shouldn't he?

WORKMAN: I walked a mile and a half for a shandy ... and no fags either ...

ALFRED: Always get fags in the Carpenters' Arms ...

TED: Information supplied free about every pub from here to Barnes.

ALFRED: Well you got to look after yourself haven't you?

WORKMAN: And only *half* a shandy too ...

NARRATOR: There are different kinds of worries in Lily's kitchen.

[KITCHEN NOISES]

LILY (*at door*):   Come on, Len. Come on, Carole. Breakfast's ready.

CAROLE (*from upstairs*):   Mummy, Len's floating ships in the basin.

LILY: Come on both of you or it'll get cold ...

CAROLE (*from upstairs*):   Mummy, Len's throwing water at me ...

LILY: Stop it at once, Len ... Oh, dear.

[NOISE CHILDREN RUNNING DOWNSTAIRS]

CAROLE: And he said a rude word and he said ...

LILY: Sit down at once, both of you, I don't want to hear what Len said and I don't want to hear anybody telling tales either ... You're one as bad as the other ...

LEN: Tell tale, tell tale ...

LILY: Eat up now, you're late ...

CAROLE: Mummy, why can't I wear my hair long and straight and half of it right across my face so that I look out mysterious...

LILY: You've got nice curly hair, you don't want to make it straight and you don't want to look mysterious either ...

LEN: If Carole's going to have her hair all silly like that, can I go bald then ...

LILY: Eat your breakfast and don't talk so daft.

LEN: Bald like Uncle Vernon ...

LILY: If Uncle Vernon heard you talk like that ... and eat properly, Carole, don't put your finger in your porridge, what d'you think spoons are for?

LEN: Eating jelly.

LEN (*at door*):   Goodbye, mummy.

CAROLE: 'Bye, mummy.

LILY: Goodbye, darlings ... Don't run across the road.

[DOOR SLAMMING]

LILY: Oh dear, sometimes I think they'll be the death of me if they didn't look so pretty when they were being naughty. Not that they're really very pretty I suppose, to anyone else except Ted and me: of course, Carole's got very good colouring and *lovely* hair, and she's got quite the sweetest eyes I ever saw, and good features, too: and of course boys are different, I mean they don't *have* to be goodlooking, but there isn't any boy in the street that's half as intelligent and he's got such a *wicked* smile ... Oh dear, I suppose there never *were* such children ... all mothers are the same. Len looks like Ted must have looked when he was a little boy. Just like in that photograph his mother showed me, the one she wouldn't part with for anything, in a sailor's suit with a funny hat and smiling just like he does now when he's trying to get his own way ...

MRS COOLEY (*off*):   Are you in, dear?

LILY: Oh come in, Mrs Cooley, I was standing here all by myself daydreaming and all the washing-up to be done and housework and shopping and everything ...

MRS COOLEY: The back was open so I just dropped in for a moment. Mrs Mackenzie twenty three's gone to hospital, I saw the ambulance.

LILY: Poor Mrs Mackenzie ...

MRS COOLEY: Well, my dear, we all knew it wasn't long before she'd got to, and I was saying to Mrs Mizler, if there's one thing you can't afford to play with, that's your health, and the way Mrs Mackenzie was going on everyone knew it was only a matter of months ... I told her at the beginning of the summer ... I said, pains like you're suffering, Mrs Mackenzie, aren't natural ... but there, the very next day she was going to the West End for a little jaunt with three children under seven and Mrs Walker from King Street who should know better ...

LILY: Poor Mrs Mackenzie. Is anyone looking after the children now she's in hospital?

MRS COOLEY: That's just what I'm going over to see myself ... but I thought I'd drop in for a moment and tell you the news and ask you if you could spare some salt until tomorrow, there's not a pinch in the house and really I can't go up to the shops now with having to look at poor Mrs Mackenzie's children and everything and as I thought you wouldn't mind ...

NARRATOR: Of course they don't mind in the kitchens of Montrose street ... sharing and sharing alike with bits of things ... with keeping an eye on the children ... with trying to keep life friendly and straight. They're women working together ... just as Ted is working now, with Alfred and Stanley and the rest of them ... working on demolition.

[NOISE OF DRILLS AND DEMOLITION FADE NOISE INTO BACK-GROUND]

ALFRED: Gives you a funny feeling, knocking down air-raid shelters. I helped to build this one.

WORKMAN: Looks a bit ricketty, too ...

TED: I used to make wireless sets and as soon as I'd finished 'em I'd pull 'em to bits. Always. Must have made scores of sets and never listened in more than a couple of minutes.

ALFRED: That's different.

TED: Course it's different. I used to try to get Moscow and South America on sets I made. Only got Germany on air-raid shelters. But I learned something new all the time I was fiddling about with coils and condensers and things. There was some point pulling them to bits and starting again ...

[A CRASH]

ALFRED: One for old Hitler ...

[ANOTHER CRASH]

WORKMAN: One for old Franco ...

TED: ... Hope we all learned something new now. Knock all the shelters and pillboxes to bits, and start all over again. But not to build new shelters. We've had enough of that.

ALFRED: Don't no need no shelters for atom-bombs. Give me a nice old fashioned 200 pounder.

TED: If a bomb had your name on it, you had it coming and that's all. Atom-bombs got everyruddybody's name on 'em, that's the difference. But there aren't going to be any atom bombs. There can't be. It doesn't make sense. We're not children.

ALFRED: I feel young enough sometimes, on a Saturday night.

TED: No, I mean, *we're* the Government, aren't we. It's we who got to say, 'No, there's not going to be any funny business any more.' And just *see* that there isn't either. If people all over the world say, 'We don't want atom bombs, we want all the things that atomic energy can make not what it can bust up,' then that's how it's going to be.

ALFRED: You shouldn't talk politics when you're working ...

TED: If a man can't talk politics when he's got a pneumatic drill in his hand, when can he then ...

[UP NOISE OF DRILLS ETC., MUSIC WHILE YOU WORK]

NARRATOR: Mrs Lily Jackson is working too.

LILY: Empty the teapot – must have a new one –
only this morning the kitchen was *so* neat –
soak the frying-pan – wish it wasn't fish –
oh *why* do people have to eat –
Why do men put fag ends in their saucers –
knives and forks and plates and cups –
think of all the breakfasts in Montrose Street –
and think of all the washing-ups –
I won't scrub the floor this morning –

I wish the plumber'd come about the sink –
I'll just sweep the breadcrumbs up and then –
another cup of tea I think ...
Women shouldn't grumble, only to themselves,
Mother always used to say –
now it's make the beds and tidy up the bedrooms –
oh, the same thing every day –
clear up after the children –
they fling their clothes *any*where –
and the *mess* they make in the bathroom –
I think there's time to do my hair –
Wish I had a proper hair-do –
found a grey hair yesterday –
troubles and grey hairs never come singly
mother always used to say –
And now it's nearly time for shopping –
Let's see, is my hat all right? –
and the new points begin *next* Monday –
have a look in my purse – bit tight
but I *think* I'll manage if I'm careful –
hope Ted's not tired of stews –
got my basket and the doorkey? –
and now I'm all ready for the queues.

[NOISE OF TRAFFIC WOMEN'S VOICES BACKGROUND: CHATTER]

1ST SHOPPER: Last week there was bananas in Humphries ... saw
them with my own eyes ...
2ND SHOPPER: Keeps 'em for his regular customers, so he says ...
1ST SHOPPER: All gone when I got there, of course ...
2ND SHOPPER: If I'm not a regular customer, Mr Humphries, I said,
who is then? Mrs Miniver?
1ST SHOPPER: That's right, dear ...
3RD SHOPPER: Pity the men can't queue a bit ...
1ST SHOPPER: How long you been queuing, dear?
3RD SHOPPER: I've been here half an hour.
2ND SHOPPER: I been queuing for six and a half years.

4TH SHOPPER: You're right there, too, why shouldn't the men do their bit of queuing? They eat most don't they?

LILY: Oh, men have got to line up too, give them their dues ... buses, and tobacco, and ...

2ND SHOPPER: It's all right for you to be so considerate, you're two in front of me ...

1ST SHOPPER: Still, mustn't grumble ...

2ND SHOPPER: Ho! Mustn't grumble, hear that, Mrs Armstrong! Who's grumbling? Everything's *lovely*. Mind your cabbage, Flo ...

[UP NOISE OF WOMEN GRUMBLING]

NARRATOR: But you must be polite in the grocer's ...

LILY: How much does all that come to, Mr Brookes?

MR BROOKES: Let's see now – that'll be ...

LILY: I don't suppose it's worth asking if you've got such a thing as a jelly, Mr Brookes? You know what children are in this hot weather and ...

MR BROOKES: Show me a jelly, Mrs Jackson, anywhere in the shop, you can have it, you can have it free, I'd be *pleased* to see a jelly, I'd be *delighted* ... do you know, Mrs Jackson, I'm not telling you a word of a lie when I tell you my wife's *mad* for a jelly but ...

NARRATOR: And so on, and so on ... and – on to the butcher's.

BUTCHER: Offal, Mrs Jackson? Now you're asking. As far as *I* can see, animals don't possess no insides these days, worth mentioning ...

[NOISE OF ROAD-DRILLS ETC.   FADE]

NARRATOR: Ted Jackson's gang has broken off for lunch. They are sitting in Joe's Eating House: the Komfy. It is one long, narrow room, opening on the street, with cubicles on each side, and in each cubicle is a wooden bench and a plain wooden table. On the walls, pre-war notices which nobody has bothered to take down, announce unobtainable food. The men are drinking large cups of dark brown tea, their parcels and tin boxes open beside them.

ALFRED: My daughter says, what'll happen when there's television in every house? Won't there be any more cinemas then? My daughter says, when her young man asks her to go to the pictures, all they'll do is go and sit in the parlour with his old man and the missus. How can they hold hands then?

TED: You tell your daughter – who's her young man now? young Arthur? – there'll always be communal places, there'll always be . . .

ALFRED: My daughter don't want communal places, Ted, she wants to go to the pictures. No, young Arthur's finished. It's young Herbie Phillips now, the chap who was a prisoner of war. You know, the chap who used to be errand boy for Wilson's and then the next we heard of him he was a commando. Funny, isn't it.

WORKMAN: Wonder if they let him keep his tricycle . . .

TED: There was a chap who was a prisoner with me – used to be a shopwalker in one of these big stores I've forgotten which. You know, 'This way to the underwear, Madam' . . . and there he was with a damned great bayonet scar half across his face . . . wonder what he's doing now . . . what's a chap like that do, scar or no scar, when *he* comes back? No shops for him again: he was one of the toughest fellows I ever saw . . . he used to sit there half the day, just staring, and moving his great torn fingers just like *this* . . . as though he were trying to strangle something . . .

WORKMAN: How long was you a prisoner?

TED: Three years. One year on my back, flat out, and two years thinking . . .

ALFRED: Funny when it's so hard to get soap that that's what old Joe puts in the tea, isn't it. That's what it tastes like . . .

TED: I used to think about things I didn't *know* I knew . . . things used to come into my head that I knew I wasn't clever enough to think . . . but they came all right. I'm in the building trade, I used to say to myself, I'm married, I live in Shepherds Bush, I got two kids, I'm not a philosopher, I used to say . . . I'm a Londoner, I am . . .

NARRATOR: Lily Jackson is having *her* lunch alone in the tidy kitchen. The kids are having their lunch at school – Lily's made a cup of tea for herself and a sandwich. She's looking through the window at the grey small square of garden where the clothes are blowing on the line. Beyond them are the roofs of the world.

LILY: Three years were an awful long time. Oh, every time I thought how long they were for me, I knew, I knew they were longer for Ted. Before they said on the wireless he was a prisoner of war, oh long before, I knew he wasn't dead. I never had to tell lies to myself, like poor Sally Peters up the street. I knew he was thinking of me. I used to hear his voice in the silly old dance tunes they played on

85

the wireless, but the words weren't silly any more. 'I love you, darling mine,' was always him saying it to me. 'In the silence of my lonely room I think of you, night and day,' he used to say. Oh I knew he wasn't alone, all right, there were thousands and thousands. But they were all alone too. Walking down Montrose Street with Carole and Len, he was walking with me. I remembered everything he ever said to me from the day we met in the dance hall down Hammersmith till the day he asked me to marry him and I couldn't say yes or anything because people were looking at us in the park and then an old man sat down next to us on the bench and said it was very cold for August, and he couldn't understand why we both burst out laughing and went on laughing and laughing till we nearly cried, and then Ted kissed me, kissed me with the old man staring, and then the old man said, 'and what's more it's going to rain ...'

[KNOCK ON DOOR]

GWEN (*at door*):   Anyone at home?

LILY: Come in, Gwen love. Take your things off.

GWEN: Don't be silly. I've only got a summer frock on.

LILY: Well come and sit down in the front room, the kitchen's like an oven ...

GWEN: Just for a minute then ...

LILY: I haven't seen you for weeks, Gwen ... Willy okay?

GWEN: Same as usual. Trying to get some back pay from the Army. I just wondered if you're not too busy you'd like to come down the Broadway. I got two coupons left and I want to buy a pair of black gloves ...

LILY: Gwen, whatever for?

GWEN: Willy's Auntie Beryl's died – you know, the one who gave us the dinner-set – and the funeral's tomorrow. I haven't got anything black at all only that grey dress I had last winter.

LILY: No I can't come really. I've got such a lot of mending and they'll be out of a school in an hour and there's ironing too ...

GWEN: Oh come on, I'll stand you an ice ...

LILY: I'll have to spend the whole evening mending if I do ... oh, all right then ... perhaps I'll catch a glimpse of Ted ... he *hates* me watching him working ...

GWEN: Well, you know where he is, anyway ... Once Willy's gone off in the lorry, heaven only knows ...

[NOISE OF TRAFFIC]

LILY: You do look funny wearing black gloves with that cotton dress ... put them in your bag, Gwen ...

GWEN: Go on with you, I'm making a new fashion ... Not bad for four and eleven three is it? Where shall we have our ice?

LILY: Let's buy one off that chap over there ...Look, there's choc ices ...

GWEN: What, me with a choc ice and my black gloves on? Think of my colour scheme! Okay. Two please.

LILY: Makes me feel like a kid walking along the street with a wafer in my hand ...

GWEN: Go on, you don't look so old anyway ... not a day over sixty.

LILY: Oh, look, look! There's Ted.

GWEN: Where?

LILY: On top of that old shelter there ...

GWEN: Well if it isn't! Making a nice little ruin, isn't he?

[NOISE OF DRILLS]

ALFRED: Don't look now, Ted, but there's a young woman waving at you ... Blimey, there's *two* young women waving now ...

[UP NOISE OF DRILLS: NOISE OF TRAFFIC BACKGROUND]

NARRATOR: Two young women, wave their ices,
               Lily and Gwen, waving at men!
               Then up the street, past the jostling shops,
               Cafes and stalls and queues and cups,
               Dairy, jewellers, sixpenny store –
               Go on, Gwen, not sixpenny any more –
               Two young women, Hammersmith's nice
               With a saucy little hat & a sixpenny ice ...
               Two young women going home – ...

GWEN: Here we are then. Forty nine. Nice of you to have come with me, Lil.

LILY: Thanks for the ice.

GWEN: Give my love to brother Ted. I'll come along and see you next week.

LILY: Bye-bye then.

GWEN: Abyssinyia ...

LILY: And don't throw your books everywhere, Len. Put them in the cupboard.

LEN: Can I go out on my bike now, ma?

LILY: Yes, and don't call me ma.

CAROLE: Why don't you like being called ma, mummy?

LILY: Because it's common. Now if you've finished your tea you can help me take the clothes off the line ...

CAROLE: Yes, ma.

[NOISE OF WHISTLES AND SIRENS]

NARRATOR: Now, for Ted Jackson, the working day is over; dusty and tired, he waits for his bus, in a queue. Newspaper placards announce a shocking murder: The Cabinet meets again: a film-star has 'flu: a West End play has been running for fifteen years: 'Bishop says shame to mixed bathing in the Sea': the weather is forecasted, firmly, as dry, or wet: nobody scored at Lords. And a workman wants his tea.

[KITCHEN NOISES]

TED: I can do with it, too ... old Alfred nearly fell off the wall when he saw you waving.

LILY: More stew?

TED: Yes please. It isn't a stew, it's a kind of a pie. Shepherds Bush pie, that what it is? And waving ice-cream too and Alfred and me like a couple of pieces of hot-buttered toast.

CAROLE: How could you look like toast?

TED: Don't be so literal. How's Gwen?

LILY: She's burying Willy's Auntie Beryl tomorrow.

TED: Dead, I hope?

CAROLE: I'm not so literal, I was only asking.

LILY: Oh, dear, I do like your jokes, Ted. Here's a fresh cup. Both of them.

TED: Len out on his bike? He better be careful. Saw him a couple of evenings ago racing that young Larkin's boy down Goldhawk Road. Asking for it. Pictures night tonight?

LILY: I got all that mending to do, *and* the ironing, I told Gwen if I went out with her I'd have to stay in and do it. You better go and see if there's any beer in the Black Boy.

TED: There's many a husband never heard his wife say that to him since the day they were married. Or before. Better tell Len. I'll fix that pump of his when I get back.

CAROLE: I wish there was a Black Boy for girls.

LILY: Oh Carole!

NARRATOR: And for Carole and Len the day is over. Now they must go to bed. But in the Black Boy, that favourite public house, the evening is just beginning.

BARMAID: Evening, Mr Dollery. No bitter. Only mild and bitter. Evening, Mr Jackson.

MR DOLLERY: Be mean with the mild then ...

TED: Evening, Dora. Pint of what you got. Evening, Mr Dollery.

MR DOLLERY: 'Lo, Ted. Makes a chap think, doesn't it ...

CUSTOMER: Old Stanley's gone to bed till there's Burton.

MR DOLLERY: Seen they got a new dartboard, Ted? I been measuring. The double nineteen's eighth of an inch too narrow.

TED: Too low for me. Give me the twenties. Funny thing, when we made a dartboard once in the camp none of us could remember which way the numbers went ...

CUSTOMER: Burton's proper beer, Stanley says, Bitter's drinking ...

MR DOLLERY: Eighth of a inch too narrow!

TED: ... You know, so long since we played. We made a shove-halfpenny board too. You had to hit the halfpennies with a hammer and then they'd go up and down like a Giant Racer.

MR DOLLERY: You only got to breathe on the board I had once ...

TED: Same again?

MR DOLLERY: Ta. You only got to *breathe* on the board and there they were: all five halfpennies in Annie's bed. Cheerioh.

TED: Cheerioh.

CUSTOMER: You can't job old Stanley off with mild and bitter.

TED: Closing at nine?

MR DOLLERY: Or before. Depends on the dart team. If they don't come in there'll be beer enough. But if they do come in they'll finish the beer and then they won't be able to finish their game. So they don't know what to do, if you see what I mean.

[UP MEN'S VOICES]

CUSTOMER (*with morose satisfaction*): They're having an argey-bargey ...

TED: What's the fuss, Dora?

BARMAID: Oh, one of 'em's saying you can't be a boxer if you drink and the other one's saying you ought to train on quarts and ...

NEW CUSTOMER (*pugnaciously*): Look at me. I been drinking beer heavy every day of my life, year in, year out ...

TED: Yes, but does it help your boxing?

NEW CUSTOMER: Boxing? Never boxed in my life. I'm an invalid.

[UP PUB NOISES]

NARRATOR: Carole and Len are in bed. In the kitchen, in the last light of the day, Lily and Ted are sitting quietly, together and alone. Lily is sewing.

TED: This was one of the things I used to remember. The kids are upstairs asleep; Carole's got a doll on her pillow, it's only got one arm and the sawdust runs out of its head; at the bottom of Len's bed there's soldiers and a bear and a kind of duck that makes the wrong noise when you press it: miaow, like a cat. I remembered that all right. And you and me were sitting downstairs, just like we are now. You could *hear* the chaps all round you, thinking, as they lay down with their eyes wide open. Some with their mouths wide open too, snorting like Spitfires. Dreaming away.

LILY (*softly*): You're half asleep now ...

TED: All of us thinking about home. Sentimental. Nobody called nobody sentimental then ...

LILY: You're half asleep ...

TED (*as if dreaming*): Things used to come into my head I didn't know I could think – but they came all right. I'm not a philosopher, I used to say, I'm in the building trade. Ted Jackson, thirty-five, 49 Montrose Street, Shepherds Bush, married, two children, wife's name Lily ... Lily ...

LILY: Let's go to bed.

[MUSIC]

NARRATOR: It is a summer night now in Montrose Street. And the street is sleeping. In number forty nine, all is quiet. The Jacksons are dreaming.

10
Wilfred Owen

Thomas wrote to Vernon Watkins on 27 April 1946: 'I'm going to do a programme on Wilfred Owen: though my job is the selection of the poems for professional readers to (badly, usually) read, and the interpolation of four-line comments between each' (*Letters* p. 588). This self-mockery is belied by the final script, which has much informed and sincerely expressed commentary – written, by the way, without the help of Watkins's essay on Wilfred Owen that Thomas asked to borrow (it could not be found).

The talk was recorded on 19 June 1946, for transmission in John Arlott's 'Book of Verse' series in the Eastern Service on 27 July 1946. The fee was twenty guineas.

The present text is the BBC script, with three of the longer Owen poems used to illustrate the talk omitted here (one of them, 'Strange Meeting' is already included in 'Welsh Poetry' – see script 5).

Wilfred Owen

This book is not about heroes. English Poetry is not yet fit to speak of them.

Nor is it about deeds, or lands, nor anything about glory, honour, might, majesty, dominion, or power, except War.

Above all I am not concerned with Poetry.

My subject is War, and the pity of War.

The Poetry is in the pity.

Yet these elegies are to this generation in no sense consolatory. They may be to the next. All a poet can do to-day is to warn. That is why the true Poets must be truthful.

And that is the preface, by Wilfred Owen, to a volume of his poems which was to show, to England, and the intolerant world, the fool-ishness, unnaturalness, horror, inhumanity, and insupportability of War, and to expose, so that all could suffer and see, the heroic lies, the willingness of the old to sacrifice the young, indifference, grief, the Soul of Soldiers.

The volume, as Wilfred Owen visualized it in trench and shellhole and hospital, in the lunatic centre of battle, in the collapsed and apprehensive calm of sick-leave, never appeared. But many of the poems that were to have been included in the volume remain, their anguish unabated, their beauty for ever, their truth manifest, their warning unheeded.

Wilfred Owen was born in 1893 and killed in 1918. Twenty-five years of age, he was the greatest poet of the first Great War. Perhaps, in the future, if there are men, then, still to read – by which I mean,

94

if there are men at all – he may be regarded as one of the great poets of all wars. But only War itself can resolve the problem of the ultimate truth of his, or of anyone else's poetry: War, or its cessation.

And this time, when, in the words of an American critic, the audiences of the earth, witnessing what well may be the last act of their own tragedy, insist upon chief actors who are senseless enough to perform a cataclysm, the voice of the poetry of Wildred Owen speaks to us, down the revolving stages of thirty years, with terrible new significance and strength. We had not forgotten his poetry, but perhaps we had allowed ourselves to think of it as the voice of one particular time, one place, one war. Now, at the beginning of what, in the future, may never be known to historians as the 'atomic age' – for obvious reasons: there may be no historians – we can see, re-reading Owen, that he is a poet of all times, all places, and all wars. There is only one War: that of men against men.

Owen left to us less than sixty poems, many of them complete works of art, some of them fragments, some of them in several versions of revision, the last poem of them all dying away in the middle of a line:

'Let us sleep now ...' I shall not try to follow his short life, from the first imitations of his beloved Keats to the last prodigious whisper of 'sleep' down the profound and echoing tunnels of 'Strange Meeting'. Mr Edmund Blunden, in the introduction to his probably definitive edition of the poems, has done that with skill and love. His collected poems make a little, huge book, working – and always he worked on his poems like fury, or a poet – from a lush ornamentation of language, brilliantly, borrowed melody, and ingenuous sentiment, to dark, grave, assonant rhythms, vocabulary purged and sinewed, wrathful pity and prophetic utterance.

But these are all words, my words. Let us hear him, before we try to see him, in some kind of flame-lit perspective, on the battlefields of France and the Earth. This poem is called 'Exposure.'

> Our brains ache, in the merciless iced east winds that
>   knife us ...
> Wearied we keep awake because the night is silent ...
> Low, drooping flares confuse our memory of the
>   salient ...
> Worried by silence, sentries whisper, curious, nervous,

But nothing happens.

Watching, we hear the mad gusts tugging on the wire,
Like twitching agonies of men among its brambles.
Northward, incessantly, the flickering gunnery rumbles,
Far off, like a dull rumour of some other war.
      What are we doing here?

The poignant misery of dawn begins to grow ...
We only know war lasts, rain soaks, and clouds sag
      stormy.
Dawn massing in the east her melancholy army
Attacks once more in ranks on shivering ranks of gray,
      But nothing happens.

Sudden successive flights of bullets streak the silence.
Less deadly than the air that shudders black with snow,
With sidelong flowing flakes that flock, pause and renew,
We watch them wandering up and down the wind's
      nonchalance,
      But nothing happens.

Pale flakes with fingering stealth come feeling for our
      faces –
We cringe in holes, back on forgotten dreams, and stare,
      snow-dazed,
Deep into grassier ditches. So we drowse, sun-dozed,
Littered with blossoms trickling where the blackbird
      fusses.
      Is it that we are dying?

Slowly our ghosts drag home: glimpsing the sunk fires
      glozed
With crusted dark-red jewels; crickets jingle there;
For hours the innocent mice rejoice: the house is theirs;
Shutters and doors, all closed: on us the doors are
      closed –
      We turn back to our dying.

Since we believe not otherwise can kind fires burn;
Nor ever suns smile true on child, or field, or fruit.

For God's invincible spring our love is made afraid;
Therefore, not loath, we lie out here; therefore were
    born,
  For love of God seems dying.

To-night, His frost will fasten on this mud and us,
Shrivelling many hands, puckering foreheads crisp.
The burying-party, picks and shovels in their shaking
    grasp,
Pause over half-known faces. All their eyes are ice,
  But nothing happens.

Who wrote this? A boy of twenty-three or four, comfortably born and educated, serious, 'literary', shy, never 'exposed' before to anything harsher than a Channel-crossing, fond of 'Endymion' and the open air, fresh from a tutor's job. Earlier, in letters to his mother, he had written from the Somme, in 1917, in that infernal winter: 'There is a fine heroic feeling about being in France, and I am in perfect spirits.' ... Or again, he talked of his companions: 'The roughest set of knaves I have ever been herded with.' When we heard the guns for the first time, he said: 'It was a sound not without a certain sublimity.'

It was *this* young man, at first reacting so conventionally to his preconceived ideas of the 'glory of battle' and such ideas – he was to slash and scorify a very short time afterwards – who wrote the poem you have just heard. It was this young man, steel-helmeted, buff-jerkined, gauntleted, rubber-wadered, in the freezing rain of the flooded trenches, in the mud that was not mud, but an octopus of sucking clay, who wrote 'Anthem for Doomed Youth'.

What passing-bells for these who die as cattle?
  Only the monstrous anger of the guns.
  Only the stuttering rifles' rapid rattle
Can patter out their hasty orisons.
No mockeries for them from prayers or bells,
  Nor any voice of mourning save the choirs, –
The shrill, demented choirs of wailing shells;
  And bugles calling for them from sad shires.

What candles may be held to speed them all?
  Not in the hands of boys, but in their eyes

Shall shine the holy glimmers of goodbyes.
　The pallor of girls' brows shall be their pall;
Their flowers the tenderness of silent minds,
And each slow dusk a drawing-down of blinds.

There is no contradiction here. The studious, healthy young man with a love of poetry, as we see him set against the safe background of school, university, and tutordom, is precisely the same as the sombre but radiant, selfless, decrying and exalting, infinitely tender humble, harrowed seer and stater of the anthem for Doomed Youth and for himself. There is no difference. Only, the world has happened to him. And everything, as Yeats once said, happens in a blaze of light.

The world had happened to him. All its suffering moved about and within him. And his intense pity for all human fear, pain, and grief was given trumpet-tongue. He knew, as surely as though the words had been spoken to him aloud, as indeed they had been though they were the words of wounds, the shape of the dead, the colour of blood, he knew he stood alone among men to *plead* for them in their agony, to blast the walls of ignorance, pride, pulpit, and state. He stood like Everyman, in No Man's Land:

It is like the eternal place of gnashing of teeth; the Slough of Despond could not be contained in one of its crater-holes; the fires of Sodom and Gomorrah could not light a candle to it – to find a way to *Babylon the Fallen.*

And out of this, he wrote the poem called 'Greater Love'.

Red lips are not so red
　As the stained stones kissed by the English dead.
Kindness of wooed and wooer
Seems shame to their love pure.
O Love, your eyes lose lure
　When I behold eyes blinded in my stead!

Your slender attitude
　Trembles not exquisite like limbs knife-skewed,
Rolling and rolling there
Where God seems not to care;
Till the fierce Love they bear

Cramps them in death's extreme decrepitude.

Your voice sings not so soft, –
    Though even as wind murmuring through raftered
      loft, –
Your dear voice is not dear,
Gentle, and evening clear,
As theirs whom none now hear,
    Now earth has stopped their piteous mouths that
      coughed.

Heart, you were never hot,
    Nor large, nor full like hearts made great with
      shot;
And though your hand be pale,
Paler are all which trail
Your cross through flame and hail:
    Weep, you may weep, for you may touch them
      not.

It was impossible for him to avoid the sharing of suffering. He could not record a wound that was not his own. He had so very many deaths to die, and so very short a life within which to endure them all. It's no use trying to imagine what would have happened to Owen had he lived on. Owen, at twenty-six or so, exposed to the hysteria and exploded values of false peace. Owen alive now, at the age of fifty-three, and half the world starving. You cannot generalize about age and poetry. A man's poems, if they are good poems, are always older than himself; and sometimes they are ageless. We know that the shape and the texture of his poems would always be restlessly changing, though the purpose behind them would surely remain unalterable; he would always be experimenting technically, deeper and deeper driving towards the final intensity of language: the words behind words. Poetry is, of its nature, an experiment. All poetical impulses are towards the creation of adventure. And adventure is movement. And the end of each adventure is a new impulse to move again towards creation. Owen, had he lived, would never have ceased experiment; and so powerful was the impetus behind his work, and so intricately strange his always growing mastery of words, he would never have ceased to influence the work of his contemporaries. Had he lived, English poetry would not be the same. The course of poetry is dictated by accidents. Even so, he is one of the four most profound influences upon the poets who came after him; the other three being Manley Hopkins, the later Yeats, and Eliot.

But we must go back, from our guesses and generalizations and abstractions, to Owen's poetry itself; to the brief, brave life and the enduring words. In hospital, labelled as a 'neurasthenic case', he observed, and experienced, the torments of the living dead, and he has expressed their 'philosophy' in the dreadful poem, 'À Terre'.

['À Terre' was read.]

To see him in his flame-lit perspective, against the background, now, of poxed and cratered war-scape, shivering in the snow under the slitting wind, marooned on a frozen desert, or crying, in a little oven of mud, that his 'senses are charred,' is to see a man consigned to articulate immolation. He buries his smashed head with his own singed hands, and is himself the intoning priest over the ceremony, the suicide, the sunset. He is the common touch. He is the bell of the church of the broken body. He writes love-letters home for the illiterate dead. Ignorant, uncaring, hapless as the rest of the bloody troops, he is their arguer shell-shocked into diction, though none may understand. He is content to be the unhonoured prophet in death's country: for fame, as he said, was the last infirmity he desired. Listen to these verses from 'Insensibility'.

['Insensibility' was read.]

None of the poems you have heard were published while Owen was alive; indeed, he saw little or nothing of his in print. But I don't want to give the impression that he wrote always in intellectual loneliness, or that he carried his poems about with him like dark, incommunicable secrets. Siegfried Sassoon has described how, when he was in a nursing-home for what were then called 'shell-shock cases,' Owen, a stranger, came into his room with a number of Sassoon's newly published book of poems, and, shyly, asked him if he would autograph them. And Sassoon and Owen talked about poetry; Sassoon, as he himself said, rather laying down the law to this unassuming, shy young man. And Owen, on leaving, gave him some poems and asked

100

him if he'd have a look at them and tell him if they were any good. And Sassoon saw that they were good. And so did several other poets and men of letters to whom Sassoon sent them. And arrangements were made for a book of them to be published. Owen never saw that book.

There are many aspects of Owen's life and work upon which I haven't touched at all. I have laboured, in these notes or pieces between poems, only one argument, and that inherent in the poems themselves. Owen's words have shown, for me, and I hope (and know) for you, the position-in-calamity which, without intellectual choice, he chose to take. But remember, he was not a 'wise man' in the sense that he had achieved, for himself, a true way of believing. He believed there was no one true way because all ways are by-tracked and rutted and pitfalled with ignorance and injustice and indifference. He was himself diffident and self-distrustful. He had to be wrong; clumsy; affected often; ambiguous; bewildered. Like every man at last, he had to fight the whole war by himself. He lost, and he won. In a letter written towards the end of his life and many deaths, he quoted from Rabindranath Tagore: 'When I go hence, let this be my parting word, that what I have seen is unsurpassable.'

He was killed on 4th November 1918. This is his last, and unfinished poem, found among his papers after his death, 'Strange Meeting'.

['Strange Meeting' was read.]

11
Margate – Past and Present

Thomas wrote to Laurence Gilliam, Head of Features, who had praised 'The Londoner' (script 9): 'I'm so glad you liked the "Portrait of a Londoner" programme, and I'll let you know some script-suggestions as soon as I can. If, in the meantime, you think of any that I could have a shot at, I'd be very grateful' (*Letters* p. 598). This was on 23 July 1946; and the Margate assignment was presumably offered to Thomas to keep him busy, though the BBC files seem to lack information about the circumstances and payment received. The play was rehearsed and recorded on 22 September 1946; Thomas's visit to Margate was apparently at the beginning of the month. Edith Sitwell provided the following delectable vignette to Wynford Vaughan Thomas when interviewed for a Dylan Memorial programme in 1963:

> One day he came to lunch with me – that was the only time when I have seen him a little, perhaps a little over – d'you see? And he said, 'I'm sorry to smell so awful, Edith, it's Margate.' 'Oh,' I said, 'Yes, of course, my dear boy, naturally it's Margate. Of course, I quite understand that.' He'd just been to Margate.

'Margate – Past and Present' was not actually done for broadcasting by the BBC but for station WOR in New York in exchange for a feature about Coney Island. Elizabeth Lutyens wrote music for the production; the cast included Sheila Sim, Howard Marion Crawford, Preston Lockwood, and Gladys Young. Thomas did not take part.

Margate – Past and Present

[MUSIC]

1ST VOICE: Well, where do we begin? Got to begin somewhere . . .

2ND VOICE: Begin in a railway carriage.

[BACKGROUND TRAIN NOISE]

1ST VOICE: Is the train moving?

2ND VOICE: Of course it's moving – are you deaf? The fuming, snorting iron steed with her attendant gallimaufry . . .

1ST VOICE: . . . wrong word . . .

2ND VOICE: . . . of green gay coaches is racing proudly along the glistening rails, her wreaths of tasselled smoke garlanding the . . . sorry, it's an electric train.

1ST VOICE: Where's it going?

2ND VOICE: Margate, stupid.

1ST VOICE: Who's in the carriage we're beginning in?

[MURMUR OF VOICES IN CARRIAGE]

2ND VOICE (*quickly*):   There's a stout, badgered lady with a cluck of children and a thermos-flask wrestling with a sunshade fallen off the rack and a crushed bag of dried-egg sandwiches. There's a small, flat lady with a baffled expression, as though she'd been slammed in a door once and couldn't remember which door, reading the new best-seller.

1ST VOICE: What's it called?

2ND VOICE (*quickly throughout*):   'Forever Wind.' And a plum-coloured man with a panama hat and a beer-bottle in his pocket, failing, out loud, to do the children's crossword puzzle. And a floral woman of indeterminate age, anything between fifty and fifty-one, knitting in the corner.

1ST VOICE: What's she knitting?

2ND VOICE: It looks like something for a horse. And a small boy counting the telegraph posts. And two girls giggling.

1ST VOICE: What about?

2ND VOICE (*exasperated*):   How do I know? Life, death, Einstein, what the lodger said. And a young American called Rick, aged about thirty maybe.

1ST VOICE: What's Rick doing?

2ND VOICE: Looking out of the window, thinking.

1ST VOICE: What's he thinking?

2ND VOICE: Listen, curiosity.

[UP TRAIN NOISE, THEN INTO BACKGROUND AGAIN]

VOICE OF RICK'S THOUGHTS: What's it the kids over here used to tell me the wheels of a train were always saying?

> Manchester, Manchester,
> To buy a pocket handkercher.
> Manchester, Manchester ...

You can pretend the train's saying anything you like, if you try hard enough.

> Going to Margate, see my Molly
> Going to the seaside, ain't it jolly.

(*in surprise*)   That's *good!*

> Going to Margate see my fiancee
> Going to Margate ...

Pity her name's Molly not Nancy, then it would rhyme okay. Have a look at her photograph again. Where's my wallet? Here ... anybody looking? I don't care ... pretend I'm looking for my ticket or something. Photograph's getting kind of worn at the edges. Wish it was in colour. What colour's her hair? Red, dark red, red as ... I don't know ... just red as her hair. Won't need a photograph of her, soon.

105

CROSSWORD MAN: What's an animal in three letters ending in N.U.?

RICK: Gnu – G.N.U.

CROSSWORD MAN: G doesn't fit. It's got to be a B. Is there a bnu? Have a drink ... d'you mind the bottle?

RICK: Thanks. What kind of beer's this?

[NOISE OF DRINKING]

CROSSWORD MAN: There's ladies present. It's *called* brown ale. I remember when beer was twopence a pint. Yar'd be singing 'Annie Laurie' when you'd had three pints even if you was an Irishman. Where you're going? Margate?

RICK: That's right. I'm going to meet my girl. Going to get married. I haven't seen her for a year.

[THE GIRLS GIGGLE]

1ST GIRL: He's a Yank.

CROSSWORD MAN: I haven't seen mine for twenty years. She gave me the dodge in a teashop in Cardiff.

2ND GIRL: No, he's not a Yank. He's not in uniform.

CROSSWORD MAN: Or perhaps it was Bradford. I was a commercial then. Said she was going to the toilet and nipped out the side door. It wasn't fair. That's a man's trick.

[UP TRAIN NOISES, THEN BACKGROUND]

RICK: Where are we now?

WOMAN: Rochester.

RICK: Say, that's a city back home. Washing hanging by the graveyard; muddle of roofs and cranes and trains; a bit of a castle, bridges, ships in the mud; warehouses. chimneys ... That's a sea plane there. Are we getting any nearer? How far's Margate from London? 74 miles. Can't smell the sea yet, only smoke and tobacco and scent and ...

1ST CHILD'S VOICE: Ma! Arnold's putting sherbert in my bucket!

RICK'S THOUGHTS: Funny to see Molly again. Like meeting a stranger you're crazy about. She's bound to recognise me, isn't she? She's never seen me only when I was a sergeant. Wonder what her folk are like.

106

2ND CHILD'S VOICE: It's my sherbert, isn't it? I can put my sherbert in Gillian's bucket, can't I, Ma?

RICK'S THOUGHTS: Wonder if Molly's folk ever thought I'd really come back to England and marry her and take her home? Wonder if Molly ever thought I'd let her down. Oh no, she *couldn't*. Perhaps her mother won't like me. I don't know any show-people. Sittingbourne. Looks far from the sea enough – coal trucks, sidings, spire, roofs. A man tapping the wheels. Guess it's a skilled occupation, but nobody'd know it. Or perhaps you're born with it ... 'What d'yer want to be when you're grown up, son?' 'I want to be a tapper, dad.' What am I thinking about? Flat, green country, fields, trees, hedges. Where's the sea? Oh, come on, Margate.

[THE GIRLS GIGGLE AGAIN]

1ST GIRL (*shyly*):   Are you an American?

RICK: New York City.

1ST GIRL (*aside*):   There, I told you so.

RICK'S THOUGHTS: Perhaps her people don't like Americans ...

2ND GIRL: Have you been to Hollywood?

RICK: Sorry, miss. And I don't know Ingrid Bergman either. I'm a mechanic.

CROSSWORD MAN: Here, look, I've changed a letter. This animal's a 'rnu' now. Have a drink. Ever heard of a 'rnu'? When you goin' to get married?

RICK: Soon as I can. Couple of weeks. Taking her back home. Her father and mother run a boarding house for show-people. They used to be show-people too. Name of McFee. Ever come across them?

CROSSWORD MAN: My wife ran away with a MacPherson.

RICK'S THOUGHTS: Molly'll be waiting for me. What'll we say? 'Good-morning, Molly.' 'Good-morning, Rick.' All stiff and formal. 'How d'you do, Miss McFee, I hope you're well, when do we get married?' Say, where *is* the smell of the sea? Maybe I got catarrh.

1ST CHILD: Ma! Arnold's thrown my whistle out of the window!

RICK: Birchington-on-Sea, Westgate-on-Sea, oh come on, Margate.

PORTER'S VOICE.   Margate!

[STATION NOISES BACKGROUND]

107

RICK'S THOUGHTS: How can I see her in this crowd? Don't know what she's wearing. Used to have a yellowish kind of dress, I'd know it anywhere. Why don't they get out of the way. Can't they see this is important? Oh please God she knows me when she sees me ... please God ...

MOLLY: Rick! Rick!

RICK: Molly!

[MUSIC   FADE   MUSIC IN BACKGROUND]

MOLLY: And all the time, Rick darling, ever since your last letter, I was thinking, 'Oh, what if he doesn't recognise me at all, and I have to go up to him and say "Good morning, Mr Johnson, d'ya remember me, I'm the girl with the carroty hair you're going to marry, remember?"'

RICK: I was going to say, 'Good morning, miss, d'ya remember that ugly guy with the three stripes and the kind of indiarubber nose – he met you in that dance hall in Hammersmith, remember, and he met you every night for two weeks, and he said he loved you, and if you'll pardon me, miss, I'm him.'

MOLLY: And now we're walking along the Front together just as though we'd always been ... Walking along the Front, arm-in-arm ... Oh, Rick.

RICK: We're not the only ones, either. Is everybody going to get married round here? Look at that couple, will you? How much do you bet she isn't his sister? See this giggle of girls coming towards us with cellophane hats? 'Kiss Me Quick' 'I'll Have to Ask Me Dad' 'I'm No Angel' 'Can I Do You Now, Sir.' Nice literature they wear on their hats these days.

[GIGGLE OF GIRLS PASSING]

RICK: Your mother and father all prepared for the worst, Moll? They'd better be. I'm scared. I never met any show-people before, *personally*. Your mother wasn't a weight-lifter in civil life was she?

MOLLY: They've got tea waiting. You'll like them, Rick. I know you will.

RICK: I bet I will. It's the other way round gets me ... Let's walk nice and slow, shall we? Very slow ...

MOLLY: There's the pierrots, Rick. D'you like pierrots?

RICK: As I'm feeling now I could stand here and watch pierrots for the next twenty-four years. What are they singing?

[BIT OF PIERROT SHOW]

MOLLY (*laughing*):   Come on, darling.

RICK: Any more pierrots? No? Let's play a wheel-game then. There's hundreds over there in those cafes and places. Quicksnack, Sportamatics, Arcadia, Continental, Hippodrome, Funland, Merrydrome, Rendezvous. Just like home. I want to procrastinate. I like that word. Anything to ride on?

MOLLY: You're not going to Dreamland now.

RICK: Never felt more awake in my life.

MOLLY: No, you silly, Dreamland's where there's all the roundabouts and chairaplanes and swings and dodgems.

RICK: That's an idea – let's dodgem.

MOLLY: I'll take you to Dreamland tonight.

RICK: That sounds like a theme-song. Say, here's a roundabout.

[ROUNDABOUT MUSIC]

MOLLY: Go on, you're too big.

RICK: Kiddies Jolly Joyride. Where's the dragons and the zebras and griffons and things. It's all little buses and cars and tanks and planes and motorbikes ... Where's the little atom-bombs? I'm coming, I'm coming. See that old boy digging a sandcastle ... bowler hat, glasses, bathing-trunks and a tummy like a bass drum. Funny, it's always the people who look funniest have the most fun, isn't it? What's that guy selling?

MOLLY: Cockles. Cockles and winkles and whelks and oysters and prawns and shrimps, but there's only cockles and winkles and whelks, really.

RICK: Two of winkles, please.

[NOISE OF VOICES ROUND WINKLE-STALL]

MOLLY: Don't you want a hamburger?

RICK: I want winkles. I'm cosmopolitan. I like that word, too.

[BIT OF DIALOGUE WITH WINKLE-MAN ETC. MUSIC]

RICK: Winkles make you hungry. What shall we eat? What's on the menu?

MOLLY: You know very well you're coming home to tea.

RICK: Fish and chips, sausage pat, Vienna steak, savoury pie, prunes and custard. Which way's home, Molly? I like the way the little boats are bobbing. See them pulling at the ropes, just like little coloured dogs. When are we going to be together, Moll? Really together? I like the way that boat – what's it called? 'The Golden Spray' – I like the way it's kind of riding and rocking on the water like a big boozed bird. There's everything in the world I've got to tell you, Moll, when we're together. Can't tell you now. I like the way the kids are hullaballooing on the sand, and the old guys in the deck-chairs with newspapers over their faces, and the girls all jumping and jaunty, and – oh look – a bunch of old ladies, all fat as barrels, lifting their dresses and paddling, and screaming!

MOLLY: I like the way you like things. We're nearly there. Here we are, dear. Number 47.

RICK (*under his breath*): Here we go. Heaven help poor Americans on a night like this.

[FADE FADE IN NOISE OF KNIVES, FORKS, ETC., PLATES BEING PUSHED AWAY]

RICK: You sure make swell pastry, Mrs McFee.

MCFEE: You can call her mother now – can't he, Flo?

MRS MCFEE (*in a very deep husky voice*): Son-in-law or no son-in-law, he don't call me mother.

MOLLY: He isn't your son-in-law yet, Ma. Perhaps he's changed his mind.

RICK: If you can cook like your mother, Moll ...

MCFEE: We used to work the shows with a man that could eat twenty sausages for breakfast, didn't we, Flo?

MRS MCFEE (*very deep, very husky*): And a egg.

MOLLY: Dad, you're not attending to your guest. Go on, pass him the beer.

MCFEE: Help yourself, Rick. Funny names Americans have, don't they, Flo?

MRS MCFEE: Gives you wind.

RICK: Beg your pardon, Mrs McFee?

MRS MCFEE: Gives you wind.

MCFEE: Flo means bottled beer gives you wind, don't you, Flo?

RICK: D'you ever feel like going back into show-business, Mr McFee?

MRS MCFEE: And palpitations.

RICK: I mean, it must have been a bit kind of odd at first, settlin' down in one place, running a boarding house.

MOLLY: But they're all show people stay here. They're all old friends. We've got a telephasist on the first floor and Madame Zaza's in the attic.

RICK: I think I like the sort of house where there's Madame Zaza in the attic.

MCFEE: Mind, I never thought we could settle down in a house, did you, Flo? Let alone a boarding-house. We lived in a caravan when we was married. And as soon as the Margate season was over, we'd be off. Olympia in Earl's Court – that's in London. Or round the provinces doing the little fairs.

MRS MCFEE: We 'ad a midget in the box-room once.

RICK: There's no freaks in Margate now, are there, Molly? Back in Coney Island, we've got a poor old girl called The Elephant Woman, but I guess they're mostly dying out.

MOLLY (*laughing*):   Who are, darling, Elephant Women?

RICK: No, I mean freaks altogether.

MCFEE: He hasn't seen Madame Zaza, has he, Flo? Seventeen stone and five feet high in her stockinged trotters.

RICK: How many boarding houses are there in Margate, Moll?

MOLLY: Rick, you sound like a chap on the wireless, you know, one of the Americans that stops people at corners and asks them things.

MCFEE: I got a book on Margate somewhere, haven't I, Flo? Know where it is?

MRS MCFEE: In the dog's bed.

RICK (*softly, to himself*):   ... In the dog's bed? Sure, that's right, in the dog's ...

MOLLY: Here it is, Dad ... oh, it's all bitten.

RICK: I like bitten books. Let's have a look. Index. Population, page thirteen ... 11, 12, here it is.

VOICE OF INFORMATION: Population of Margate, about 30,000.

RICK: Say, this is almost a village: there's back in Coney Island ...

VOICE OF INFORMATION (*nettled*):   Don't boast, don't boast. (*Officially*

111

informative again)   At a rough estimate about 80% of the population are engaged in some way or another in entertainment, including those who accommodate, cater for, or entertain the visitors, and those who are responsible for transport and lighting. One proportion of entertainment establishments is about 300% greater than in an ordinary residential town.

RICK: Let's see – page fifteen: accommodation: here's a bunch of figures.

VOICE OF INFORMATION: Number of hotels – 240. Number of boarding houses – 1,300. Number of apartment houses – 5,000. The number of beds available to visitors to Margate is, in hotels 10,800, in boarding houses 39,000, in apartment houses 23,000. That makes all together –

RICK: Wait a minute: 10,800, 39,000 and 23,000 – that makes the number of beds –

VOICE OF INFORMATION (*sharply*):   72,800 Margate beds.

RICK: Margate's got a history, too. D'you ever read this book, Mr McFee?

MCFEE: I read Westerns.

RICK: Page 25: Margate was –

VOICE OF INFORMATION (*firmly*):   Margate, under Queen Elizabeth, was a small fishing village with twenty small hoys –

RICK: Small what?

VOICE OF INFORMATION (*sharply again*):   Hoys! Small vessels. In the coasting and river trades. In the 18th century Margate first became known as a bathing place. At the end of the 18th century, the discovery was made that sea-air was good for you –

RICK: Didn't people *breathe* before?

VOICE OF INFORMATION: And Benjamin Beale, a Quaker, introduced bathing machines.

RICK: Good work, Ben.

VOICE OF INFORMATION: At the beginning of the 19th century there was a popular ballad that began

BROADSHEET VOICE: Now's the season for laughing and jollity
Crowding together all stations and quality
Margate ahoy as I merrily holla ye,
All come aboard while the sea-breezes blow.

MOLLY: You read it and improve your mind, darling. I'll clear up the things, and then we'll go to Dreamland and you can go on the scenic railway and ...

[NOISE OF CLEARING UP OF PLATES ETC.]

MRS MCFEE: Rover always takes a book to bed.

MCFEE: Funny what people do for pleasure, paying a tanner to go on a thing that wobbles your inside and turns you upside down and whizzes you giddy and – there used to be a giant racer down in South Wales, remember, Flo? It *looked* dangerous, it *sounded* dangerous, and it *was* dangerous, too. Very popular.

RICK: Here's another thing in this book.

VOICE OF INFORMATION: 'After tumbling and rumbling, tacking and re-tacking, we reached Margate, to the great joy of Neptune's patients ... the few who were not affected by the tow'ring motion experienced from hunger pains that need not be described ... It was impossible to land at the pier, through the lowness of the tide, and boats put off, to our relief, for, to say truth, the Margatians are a friendly sort of people whenever they can use a Wrecking Hook or make demands upon the purse.'

[A BELL RINGS]

MRS MCFEE: That's Madame Zaza now. She used to 'ave a whistle.

[NOISE OF MRS MCFEE WALKING ACROSS ROOM, OPENING AND SHUTTING OF DOOR]

MCFEE (*conspiratorially*):   There's a pub at the corner of Dreamland, the 'Oyster Bar' – see you there just before closing time. Molly'll show you.

MOLLY: Ready, Rick? Finished your little guide-book?

RICK: Ready, Moll. Rover's ate all the last pages. I guess he's about the best-read dog in Margate.

MCFEE: The 'Oyster Bar' – don't forget.

MOLLY: Come on, darling.

RICK: Okay. Hang on, Dreamland, we're coming.

[UP DREAMLAND FAIRGROUND NOISE   DOG RACE DISC]

RICK: Nice voice! Sounds as if he'd been eating hedgehogs. Hedgehog

113

pie and gravel in the gravy. Here's another spin-game. We're going to have sixpennyworth each, Mrs Rockfeller. Why do you call sixpence a tanner, by the way? Jack Waller's film stars. Here goes.

JACK WALLER: This prize is guaranteed to cook without burning or sticking. This is a guarantee. I guarantee that you'll never have a sticky bottom if you cook with that frying pan. [LAUGHTER] Put that underneath your pillow at night and you'll wake up next morning with a permanent wave. Here's a prize – you get half a dozen of these egg-cups with a recess there for the salt. That's the latest design, that's in case they ration it. You get the half dozen and the tray as one prize. At 6d. a ticket that works out 1d. each for the egg-cups and sweet fanny nothings for the tray. Here's another prize – one of our tea-strainers. [LAUGHTER] I am sorry to say that these are second prizes – they've all got holes in them. Here's a pair of Army socks – no coupons. [CHORUS OF APPROVAL] Now I've done hundreds and hundreds of miles in these socks – on a bike. And believe you me, if you suffer with perspiring feet, if you wear these socks I'll gamble that your feet will smell like violets. Ladies, you can also wear these as bedsocks to save scratching the old man. Here's another prize, the boozer's set. Half a dozen glasses and a jug. I've got a prize here I'll show you – here it is. A utility pot. That's a kettle, or a tea-pot or a stewpot. You can take the lid off and it even goes under. [LAUGHTER] Just a minute, just a minute, please. This goes under the tap and you fill it with water to make your tea with it. Now if you watch the lights – you're watching the remaining light – if you hold the corresponding ticket, you're the winner. It's gone quiet, hasn't it? This time it's a bloke after my own heart – it's Jack Buchanan. There's the winning ticket, now here's the prize. This is Jack Waller's famous film stars. We've been here over 20 years and we've only moved down here to save you carrying your prizes too far. Now if you watch the lights – we're sold out as usual with prizes like this, they speak for themselves. Right-ho. Who's going to work the doofer? Lady? Right-ho.

[BACKGROUND BINGO]

MOLLY: Oh Rick! And I might have won a china dog, or a paper hat anyway.

RICK: Back in Coney Island – there I go again! – back home for one nickel you can win anything from a ham to three pairs of nylon stockings or a giant baby panda. I want some winkles. I'm a winkle fan.

MOLLY: I'm going to have an ice. Two cornets please.

RICK: Make mine alcoholic. What's that kid eating?

MOLLY: Cotton candy.

RICK: Looks kind of antiseptic to me. At home it's all ...

MOLLY: There you go again.

RICK: ... taffy and popcorn and water-melon and hot buttered corn-in-the-cob. Say, I'm making myself hungry.

MOLLY: D'you want to go on the chairaplanes?

RICK: Sure.

MOLLY: Want to go on the dodgems?

RICK: Sure.

MOLLY: And the swings? And the gondolas? And the whip? And the crazy house?

RICK: Sure. Let's go on all of 'em. Especially the crazy house. Tell me, Moll, what did your mother do when she was in show-business? Oh boy, here's the shooting gallery! Like to see old-fashioned lynx hitting the bull's eye? No? 'Distorting Mirrors' – that's for us. In we go.

[DISTORTING MUSIC. LAUGHTER AND SQUEALS ETC. OF DISTORTED PERSONS]

MOLLY: Oh Rick, Rick, look! I'm like Madame Zaza! I'm round!

RICK: I'm Humpty Dumpty! Say, look at me! I go out where I ought to go in! I'm globular – I like that word. I'm spherical, I'm a void – no, I'm not, look at me now, I'm a drainpipe. Hold me, honey, I'm dwindling!

CHILD'S VOICE: Mummy, Mummy, where's my feet?

RICK: Hear that? She wants to know where her feet are. I think I must have swallowed them! I look like an ostrich. No, I don't! Half of me looks like Charles Laughton and the rest's like a tarantula.

CHILD'S VOICE: Mummy, you look like a weazel!

RICK: What *is* this? A menagerie? One minute you look like something out of Oscar Wilde and the next you're like a walrus. Not you, Molly, just everybody.

MOLLY: I wish I could stay looking like this ...

RICK: Somebody ought to censor me! I'm downright indecent! Is *that* my face?

CHILD'S VOICE (*in terror*): Mummy, I got a nose like Uncle Arthur's!

[FAIRGROUND NOISES AGAIN]

RICK: Somebody told me about a book called 'Dante's inferno'. I wonder who wrote it. He ought to have had a look in those mirrors! Bet you I scoop a prize on this spinner. 'Dog Races!' Goodie! So long as Rover isn't running! Who taught your dog to read, anyway?

[UP DOG RACES]

RICK: My mother always told me not to gamble! Let's try 'Noah's Ark'.

[UP NOAH'S ARK]

RICK: Let's have another shot. This gets right into my blood, just like London beer.

MOLLY: No, no more.

RICK: No more 'Noah's Ark'? What's the time? Gee, the old man'll be waiting. I like 'Noah's Ark'. I'd like to live in Noah's Ark. Just old Noah and Mrs Noah and you and Shem and Japhet – and me, I'm Ham. I'm thirsty too ...

[UP PUB NOISE]

RICK: Same again, Mr McFee? Okay. Same again, Joe.

BARMAN (*in a flat, weary voice*): You can't have the same – you can have similar.

RICK: Three similars. And what's yours, Mr Wimbush?

MR WIMBUSH: Black and tan.

MCFEE: That's stout and bitter.

RICK: And a black and tan please. Would anybody dare order a drink called that in Dublin?

MCFEE: I had good gaff in Dublin once.

RICK: Gaff?

MOLLY: A gaff's a showground.

MCFEE: You give me Dublin on a burster and I'll bet you a tosheroon I'd have a edge around me like a football scrum in a couple of minutes.

116

RICK: Wish I knew English.

MOLLY: A burster's a good showday, and a parney's when it's raining, and a tosheroon is half-a-crown, and get an edge is get a crowd around you and –

MR WIMBUSH (*tolerantly*):   He'll learn.

MCFEE: There's punters and mug-punters and steemers and grafters, and chalk in your swag, and you've got a caser in your pocket if you're lucky or a sprazz, or a keybosh ... it's all very easy really once you know.

RICK: Like knocking out Joe Louis.

BARMAN (*in his flat, weary voice*):   Time, gentlemen and others ...

BARMAID'S VOICE (*from further away*):   Time, gentlemen!

ANOTHER BARMAN'S VOICE: Time!

BARMAN: Time, please.

MR WIMBUSH: It's time.

BARMAID'S VOICE: Time, gentlemen ...

RICK: I guess they're hinting that it might be time.

[UP NOISE OF PUB, VOICES]

MOLLY: Rick and me are going a walk, Dad. Before we go home. Goodnight, Mr Wimbush.

RICK: Goodnight, Mr Wimbush.

MR WIMBUSH: Abysinnia.

[FADE PUB VOICES. NIGHT MUSIC]

MOLLY: I like Dreamland in the dark. I always like showgrounds when the lights are all gone out. When I was a little girl I used to creep out of the caravan. There were big red flowers painted all over the sides, and little yellow curtains, oh Rick, it was all so nice and bright and comfy and warm, just Ma and Dad, and Ernie and me. Ernie's dead. I showed you Ernie's picture, remember? I wish he wasn't dead. He was older than me, nearly seven years. He was just, he was just my brother – I don't think I hardly knew him, properly, at all. You don't know your brother when you're all that younger. He was just my brother; he used to order me around and everything. I think he liked me though. *I'd* like him now. Why did he have to

117

die? He was only twenty-five when he was killed. Ernest Terence Ian McFee, I used to call him Terence sometimes, when I wanted to make him mad. He hated that. I used to sneak out of the caravan when they were all asleep and go round the stalls and roundabouts and look at all the horses and wooden camels and things all like they were dead under the white sheets. I think a big showground's the quietest place on the earth when the crowd's have gone home, no lights, no noise, no nothing. It's suddenly so *dead, dead quiet* after the hurdygurdies and the barkers and the squealing and the screaming and everything. Dreamland was like this all the time when the war was on. And the town too. I came back for a couple of days to see Dad. He was in the Home Guard; everybody else was evacuated, nearly. There were guns and planes alright, but the town was *dead, dead quiet*. You'd walk along the front on an August afternoon, beautiful weather, sun and birds and clouds and everything, and see the streets were empty and all the boarding houses were shut and shuttered and *dead*. All the aspidistras in the winders were dead too – nobody water'd them for three years. The gardens were kind of jungles – up to your head. And grass on the pavements. There were flowers growing in the middle of the road. All the garden paths were covered in brambles. Nobody about. Nobody. Then a couple of soldiers a long way away, turning the corner of a street. Then nobody again. And then the guns. We turn here, by the hoopla. This way. Funny place in the night ... isn't it, darling ... Funny place in the night ... I love you, Rick ... [FADE]

1ST VOICE: Well, where do we end? Got to end somewhere. Do we end in Dreamland, in the dark?

2ND VOICE: End at the foot of the stairs in the dim-lit hallway of the McFee's boarding-house. End with Molly and Rick saying goodnight.

MOLLY: Goodnight, Rick darling.

RICK: Goodnight, Molly darling.

MOLLY: Sleep well.

RICK: It'll be nice not to have to say goodnight to you. (*Softly*) Say, Molly, I like your people. I like your Mum and Dad.

MOLLY: They like you too, darling.

RICK (*very softly, rather shyly*):   I've been meaning to ask: what did your mother do when she was in show-business ...?

MOLLY: She threw knives at Daddy.
RICK: Oh! Goodnight darling.
MOLLY: Goodnight.

[KISS   MUSIC]

12
How to Begin a Story

This irreverent piece is like the continuation of a conversation between Thomas and Roy Campbell, poet, friend, and BBC producer. They cooked it up together for the Home Service 8 October 1946. Thomas's fee was ten guineas.

It was printed in *The Listener* (17 October 1946), where Martin Armstrong's column in the same issue contained a short notice:

> At a party some frivolity is welcome and he was fairly bristling with it; in fact I thought he was rather too conscientiously bent on being funny, although now and then he brought it off triumphantly.

How to Begin a Story

The way to begin a story depends not so much upon what you mean by a story as upon the story itself and the public for which it is intended. That this goes without saying need in no way deter me from saying it: these are notes in the margin of a never-to-be-written treatise and are free as the London air, though not so smutty.

It would, for example, be wrong, however pleasant, to begin a story for *Little Tim's Weekly* in the style of a sentimentally savage, gauchely cynical, American underworld novel salted with sex-slang, peppered with lead, sugared with stiffs and stiff with cigars and sugars: the kind of novel beneath whose hard and sinister shell lurks no embryonic bird of prey, great Chicago auk or fabulous Brooklyn roc, but a backward, shy and shabby backwood sparrow twittering for crumbs and buddies. Those flash, brash, cigar-mashing floozy-flayers and anti-social bad babies who, in recent gangster-films, confess, at some Ufa-lighted moment in abattoir, railway-siding, or condemned cell, that they have always been kinda unwanted and lonesome, even back in mid-western little Bloodville, and that it all began when their dipsomaniac second stepmothers put them on the fire for saying their prayers – these psychopathic gorillas coked to the gills have no place in Little Tim's cosmography, however much Little Tim would appreciate it, and the writer of children's stories should never, in any circumstances, emotional or atomic, begin with an expletive-packed and monosyllabic description of a raid by the vice-squad on a clip-joint for retired rod-men. It is legitimate to begin a children's story with a conversation between rats; but only between certain kinds of rats.

Neither should the writer of a story intended to command a steady,

122

unsensational provincial sale, and concerning the birth, education, financial ups and downs, marriage, separations, and deaths of five generations of a family of Lancashire cotton-weavers, begin with, say, the Joyceian interior monologue of a moronic haberdasher trapped in a lift full of moths, or with a twee scene, in Hopskipandjump Town or Eiderdown Land, between Gruffums, the Lion, and Hold, that Tiger.

The man who begins a story for a girl's popular weekly – 'Myrtle's' or 'Pam's,' or maybe it is 'Greta's' now, or 'Ingrid's' – with a subtle analysis of the state of mind of a neurotic young man of letters about to meet a phobia, socially, in a disused Nissen-hut, will never make the grade and is doomed to perpetual immurement in magazines with a circulation of seventeen poets and a woman who once met Kafka's aunt.

Now let us consider, most briefly, just a very few of the many favourite ways of beginning stories, and see if we can put a little new life into them.

School-stories first. Not the dull ones about the repressions and urges of sensitive plants and backward sons, and the first dawning of love and Shelley on the awakening mind, but the good, or bad, old stories which are all about tea and muffins in the cosy study, midnight spreads by candlelight in the ill-patrolled dormitory, escapes by knotted sheets to out-of-bound circuses or fairs, the ruthless ragging and baiting of unpopular masters and impecunious buffoons, the expulsion of cads for smoking in the fives-court – poor little sallow Maltravers with the dark rings already under his roué's eyes – and all the trivial tribal warfares of fantastic and ageless boys.

The onomatopoeic, gemmed and magnetic, time-honoured opening cannot be bettered:

'Leggo!'
'Geroff!'
'Yaroo!'

And then, of course:

These stentorian cries echoed down the corridor of the Upper Shell.

The novice should begin *every* school story with exactly those words. In the next sentence he must introduce his principal characters, a bunch of bold, breathless, exclamatory, ink-stained, beastly, Dickensian-surnamed boys with their caps awry, their lines undone, pets in their desks, paper-pellets in their pockets, and barbarous though innocuous oaths on their unrazored lips.

But let us introduce a new element:

> 'Leggo!'
> 'Geroff!'
> 'Yaroo!'

These stentorian cries echoed down the corridor of the Upper Shell as Tom Happy and his inseparables, known to all Owlhurst as the 'Filthy Five', lurched arm-in-arm out of Mrs Motherwell's fully-licensed tuckshop.

There you have a beginning at once conventional and startling. The reader is at your mercy. And you can continue, within the accepted framework and using only the loudest, minutest, and most formal vocabulary, to describe such goings-on as the formation, by Tom Happy, of the Owlhurst Suicide Club and the setting-up of a hookah in the boothole.

Then there is the story of rural life. I don't mean the depressing tale, told through four interminable seasons, of rugged toil and weather-beaten love on an isolated farm of that part of Sussex where you can't hear the thrushes for the noise of typewriters; nor the earthy, middenish record, stuffed with nature lore and agricultural information, studded – if that is the word – with all too precise observations of animal behaviour, whiskered with 'characters,' riddled with unintelligible snatches of folkverse and altogether jocular as a boot, of how a middle-aged literary man 'discovered' the country and his soul, price eight and six. No; I mean the kind of story set in a small, lunatic area of Wessex, full of saintly or reprehensible vicars, wanton maidens, biblical sextons, and old men called Parsnip or Dottle. Let us imagine a typical beginning:

> Mr Beetroot stood on a hill overlooking the village of Upper Story. He saw that there was something wrong in it. Mr Beetroot was a retired mole-trapper. He had retired because he had trapped all the moles. It was a fine winter's morning, and there were little clouds in the sky like molehills. Mr Beetroot caught a rabbit,

taught it the alphabet, let it go, and walked slowly down the hill.

There we have firmly fixed the location and mood of the story, and have become well, if briefly, acquainted with Mr Beetroot, a lover of animals and addicted to animal education.

The common reader – legendary cretin – now knows what is coming to him: Mr Beetroot, that cracked though cosmic symbol of something or other, will, in the nutty village, with dialect, oafs, and potted sermons, conduct his investigation into unreal rural life. Everyone, in this sophisticatedly contrived bucolic morality, has his or her obsession: Minnie Wurzel wants only the vicar; the vicar, the Reverend Nut, wants only the ghost of William Cowper to come into his brown study and read him 'The Task'; the Sexton wants worms; worms want the vicar. Lambkins, on those impossible hills, frolic, gambol, and are sheepish under the all-seeing eye of Uncle Teapot, the Celestial Tinker. Cruel farmers persecute old cowherds called Crumpet, who talk, all day long, to cows; cows, tired of vaccine-talk in which they can have no part, gore, in a female manner, the aged relatives of cruel farmers; it is all very cosy in Upper Story. But so the reader – cretinous legend – thinks. The beginner, beginning a story of this kind, would be wise to ...

I see there is little, or no, time to continue my instructional essay on 'How to Begin a Story.' 'How to End a Story' is, of course, a different matter ... *One* way of ending a story is –

13
What Has Happened to English Poetry?

Thomas received a fifteen-guinea fee for appearing in the 'Freedom Forum' series as the archetypal Modern poet in discussion with Edward Shanks as the archetypal Georgian poet. The producer of the series, Anthony McDonald was in the chair. Recorded on 11 October 1946, the discussion was broadcast in the North American Service 16, 18, and 19 October 1946, and in the African Service 22 October 1946.

The extant BBC script is a transcription from a disc no longer in existence. The stenographer did not attempt to assign the speakers' names to the round-table exchanges, so the present text has an element of tentative guesswork in this regard. Editorial latitude seemed called for in omitting segments where it would not be useful to even guess at the identity of the speaker.

What Has Happened to English Poetry?

ANTHONY MCDONALD: This is Freedom Forum coming to you from the British Broadcasting Corporation in London. Today, we're going to talk about what has happened to English poetry, and I've got two distinguished poets here to discuss it, one of the old school, shall we say, Edward Shanks, who was writing at the end of the First World War, and then on for some years, and has been associated in most people's minds with the Georgians, and the other, Dylan Thomas, who most people regard as one of the moderns, though perhaps he regards himself as outside the general run of the moderns, I don't know. At all events, he's writing now, and has been for some years. With myself, Anthony McDonald, in the chair.

EDWARD SHANKS: Well, I should regard myself rather as an ex-poet, and I was most interested here in meeting you, Thomas.

DYLAN THOMAS: Thank you.

EDWARD SHANKS: And I was interested in the title that's been given to this discussion, 'What has happened to English Poetry,' and that reminded me of the story of an English novelist who suddenly came into prominence and visited New York, and there he met a lady at dinner who said to him: 'Oh, Mr So-and-so, you know I always used to go to London for a part of every year and I do so miss it, do tell me what's happened.' And he said: 'I've happened.'

ANTHONY MCDONALD: Yes, I think I know who your novelist friend was – he must have been on the wrong side of the road, even on the Angel Pavement.

128

EDWARD SHANKS: Perhaps, well – if I'd tried to imitate his voice it might have been even easier to recognise. But, I was talking to some friends this morning, about this discussion, and I asked one of them to read one of your books, Thomas, and he said: 'Yes, well – that's what's happened to English poetry. I think it's a disaster.' I wouldn't like to put that as my position, but...

DYLAN THOMAS: You've rather stolen my introductory thunder – not that it was very thunderous, because I too was saying just before we came along to this studio – I was asking a friend of mine whether he knew you, Shanks, and he said, 'Well of course I know his verses. Is he still alive?' (*Laughter*)

ANTHONY MCDONALD: Well, that I think is sufficiently insulting for both of you to start with. Let me see if I can find any agreement between you at all. Do you both agree, for example, that a major change has taken place in this century in English poetry?

DYLAN THOMAS: Well of course there has. Just as there's been a major change in how people live. Poetry changes only according to how you can deal with change. People very often talk about poetry as though it's only about something that you read in books, it's just a matter of words put down in certain order, usually bad, on sheets of paper, – well, it isn't. It's something produced with a great deal of trouble by ordinary human beings who alter as the society in the circumstances under which they live – as that alters so they do.

ANTHONY MCDONALD: Yes, but do the fundamentals change?

DYLAN THOMAS: I don't think so, unless the wish for self-destruction has grown up considerably in the last few years.

EDWARD SHANKS: I think the crisis in English poetry came with the climax of Swinburne, and Swinburne burnt up all that was left of the old romantic tradition, and he wrote that kind of verse with such extraordinary virtuosity that there was nothing left to be done; there was no influence that could pass on: and then English poetry passed into the trough and it's been trying to struggle out of it in various ways ever since.

DYLAN THOMAS: No, but surely Swinburne's subjects were again only life, death, and all the usual ones that poets have been bothering about ever since?

EDWARD SHANKS: Yes, I suppose that's how it might have been; but however, there it was. You can see it in the nineties – those people trying to get back somehow and they were trying to get at secondhand the inspiration from the earlier English people that had come round by way of France through Verlaine and Baudelaire, and they were trying to do it in the nineties; it was a minor revival and it produced some good brains: and then it faded away again and it came round again through the Georgian revival – people were looking round for something new and not able to find it. My view is that your generation – the generation we're talking about – a good many of them older than you are – took violent means to find something new.

ANTHONY MCDONALD: Yes; even when I heard your last sentences I was thinking of what you could mean by the Georgian revival.

DYLAN THOMAS: A revival of rather tepid poets, sitting in deck chairs – outside public houses in the country: or inns, I'm sorry. Sitting outside inns and writing poems about how lovely it was to see a cow or a bull or even an obscure bird for perhaps the third time.

ANTHONY MCDONALD: But I think Shanks himself has crystallized the whole objection. Do you remember?

EDWARD SHANKS: Well, let me see, though I don't think it's usually known, I did invent the term 'The week-end school of poetry'; and I meant it as much for myself as for anybody else.

DYLAN THOMAS: I told you at the beginning you'd stolen my thunder.

ANTHONY MCDONALD: I think Shanks is right to some extent when he says that from the end of Swinburne on, people were looking for something new.

EDWARD SHANKS: Well, Yeats, who went on, not very often, I don't think, using Swinburnian rhythms: not Swinburnian rhythms: Swinburnian metres I meant to have said.

130

DYLAN THOMAS: No, they weren't. I don't think you'd find the Swinburnian metre anywhere.

EDWARD SHANKS: I think in some of those plays – the early Yeats.

DYLAN THOMAS: Yes, but then it didn't take very long for Yeats also to find out that this was a humbug – I must use the same word – that this was a humbug re-emerging; and he changed – he didn't change quickly. I think a lot of people say that suddenly he realised 'Oh, this is old faked stuff that I'm writing now – now I'm going to write: now I'm going to be contemporary.' He was always contemporary.

EDWARD SHANKS: Yes; I think Yeats felt that the metres – that the style that he was using was you might say 'haunted'; and that he was living in somebody else's house and not his own, and he was determined to build his own house and live in it; and I think that is what the poets of your generation have done.

DYLAN THOMAS: Lived in Yeats's house?

EDWARD SHANKS: No, no, they've tried to build their own house. Looking around for something new –

DYLAN THOMAS: It may be a shack but –

ANTHONY MCDONALD: Well, surely that's all right, isn't it, and one of the objections which is always taken to modern verse – meaning verse for the last ten, fifteen, twenty years has been 'ivory tower' or even 'Communism lookout'; or even people who didn't live in the ivory tower or the Communist lookout, but lived in the tops of pylons.

DYLAN THOMAS: Yes, but the fact that you say that people are trying to build their own houses – which, after all, I mean in that sense as I imagine you're using it – a house is only something to put around you to keep the weather out, something in which you can work and live and breathe and all the other things. Well, if one of your major arguments against this kind of poetry is that one of the main things modern poets do is try to build these little houses on the great track, on the great huge road – the great traditional road of English poetry, or on sides of it rather, let us have the life blood of everything, the life blood of everybody which is the life blood of poets also. So let them go along, they can live spattered and scattered up˙and down it, in their little houses.

EDWARD SHANKS: I didn't think I was advancing a major argument, I thought I was throwing you a bouquet.

ANTHONY MCDONALD: But in what way do you feel that your mission has changed, do you feel that, before nineteen hundred, poets were writing as a means of communication whereas since then the stress has been on self expression in poetry, or the other way round, or hasn't there been a change?

EDWARD SHANKS: I don't think that either Thomas or I would agree that the mission has changed at all, that the job has changed at all.

ANTHONY MCDONALD: Do you agree with that?

DYLAN THOMAS: I do, the job has always been the same.

ANTHONY MCDONALD: Self-expression?

DYLAN THOMAS: Well, self-expression and – with this added difference I mean with the added difference now as we are talking about modern poetry, with this difference that modern poets even though they might write obscurely, or what seems obscure, that even though they write in the most condensed language, they are really more concerned with how everybody feels inside themselves than the majority of poets in the past. That they indentify themselves with this legendary creature who is only ourselves after all, this legendary creature called 'the common man'.

ANTHONY MCDONALD: The spirit of the man?

DYLAN THOMAS: They are seeking to interpret the spirit of the people as they feel it in themselves.

EDWARD SHANKS: Didn't Wordsworth have that idea rather?

DYLAN THOMAS: Yes.

EDWARD SHANKS: Incidentally, Wordsworth was the most lucid of all poets, you may consider him dull but you never can say he is difficult to understand.

132

DYLAN THOMAS: No, well I sometimes find it difficult to understand one thing in Wordsworth, why, when he wanted to interpret the common people – the common people that Wordsworth meant, the peasants weren't they, the Cumberland peasants mostly and what not?

EDWARD SHANKS: Yes.

DYLAN THOMAS: Well, why he should have to express their aspirations and hopes and loves and fears in such platitudinary language and in such flat language whereas one of the jobs of the modern poet as I see it, is to take the hopes and aspirations – not to *take* them because you have got them there anyway – of a garage hand and express it in language that a garage hand cannot possibly understand.

ANTHONY MCDONALD: I think that's a very fair criticism, Thomas. However let's go on to another thing I wanted to ask you. Well, leaving out of account, or having dealt with the change, if any, in the poet's job, what about the subject matter out of which he makes his poetry, do you feel that has changed?

DYLAN THOMAS: Well, in one way, yes. I think it has changed only in the sense that he can write about anything now. Well, perhaps he wasn't barred by any exterior rules, but something inside himself, by the habits, the ingrained habits.

ANTHONY MCDONALD: What about technique, the mere matter, the mere question of the rhymes and the metres, of all the other aspects of technique that you use? It's silly to ask you whether that's changed, but of course it's changed, since 1904. Why?

DYLAN THOMAS: Well, I think the technical apparatus of poetry has changed, but it's changed – it's changed almost imperceptibly really. Of course, I think when you look for revolutionary changes in actual structure of verse – and I'm sure this is going to be entirely disagreed with – when you look for revolutionary changes in structure in verse, you probably look at bad poets not good ones.

EDWARD SHANKS: Yes, well, of course, Bridges tried to make a revolution or a change.

DYLAN THOMAS: Of course, you could claim that he was a good poet.

133

EDWARD SHANKS: He was a good poet, and the attempt was a complete failure.

DYLAN THOMAS: A complete failure, yes. I was only saying that the real revolutionary changes in the technique of verse are provided by failures not by . . .

ANTHONY MCDONALD: But it is true that you don't pay as much lip service, you moderns, do you, to rhyme or metre as the traditionalists did?

DYLAN THOMAS: Oh, I think we do, entirely as much.

EDWARD SHANKS: Oh, now really, I must disagree with that. You don't.

ANTHONY MCDONALD: Well maybe you do, and maybe you're a traditionalist, after all Thomas. (*Laughter*)

DYLAN THOMAS: I think we're all traditionalists.

ANTHONY MCDONALD: Well –

DYLAN THOMAS: Well, we're bound to be traditionalists if we're going to be any good at all. We're bound to continue in the one stream of English verse, stream, road, river, path, whatever word we want to use we're still bound to continue in that, however much we might disagree on the way. And it's all the same language, and that's what we've got to use. And as a matter – harking back to that failure thing – you know the failure of technical devices and things like that – well I don't know whether you, Shanks, will agree with me that one of the profoundest influences on what we are now calling modern verse is Gerard Manley Hopkins.

ANTHONY MCDONALD: Well, Thomas, it's quite clear that you think that any changes that have taken place are only very minor ones, and that poetry is still really fundamentally in the great tradition. Shanks, what do you think – where do you think it's going?

EDWARD SHANKS: Well, my reply to that is conditioned by my view of our current history. And as I do think that we're passing into the decline of our civilisation, I assume that after Thomas and his friends have got through their period of – you'll forgive me saying won't

134

you – eccentricity, we shall have a sort of golden age, a sort of Augustan age with a Virgil and a Horace or something like that, and after that no more that matters very much.

ANTHONY MCDONALD: Do you agree with that, Thomas, or do you think you're going to develop a Virgil?

DYLAN THOMAS: I'm – well of course I don't believe it.

EDWARD SHANKS: I wouldn't be in the slightest degree surprised to find Thomas the new Virgil.

14
Holiday Memory

After its broadcast on the Third Programme on 25 October 1946, 'Holiday Memory' was referred to by N. G. Luker, Assistant Director of Talks, as 'one of the half dozen best talks I have ever heard' (memo to the producer, James Langham). Thomas was asked to re-read it for the BBC Archives on 6 December 1946; that reading survives and has been used to confirm the accuracy of the present text, based on the BBC script and the printing in *The Listener* (7 November 1946).

Edward Sackville-West included the following review in his 'Radio Notes' *New Statesman* (2 November 1946):

> Dylan Thomas's recollections of a seaside holiday prompted me to wonder why this remarkable poet has never attempted a poetic drama for broadcasting: he would seem to have all the qualities needed. Even more of a feast than his Christmas memories, this latest broadcast had far more the effect of poetry than of prose. A verbal steeplejack, Mr. Thomas scales the dizziest heights of romantic eloquence. Joycean portmanteau words, toppling castles of alliteration, a virtuoso delivery which shirked no risk – this was radio at its purest and a superb justification of its right to be considered as an art in itself.

Holiday Memory

August Bank Holiday. A tune on an ice-cream cornet. A slap of sea and a tickle of sand. A fanfare of sunshades opening. A wince and whinny of bathers dancing into deceptive water. A tuck of dresses. A rolling of trousers. A compromise of paddlers. A sunburn of girls and a lark of boys. A silent hullabaloo of balloons.

I remember the sea telling lies in a shell held to my ear for a whole harmonious, hollow minute by a small, wet girl in an enormous bathing-suit marked 'Corporation Property'.

I remember sharing the last of my moist buns with a boy and a lion. Tawny and savage, with cruel nails and capacious mouth, the little boy tore and devoured. Wild as seed-cake, ferocious as a hearth-rug, the depressed and verminous lion nibbled like a mouse at his half a bun, and hiccupped in the sad dusk of his cage.

I remember a man like an alderman or a bailiff, bowlered and collarless, with a bag of monkey-nuts in his hand, crying 'Ride 'em, cowboy!' time and again as he whirled in his chairoplane giddily above the upturned laughing faces of the town girls bold as brass and the boys with padded shoulders and shoes sharp as knives; and the monkey-nuts flew through the air like salty hail.

Children all day capered or squealed by the glazed or bashing sea, and the steam-organ wheezed its waltzes in the threadbare playground and the waste lot, where the dodgems dodged, behind the pickle factory.

And mothers loudly warned their proud pink daughters or sons to put that jellyfish down; and fathers spread newspapers over their faces;

138

and sand-fleas hopped on the picnic lettuce; and someone had forgotten the salt.

In those always radiant, rainless, lazily rowdy and sky-blue summers departed, I remember August Monday from the rising of the sun over the stained and royal town to the husky hushing of the roundabout music and the dowsing of the naphtha jets in the seaside fair: from bubble-and-squeak to the last of the sandy sandwiches.

There was no need, that holiday morning, for the sluggardly boys to be shouted down to breakfast; out of their jumbled beds they tumbled, scrambled into their rumpled clothes; quickly at the bathroom basin they catlicked their hands and faces, but never forgot to run the water loud and long as though they washed like colliers; in front of the cracked looking-glass bordered with cigarette-cards, in their treasure-trove bedrooms, they whisked a gap-tooth comb through their surly hair; and with shining cheeks and noses and tide-marked necks, they took the stairs three at a time.

But for all their scramble and scamper, clamour on the landing, catlick and toothbrush flick, hair-whisk and stair-jump, their sisters were always there before them. Up with the lady lark, they had prinked and frizzed and hot-ironed; and smug in their blossoming dresses, ribboned for the sun, in gym-shoes white as the blanco'd snow, neat and silly with doilies and tomatoes they helped in the higgledy kitchen. They were calm; they were virtuous; they had washed their necks; they did not romp, or fidget; and only the smallest sister put out her tongue at the noisy boys.

And the woman who lived next door came into the kitchen and said that her mother, an ancient uncertain body who wore a hat with cherries, was having 'one of her days' and had insisted, that very holiday morning, in carrying all the way to the tram-stop a photograph album and the cut-glass fruit-bowl from the front room.

This was the morning when father, mending one hole in the thermos-flask, made three; when the sun declared war on the butter, and the butter ran; when dogs, with all the sweet-binned backyards to wag and sniff and bicker in, chased their tails in the jostling kitchen, worried sandshoes, snapped at flies, writhed between legs, scratched among towels, sat smiling on hampers.

And if you could have listened at some of the open doors of some of the houses in the street you might have heard:

'Uncle Owen says he can't find the bottle-opener...'

'Has he looked under the hallstand?'

'Willy's cut his finger...'

'Got your spade?'

'If somebody doesn't kill that dog...'

'Uncle Owen says why should the bottle-opener be under the hall-stand?'

'Never again, never again.'

'I know I put the pepper somewhere...'

'Willy's bleeding...'

'Look, there's a bootlace in my bucket...'

'Oh come *on*, come on...'

'Let's have a look at the bootlace in your bucket...'

'If I lay my hands on that dog...'

'Uncle Owen's found the bottle-opener...'

'Willy's bleeding over the cheese...'

And the trams that hissed like ganders took us all to the beautiful beach.

There was cricket on the sand, and sand in the sponge cake, sand-flies in the watercress, and foolish, mulish, religious donkeys on the unwilling trot. Girls undressed in slipping tents of propriety; under invisible umbrellas, stout ladies dressed for the male and immoral sea. Little naked navvies dug canals; children with spades and no ambition built fleeting castles; wispy young men, outside the bathing-huts, whistled at substantial young women and dogs who desired thrown stones more than the bones of elephants. Recalcitrant uncles huddled over luke ale in the tiger-striped marquees. Mothers in black, like wobbling mountains, gasped under the discarded dresses of daughters who shrilly braved the goblin waves. And fathers, in the once-a-year sun, took fifty winks. Oh, think of all the fifty winks along the paper-bagged sand.

Liquorice allsorts, and Welsh hearts, were melting, and the sticks of rock, that we all sucked, were like barbers' poles made of rhubarb.

In the distance, surrounded by disappointed theoreticians and an ironmonger with a drum, a cross man on an orange-box shouted that holidays were wrong.

And the waves rolled in, with rubber ducks and clerks upon them.

I remember the patient, laborious, and enamouring hobby, or profession, of burying relatives in sand.

I remember the princely pastime of pouring sand, from cupped hands or buckets, down collars and tops of dresses; the shriek, the shake, the slap.

I can remember the boy by himself, the beachcombing lone-wolf, hungrily waiting at the edge of family cricket; the friendless fielder, the boy uninvited to bat or to tea.

I remember the smell of sea and seaweed, wet flesh, wet hair, wet bathing-dresses, the warm smell as of a rabbity field after rain, the smell of pop and splashed sunshades and toffee, the stable-and-straw smell of hot, tossed, tumbled, dug, and trodden sand, the swill-and-gaslamp smell of Saturday night, though the sun shone strong, from the bellying beer-tents, the smell of the vinegar on shelled cockles, winkle-smell, shrimp-smell, the dripping-oily backstreet winter-smell of chips in newspapers, the smell of ships from the sun-dazed docks round the corner of the sand-hills, the smell of the known and paddled-in sea moving, full of the drowned and herrings, out and away and beyond and further still towards the antipodes that hung their koala-bears and maoris, kangaroos, and boomerangs, upside down over the backs of the stars.

And the noise of pummelling Punch, and Judy falling, and a clock tolling or telling no time in the tenantless town; now and again a bell from a lost tower or a train on the lines behind us clearing its throat, and always the hopeless, ravenous swearing and pleading of the gulls, donkey-bray and hawker-cry, harmonicas and toy trumpets, shouting and laughing and singing, hooting of tugs and tramps, the clip of the chair-attendant's puncher, the motor-boat coughing in the bay, and the same hymn and washing of the sea that was heard in the Bible.

'If it could only just, if it could only just?' your lips said again and again as you scooped, in the hob-hot sand, dungeons, garages, torture-chambers, train tunnels, arsenals, hangars for zeppelins, witches' kitchens, vampires' parlours, smugglers' cellars, trolls' grogshops, sewers, under a ponderous and cracking castle, 'If it could only just be like this for ever and ever amen.' August Monday all over the earth, from Mumbles where the aunties grew like ladies on a seaside tree to brown, bear-hugging Henty-land and the turtled Ballantyne Islands.

'Could donkeys go on the ice?'

'Only if they got snowshoes.'

We snowshoed a meek, complaining donkey and galloped him off in the wake of the ten-foot-tall and Atlas-muscled Mounties, rifled and pemmicanned, who always, in the white Gold Rush wastes, got their black-oathed-and-bearded Man.

'Are there donkeys on desert islands?'

'Only sort-of donkeys.'

'What d'you mean, sort-of donkeys?'

'Native donkeys. They hunt things on them!'

'Sort-of walruses and seals and things?'

'Donkeys can't swim!'

'These donkeys can. They swim like whales, they swim like anything, they swim like——'

'Liar.'

'Liar yourself.'

And two small boys fought fiercely and silently in the sand, rolling together in a ball of legs and bottoms.

Then they went and saw the pierrots, or bought vanilla ices.

Lolling or larrikin that unsoiled, boiling beauty of a common day, great gods with their braces over their vests sang, spat pips, puffed smoke at wasps, gulped and ogled, forgot the rent, embraced, posed for the dicky-bird, were coarse, had rainbow-coloured armpits, winked, belched, blamed the radishes, looked at Ilfracombe, played hymns on paper-and-comb, peeled bananas, scratched, found seaweed in their panamas, blew up paper-bags and banged them, wished for nothing.

But over all the beautiful beach I remember most the children playing, boys and girls tumbling, moving jewels, who might never be happy again. And 'happy as a sandboy' is true as the heat of the sun.

Dusk came down; or grew up out of the sands and the sea; or curled around us from the calling docks and the bloodily smoking sun. The day was done, the sands brushed and ruffled suddenly with a sea-broom of cold wind.

And we gathered together all the spades and buckets and towels, empty hampers and bottles, umbrellas and fish-frails, bats and balls and knitting, and went – oh, listen, Dad! – to the fair in the dusk on the bald seaside field.

Fairs were no good in the day; then they were shoddy and tired; the voices of hoop-la girls were crimped as elocutionists; no cannon-ball could shake the roosting coconuts; the gondolas mechanically repeated their sober lurch; the Wall of Death was safe as a governess cart; the wooden animals were waiting for the night.

But in the night, the hoop-la girls, like operatic crows, croaked at the coming moon; whizz, whirl, and ten for a tanner, the coconuts rained from their sawdust like grouse from the Highland sky; tipsy the griffin-prowed gondolas weaved on dizzy rails and the Wall of Death was a spinning rim of ruin, and the neighing wooden horses took, to a haunting hunting tune, a thousand Beecher's Brooks as easily and breezily as hooved swallows.

Approaching, at dusk, the fair-field from the beach, we scorched and gritty boys heard above the belabouring of the batherless sea the siren voices of the raucous, horsy barkers.

'Roll up, roll up!' In her tent and her rolls of flesh the Fattest Woman in the World sat sewing her winter frock, another tent, and fixed her little eyes, blackcurrants in blancmange, on the skeletons who filed and sniggered by.

'Roll up, roll up, roll up to see the Largest Rat on Earth, the Rover or Bonzo of vermin.' Here scampered the smallest pony, like a Shetland shrew. And here The Most Intelligent Fleas, trained, reined, bridled, and bitted, minutely cavorted in their glass corral.

Round galleries and shies and stalls, pennies were burning holes in a hundred pockets.

Pale young men with larded hair and Valentino-black side-whiskers, fags stuck to their lower lips, squinted along their swivel-sighted rifles and aimed at ping-pong balls dancing on fountains.

In knife-creased, silver-grey, skirt-like Oxford bags, and a sleeveless, scarlet, zip-fastened shirt with yellow horizontal stripes, a collier at the strength-machine spat on his hands, raised the hammer, and brought it Thor-ing down. The bell rang for Blaina.

Outside his booth stood a bitten-eared and barndoor-chested pug with a nose like a twisted swede and hair that started from his eyebrows and three teeth yellow as a camel's inviting any sportsman to a sudden and sickening basting in the sandy ring or a quid if he lasted a round; and, wiry, cocky, bow-legged, coal-scarred, boozed, sportsmen by the dozen strutted in and reeled out; and still those three teeth remained, chipped and camel-yellow in the bored, teak face.

Draggled and stout-wanting mothers, with haphazard hats, hostile hatpins, buns awry, bursting bags, and children at their skirts like pop-filled and jam-smeared limpets, screamed before distorting mirrors, at their suddenly tapering or tubular bodies and huge ballooning heads, and the children gaily bellowed at their own reflected bogies withering and bulging in the glass.

Old men, smelling of Milford Haven in the rain, shuffled, badgering and cadging, round the edges of the swaggering crowd, their only wares a handful of damp confetti.

A daring dash of schoolboys, safely, shoulder to shoulder, with their father's trilbies cocked at a desperate angle over one eye, winked at and whistled after the procession past the swings of two girls arm-in-arm: always one pert and pretty, and always one with glasses.

Girls in skulled and cross-boned tunnels shrieked, and were comforted.

Young men, heroic after pints, stood up on the flying chairoplanes, tousled, crimson, and against the rules.

Jaunty girls gave sailors sauce.

All the fun of the fair in the hot, bubbling night. The Man in the sand-yellow moon over the hurdy of gurdies. The swing-boats swimming to and fro like slices of the Moon. Dragons and hippogriffs at the prows of the gondolas breathing fire and Sousa. Midnight roundabout riders tantivying under the fairy-lights, huntsmen on billygoats and zebras hallooing under a circle of glow-worms.

And as we climbed home, up the gas-lit hill, to the still homes over the mumbling bay, we heard the music die and the voices drift like sand. And we saw the lights of the fair fade. And, at the far end of the seaside field, they lit their lamps, one by one, in the caravans.

15
Walter de la Mare
as a Prose Writer

The ninth in the Third Programme series 'Living Writers', in which 'one contemporary writer is examined by another, with illustrations from his work', was Dylan Thomas on Walter de la Mare. Recorded and broadcast on 30 November 1946, the talk was repeated in the West Region on 8 December 1946. Thomas's fee was fifteen guineas.

The producer G. H. Phelps included this talk, along with others of the series, in the volume *Living Writers* (London: The Sylvan Press 1947). In doing so he made many cuts in the script as broadcast. However, the editing was extremely judicious; it would not be sensible, in this case, to expand the script back to its original size. The present text, therefore, is as published there, which is also the text as printed in *Quite Early One Morning*.

Walter de la Mare as a Prose Writer

What I say is, keep on this side of the tomb as long as you can. Don't meddle with that hole. Why? Because while some fine day you will have to go down into it, you can never be quite sure while you are here what mayn't come back out of it.

There'll be no partings there – I have heard them trolling that out in their chapels like missel-thrushes in the spring. They seem to forget there may be some mighty unpleasant *meetings*. And what about the furthur shore? It's my belief there's some kind of a ferry plying on that river. And coming back depends on what you want to come back *for*.

So an old, smallish man, muffled in a very respectable greatcoat at least two sizes too large for him, mutters in a dark corner of the firelit station waiting-room in Walter de la Mare's uneasy story, *Crewe*.

How many of the nasty ghosts, from the other side of the razor's edge, from the wrong room, from the chockablock grave, from the trespassing hereafter, from the sly holes, crawl over and into the seedy waiting-rooms, the creeping railway carriages, the gas-lamped late-Victorian teashops the colour of stewed tea, where down-at-soul strangers contrive their tales and, drop by drop, leak out the shadows of their grey or black, forlorn, and vaguely infernal secrets. The ghosts of Mr de la Mare, though they reek and scamper, and, in old houses at the proper bad hours, are heard sometimes at their infectious business, are not for you to see. But there is no assurance that they do not see you.

And remember, in Mr de la Mare, the scarecrow that suddenly

appears in a cornfield behind a house where lately a man has hanged himself. ' "Does the air round the scarecrow strike you as funny at all?" I asked him. "Out of the way funny – quivering, in a manner of speaking?" "That's the heat," he said, but his lip trembled.' And the shocking, hallucinatory mask of face and head lying on Mr Bloom's pillow. And the polluted, invisible presences that seep through the charnel-house of Seaton's bloated and grave-emptying Aunt. Here in this house, and in all the other drenched, death-storied houses, down whose corridors and staircases the past hisses, and in whose great mirrors you see behind you a corridor of hinted faces, and in whose lofty beds you share your sheets and nightmare with an intangible, shifted fellow or the sibilant echo of a sound you wish had never been made, most things that happen are ordinary, or very nearly ordinary, and vile. These are houses suspended in time; and timelessness erupts in them.

Mr de la Mare's *first* world of childhood is as 'phantasmal' and 'solitary' as Hans Andersen's, but rarely so cruel – or so alive. We grow to know that a huge mythological distance separates that world where Kay and Gerda breathe for ever and that in which the child-alone of de la Mare's tall tales go about their dreams, loves, and surprises. The country whose habitations, whose great sleepy meadows of March mornings, blue and tumultous and bleak, far away cold towers and pinnacles, whether of clouds or hills, valleys and spelled woods, grey-green dells, mistletoed and mustard-seeded avenues, that the children of his earliest stories people, infest, and, to high music, moon, glide, and meander through, this is a country of books. Hans Andersen's characters move in a magic that was not, beforehand, composed, pictured, or written down, but is created there and then, by their lovely motion, and for themselves alone to inhabit. But in, for example, *Henry Brocken*, the first of de la Mare's long tales, the world through which the beguiled boy wanders on his mild Rosinante is made of the trees and climates, moors, mornings and evenings, groves, hills, suns, stars, and gardens, of written, remembered words, of Bunyan's allegory and Swift's satire, of the poetry of Wordsworth, Herrick, Shakespeare, Poe, and Keats. Here enamoured Henry Brocken, in the library country, roving deep in the coils of the necromantic ball, meets Lucy Gray, Jane Eyre, Julia Electra, Dianeme, Anthea, Nick Bottom, the Sleeping Beauty, Gulliver, La Belle Dame

Sans Merci, Annabel Lee. But, overdecorated, remote, rooted in 'reverie', that favourite woollen-headed word, the adventure is all shades. *Henry Brocken* is a bookish and starry-eyed mood on a borrowed horse. The fabled earth is cloud. Clouds are reflections and echoes of seawaves that rhyme with other words. Rarely just pretty or arch, the way of the story is too often sadly sweet and single-noted.

But as Mr de la Mare went on writing, his children went on growing. They did not grow into youths but into children. They lost that lorn and dewy wonder, and when they moved, though always on odd errands, they did not rustle like the pages of an old book, turned in a lamplit brown study by a wan, near-tenuous, but inky hand. 'Home-sick,' 'forlorn,' 'lost,' and 'silent' – these words were used less often, though the nostalgia for the 'mournful gaiety' of the past, the loneli-ness, the silence, and the delirium, still were there.

It was through Mr de la Mare's perception of the very natural oddity and immediacy of childhood that a story like *The Almond Tree* emerged, most movingly, out of the tapestried and *unnatural* 'farness' of *Henry Brocken*.

Nicholas in *The Almond Tree* is, in Mr Forrest Reid's words, 'the first of a line of strange, wayward, intelligent, dangerously sensitive, infinitely alive small boys.' In later stories his name changes, he is older or younger, sadder or gayer, more darkly cunning or more coldly innocent, now embroiled and tangled in briery thickets of love, now critical and aloof, faintly smiling, in fear and evil occurrences; but always his eyes are the same. It is through these eyes we see the astonishing systems, the unpredictable order, of life on the edge of its answer or quivering on a poisonous threshold.

Only on slight occasions do Mr de la Mare's children come into contact with each other. We see them, nearly always, in their relation to abnormal men and women. And, of his children, it is only the small boys who become real. The little girls live in a distant, and more fragile, past.

A '*more* fragile' past; for he is loyal, always, to old Ways and Days, old houses, regions, customs, scents, and colours. His children loiter, wonder, and perceive, his men and women suffer, love, and are haunted, his weathers happen, his dead-behind-the-wainscot blow and scamper, in a time and place that was before he was born. The life of his countryside is that which his mother remembered hearing

148

her mother tell of, and of which she told him when he was a child. His imagined memories of childhood are all of a timeless past before his own.

Mr de la Mare's stories first appeared about 1900. One of the first reviewers to recognize his awakening genius was Francis Thompson. Through all those intermediary years he has written long and short stories, for children, about children, for grown men and dead men, for the unborn, for a livelihood, for nothing, for the best reward, through innocence and with wide and deep skill, for pleasure, for fun, from suffering, and for himself.

His influences? Sir Thomas Browne, de Quincey, Ecclesiastes, Henry James, Emily Bronte, Stevenson, Poe, Traherne. And, in later life, Julian Greene perhaps? His style? It is his stories. At the very beginning he was fond, I think, of a rather flowery verbosity; he used a lot of clichés, but they were always the right ones. There was the suggestion of something, even in a young man, old-maidenish about his attitude to the love of men for women. Country terror was a little cosy, so that you felt not that something nasty had happened in the woodshed but that there were quite hellish goings-on among the wool-baskets in the parlour. The period and place about which he writes? Somewhere in rural England, say anywhere after 1830 and just before the after-life. In his more mature dramatic stories about grown-up human relationships, he often used a convoluted monologue-manner that occasionally suggested the ghost of a landbound Conrad talking from behind a pot of ferns. A fault of the prose style, always avoided in the verse, was a gravy-like thickening of texture. And his elaborate language, fuller than ever of artifice and allusion when it was seemingly simple, did not suit, to my mind, the more-or-less straightforward, or the grotesque fairy-story. His *real* fairies are as endearing as Dracula. And his subject, always, is the imminence of spiritual danger.

16
The Crumbs of One Man's Year

After the success of 'Holiday Memory', broadcast on 25 October 1946, James Langham the producer wrote in a BBC memo: 'Dylan Thomas would appreciate the opportunity, should it occur, of giving a talk during Christmas week. It would consist of some personal aspect of Christmas and would be written in the style of "Holiday Memory".' 'Tonight's Talk' at prime time after the nine o'clock news on 27 December 1946 was 'The Crumbs of One Man's Year'. Thomas wrote to his parents about it (*Letters* p. 614):

> The day after Boxing Day I had to go to London to give my after-the-news talk. A lot of people found the talk eccentric; perhaps it was; it wasn't, certainly, what most people expected to hear after the news. I've had quite a big post from it: half of it enthusiastic, the other half calling me anything from obscurantist to poseur, surrealist comedian to Bedlamite. The Manchester Guardian reviewed it very cheeringly; the News Chronicle with boos.

The talk was printed in *The Listener* (2 January 1947), where Martin Armstrong reviewed the broadcast (p. 39):

> I have before now mentioned talks by Dylan Thomas with appreciation. Why was it, then, that I didn't very much enjoy his talk after the news on Friday night? It was not that it wasn't as good as the others, but simply that, though its subject was different, its manner, method, style and even intonations were too closely similar to the others. One does not continue indefinitely to react to certain kinds of stimuli. After a limited number of repetitions one becomes immune. Last Friday, it seems, I unwillingly achieved immunity and I couldn't shake off the impression

151

that I was listening to Dylan Thomas doing a very good and slightly malicious imitation of himself. Now what is the meaning of all this? It is, in the first place, that Dylan Thomas has invented an instrument with a restricted compass and a very special *timbre* – a sort of literary cor anglais – which is extremely effective when not overworked, but is dangerously apt to pall; and secondly, that he is beginning to make a mannerism of a highly personal intonation.

The Crumbs of One Man's Year

Slung as though in a hammock, or a lull, between one Christmas for ever over and a New Year nearing full of relentless surprises, waywardly and gladly I pry back at those wizening twelve months and see only a waltzing snippet of the tipsy-turvy times, flickers of vistas, flashes of queer fishes, patches and chequers of a bard's-eye view.

Of what is coming in the New Year I know nothing, except that all that is certain will come like thunderclaps or like comets in the shape of four-leaved clovers, and that all that is unforeseen will appear with the certainty of the sun who every morning shakes a leg in the sky; and of what has gone I know only shilly-shally snatches and freckled plaids, flecks and dabs, dazzle and froth; a simple second caught in coursing snow-light, an instant, gay or sorry, struck motionless in the curve of flight like a bird or a scythe; the spindrift leaf and stray-paper whirl, canter, quarrel, and people-chase of everybody's street; suddenly the way the grotesque wind slashes and freezes at a corner the clothes of a passer-by so that she stays remembered, cold and still until the world like a night-light in a nursery goes out; and a waddling couple of the small occurrences, comic as ducks, that quack their way through our calamitous days; whits and dots and tittles.

'Look back, back,' the big voices clarion, 'look back at the black colossal year,' while the rich music fanfares and dead-marches.

I can give you only a scattering of some of the crumbs of one man's year; and the penny music whistles.

Any memory, of the long, revolving year, will do, to begin with.

I was walking, one afternoon in August, along a river-bank, thinking the same thoughts that I always think when I walk along a river-bank

153

in August. As I was walking, I was thinking – now it is August and I am walking along a river-bank. I do not think I was thinking of anything else. I should have been thinking of what I should have been doing, but I was thinking only of what I was doing then, and it was all right: it was good, and ordinary, and slow, and idle, and old, and sure, and what I was doing I could have been doing a thousand years before, had I been alive then and myself or any other man. You could have thought the river was ringing – almost you could hear the green, rapid bells sing in it: it could have been the River Elusina, 'that dances at the noise of Musick, for with Musick it bubbles, dances and growes sandy, and so continues till the musick ceases ...' or it could have been the river 'in Judea that runs swiftly all the six dayes of the week, and stands still and rests all their Sabbath.' There were trees blowing, standing still, growing, knowing, whose names I never knew. (Once, indeed, with a friend I wrote a poem beginning, 'All trees are oaks, except fir-trees.') There were birds being busy, or sleep-flying, in the sky. (The poem had continued: 'All birds are robins, except crows, or rooks.') Nature was doing what it was doing, and thinking just that. And I was walking and thinking that I was walking, and for August it was not such a cold day. And then I saw, drifting along the water, a piece of paper, and I thought: Something wonderful may be written on this paper. I was alone on the gooseberry earth, or alone for two green miles, and a message drifted towards me on that tabby-coloured water that ran through the middle of the cow-patched, mooing fields. It was a message from multitudinous nowhere to my solitary self. I put out my stick and caught the piece of paper and held it close to the river-bank. It was a page torn from a very old periodical. That I could see. I leant over and read, through water, the message on the rippling page. I made out, with difficulty, only one sentence: it commemorated the fact that, over a hundred years ago, a man in Worcester had, for a bet, eaten, at one sitting, fifty-two pounds of plums.

And any other memory, of the long evolving year, will do, to go on with.

Here now, to my memory, come peaceful blitz and pieces of the Fifth of November, guys in the streets and forks in the sky, when Catherine-wheels and Jacky-jumps and good bombs burst in the blistered areas. The rockets are few but they star between roofs and up to the wall of the warless night. 'A penny for the Guy?' 'No, that's my father.' The great joke brocks and sizzles. Sirius explodes in the backyard by the shelter. Timorous ladies sit in their back-rooms, with the eighth programme on very loud. Retiring men snarl under their blankets. In the unkempt-gardens of the very rich, the second butler lights a squib. In everybody's street the fearless children shout, under the little, homely raids. But I was standing on a signalling country hill where they fed a hungry bonfire Guy with brushwood, sticks, and cracker-jacks; the bonfire Guy whooped for more; small sulphurous puddings banged in his burning belly, and his thorned hair caught. He lurched, and made common noises. He was a long time dying on the hill over the starlit fields where the tabby river, without a message, ran on, with bells and trout and tins and bangles and literature and cats in it, to the sea never out of sound.

And on one occasion, in this long dissolving year, I remember that I boarded a London bus from a district I have forgotten, and where I certainly could have been up to little good, to an appointment that I did not want to keep.

It was a shooting green spring morning, nimble and crocus, with all the young women treading on naked flower-stalks, the metropolitan sward, swinging their milk-pail handbags, gentle, fickle, inviting, accessible, forgiving each robustly abandoned gesture of salutation before it was made or imagined, assenting, as they revelled demurely towards the manicure salon or the typewriting office, to all the ardent unspoken endearments of shaggy strangers and the winks and pipes of clovenfooted sandwichmen. The sun shrilled, the buses gambolled, policemen and daffodils bowed in the breeze that tasted of buttermilk. Delicate carousal plashed and babbled from the public-houses which were not yet open. I felt like a young god. I removed my collar-studs and opened my shirt. I tossed back my hair. There was an aviary in my heart, but without any owls or eagles. My cheeks were cherried warm, I smelt, I thought, of sea-pinks. To the sound of madrigals sung by slim sopranos in waterfalled valleys where I was the only tenor, I leapt on to a bus. The bus was full. Carefree, open-collared, my eyes alight, my veins full of the spring as a dancer's shoes should be full of champagne, I stood, in love and at ease and always young, on the packed lower deck. And a man of exactly my own age – or perhaps he was a little older – got up and offered me his seat. He said, in a respectful voice, as though to an old justice of the peace, 'Please, won't you take my seat?' and then he added – 'Sir.'

How many variegations of inconsiderable defeats and dis-illusionments I have forgotten! How many shades and shapes from the polychromatic zebra house! How many Joseph-coats I have left uncalled-for in the Gentlemen's Cloakrooms of the year!

And one man's year is like the country of a cloud, mapped on the sky, that soon will vanish into the watery, ordered wastes, into the spinning rule, into the dark which is light. Now the cloud is flying, very slowly, out of sight, and I can remember of all that voyaging geography, no palaced morning hills or huge plush valleys in the downing sun, forests simmering with birds, stagged moors, merry legendary meadowland, bullish plains, but only – the street near Waterloo station where a small boy, wearing cut-down khaki and a steel helmet, pushed a pram full of firewood and shouted, in a dis-passionate voice, after each passer-by: 'Where's your tail?'

The estuary pool under the collapsed castle, where the July children rolled together in original mud, shrieking and yawping, and low life, long before newts, twitched on their hands.

The crisp path through the field in this December snow, in the deep dark, where we trod the buried grass like ghosts on dry toast.

The single-line run along the spring-green river bank where water-voles went Indian-file to work, and where the young impatient voles, in their sleek vests, always in a hurry, jumped over the threadbare backs of the old ones.

The razor-scarred back-street café bar where a man with cut cheeks and chewed ears, huskily and furiously complained, over tarry tea, that the new baby panda in the zoo was not floodlit.

The gully sands in March, under the flayed and flailing cliff-top trees, when the wind played old Harry, or old Thomas, with me, and cormorants far off sped like motor-boats across the bay, as I weaved towards the toppling town and the Black, loud Lion where the cat, who purred like a fire, looked out of two cinders at the gently swilling retired sea-captains in the snug-as-a-bug back bar.

And the basement kitchen in nipping February, with napkins on the line slung across from door to chockablock corner, and a bicycle by the larder very much down at wheels, and hats and toy-engines and bottles and spanners on the broken rocking-chair, and billowing papers and half-finished crosswords stacked on the radio always turned full tilt, and the fire smoking, and onions peeling, and chips always spitting on the stove, and small men in their overcoats talking of self-discipline and the ascetic life until the air grew woodbine-blue and the clock choked and the traffic died.

And then the moment of a night in that cavorting spring, rare and unforgettable as a bicycle-clip found in the middle of the desert. The lane was long and soused and dark that led to the house I helped to fill and bedraggle. ('Who's left this in this corner?' 'What, where?' 'Here, this.' A doll's arm, the chitterlings of a clock, a saucepan full of hatbands.) The lane was rutted as though by bosky watercarts, and so dark you couldn't see your front in spite of you. Rain barrelled down. On one side you couldn't hear the deer that lived there, and on the other side – voices began to whisper, muffled in the midnight sack. A man's voice and a woman's voice. 'Lovers,' I said to myself. For at night the heart comes out, like a cat on the tiles. Discourteously, I shone my torch. There, in the thick rain, a young man and a young woman stood, very close together, near the hedge that whirred in the wind. And a yard from them, another young man sat, staidly, on the grass verge, holding an open book from which he appeared to read. And in the very rutted and puddly middle of the lane, two dogs were fighting, with brutish concentration and in absolute silence.

17
Sir Philip Sidney

Thomas's friend, the poet Desmond Hawkins, was the producer of a series 'Literature in the West' in the West of England Region, Bristol. Thomas went there on 24 January 1947 to contribute a talk on Sir Philip Sidney. It was repeated in the Third Programme 22 April 1947. The fee for script and reading was twelve guineas.

Vernon Watkins wrote in the *Times Literary Supplement* (19 November 1954) that only in this broadcast

does Dylan Thomas wear for a short time a mask which does not seem to be his own. Even this is full of brilliant things, but there is less spontaneity because one feels that he would not have carried an historical background to Sidney's poetry in his head, unless he had to. Historical data did, to a certain extent, cramp his style, as though he were collaborating.

Sir Philip Sidney

It is among the arguments of the *Defence of Poesie* that the Poet is the greatest teacher of knowledge because he teaches by a divine delightfulness. 'For,' wrote Sir Philip Sidney,

> he doth not only show the way, but giveth so sweet a prospect into the way as will entice any man to enter into it. Nay, he doth, as if your journey should lie through a fair vineyard, at the first give you a cluster of grapes that, full of that taste, you may long to pass further. He beginneth not with obscure definitions, which must blur the margent with interpretations, and load the memory with doubtfulness, but he cometh to you with words set in delightful proportion, either accompanied with, or prepared for, the well-enchanting skill of music; and with a tale forsooth he cometh unto you, with a tale, which holdeth children from play, and old men from the chimney corner.

The Defence of Poesie is a defence of the imaginative life, of the duty, and the delight, of the individual poet living among men in the middle of the turning world that has, in his time, so little time for him. Sometimes melancholy, often distant, proud and politic, delicate and hot-headed, unperturbedly honest, he exercised a grave fascination upon all who met him. He deliberated upon himself with gravity, and found it delightful or distasteful as the wind of love blew, as the life of Elizabeth's court grew perilous, lax, fickle, or degraded, as shallow justice shook, as adventurers sailed with wrong maps round the real rich roaring globe.

Even when he was a child at Penshurst or in Wales, his parents,

160

seeing him such a grave boy, 'adjured him to be merry'. He was praised, while a child, by Fulke Greville, for being of 'such staidness of mind, lovely and familiar gravity, as carried grace and reverence above greater years'.

Sir Philip Sidney's mother was the daughter of John Dudley, the Duke of Northumberland who was beheaded for his part in the placing of Lady Jane Grey upon the throne of England. That little reign brought death and desolation to all his mother's kin. Sidney could never have forgotten what his mother must have told him. Lady Mary Sidney who nursed Queen Elizabeth through smallpox and who caught the disease herself so horribly that, even at home, she always wore a mask: he never could have forgotten that Guildford Dudley, his mother's brother, married Jane Grey; that on her way to be made queen, dressed in green velvet, she was so slight and small she was mounted on very high chopines to make her look taller. 'She was sixteen, Guildford was a very tall strong boy with light hair, who paid her much attention.' On her way to the scaffold she carried a prayer book, and wore black.

Sidney's father, Sir Henry, was the ablest governor of Ireland under Elizabeth. He wrote to his very young son, then a scholar at Shrewsbury School, this mature advice:

Seldom drink wine, and yet sometimes do, lest being enforced to drink upon the sudden you should feel yourself inflamed.

Be courteous of gesture and affable to all men, with diversity of reverences according to the dignity of the person: there is nothing that winneth so much for so little cost.

Give yourself to be merry, for you degenerate from your father if you find not yourself most able in wit and body and to do anything when you be most merry: but let your mirth be ever void of all scurrility and biting words to any man.

Three important events, of the little that is known, occurred in Sidney's boyhood.

He and Fulke Greville, who was afterwards to write so much and so movingly about him, entered Shrewsbury on the same day, in 1564.

In 1566, when he was twelve, he was presented with the poems of Virgil. And in the summer of that year he was summoned by his uncle, the Earl of Leicester and Chancellor of the University, to go from Shrewsbury to Oxford where he saw, for the first time, Queen Elizabeth in her, to his young eyes, uncomplicated glory.

161

Sidney, as a child, was of a charming and ingenuous appearance, as Thomas Moffett, in his recently discovered and translated *Nobilis* and *Lessus Lugubris*, testifies, he was 'endowed with gifts of nature, with a strong and almost manly voice, and, in fine, with a certain consistent and absolute perfection of mind and body. When as a three year old he beheld the moon, with clean hands and head covered he used to pray to it and devoutly to worship.' Here follows the sonnet:

> With how sad steps, ô Moone, thou clim'st the skyes,
>> How silently, and with how wanne a face,
> What may it be, that ev'n in heavenly place,
> That busie Archer his sharpe Arrowes tryes?
> Sure if that long with love acquainted eyes
>> Can judge of love, thou feel'st a Lover's case,
>> I reade within thy lookes thy languisht grace.
> To mee that feele the like, my state discries.
> Then even of fellowship ô Moone tell me,
> Is constant love deemde there but want of wit?
> Are beauties there, as proude as heere they be?
> Doe they above love to be lov'd, and yet
>> Those Lovers scorne whom that love doth
>>> possesse?
>> Doe they call vertue there ungratefulnesse?

The Earl of Leicester, then favoured by the Queen, made sure that his nephew was a pretty boy to see her, bought him damask gowns trimmed with velvet, doublets of crimson and green taffeta, jerkins of blue leather, hose of carnation, shoes of white and green and blue. And he saw Elizabeth come into Oxford, clothed in scarlet silk and gold, with headdress of spun gold, her mantle of purple and ermine, and according to some historians, she sat on a high gold seat in an open litter drawn by mules.

In 1572, when he was eighteen, he received the Queen's licence to undertake a two years' visit to the continent. Attached to the suite of the Earl of Lincoln, he went first to Paris: 'a grave and tender handsome youth', or, as his uncle Leicester wrote in a letter to Walsingham, ambassador to France, 'young and raw'. A convinced and zealous Protestant by birth, education, and inclination, he was present at the anarchic eve of St Bartholomew's Day when an unknown number of

162

thousands of Protestants perished. At Frankfurt, he stayed at the shop of the scholarly printer, Andrew Wechel, where he met the learned Protestant controversialist, Hubert Languer, to whom, he confessed, he owed all his knowledge of literature and true religion. He visited Strasbourg, Vienna, Venice, Genoa, Florence, Padua (where he studied astronomy, geometry, music, and Greek), he travelled to Poland and came home. Leicester at once placed him at court, at Greenwich, where Elizabeth at the age of forty-two was, as Sidney wrote, 'somewhat advanced in years'. He was taught to be a courtier. He was at Kenilworth, in the dazzling, rippling, musical summer of 1575 where there were unforgettable pageants for the Queen, masques and fireworks, the playing of gittern and cithern and virginals, tilts and jousts, bear-baiting, morris-dancing, tournaments, water-plays, and drinking from great livery pots of silver filled with claret and white wine.

In 1576, with the Earl of Essex, he joined his father in Ireland, and fought the boggish and cantankerous Irish, who did not think, as he did, that English law was, in all the world, the most just and agreeable.

There Essex died, leaving a message for Sidney: 'Tell him I send him nothing, but I wish him well, and so well that if God do move their hearts, I wish that he might match with my daughter. I call him son; he is so wise, so virtuous, and so godly; and if he go on in the course he hath begun, he will be as famous and worthy a gentleman as ever England bred.'

The daughter of Essex was Penelope Devereux, the Stella of the sonnets. Court life, home in England, proved expensive and lowering. His subsequent ambassadorship to the imperial court of Austria, splendid and unimportant. What he wanted, above all, was to serve the cause of Protestant religion. The Queen allowed him no opportunities. His uncle, Leicester, was disgraced, almost fatally, by the Queen's discovery of his hidden marriage. The Queen herself was about to contract an unfortunate marriage with the house of Anjou. Sidney wrote to her his charming Discourse to the Queen's Majesty touching upon the affair and graciously attempting to dissuade her from it; for which he received no thanks. He challenged the unpleasant Earl of Oxford to a duel. John Stubbes, who had written a pamphlet expressing the feelings of the common people against Elizabeth's proposed marriage, had his offending right hand cut off with mallet and butcher's cleaver. And Sidney was, fortunately, so depressed by life in London, that he retired, from unemployment at court, to the company of his sister, the Countess of Pembroke, at Wilton House, in the Hundred of Branch and Dale, Wiltshire, there to write *Arcadia*.

Wilton was begun in the time of Henry VIII, under the conduct of Hans Holbein, and finished in the time of Edward VI for the first Earl of Pembroke. The garden of Wilton that Sir Philip Sidney knew and loved can be seen in an old print. Here are the embroidered plots with their four fountains; the plots of flowers, and beyond them the little terrace. Here are groves through which passes the river Nader, and statues of Bacchus and Flora, and covered arbours, and great ponds with fountains and columns and two crowns spinning on the top of the water; and a compartment of greens, and cherry trees; and the great oval with the brass Gladiator; more arbours and turning galleries, porticos, and a terrace whose steps are sea-monsters.

Here was the most perfect house and garden for the writing of an Arcadian romance thronged with enchantments and disguised princes, murders, shepherds, sports, potions, and many kinds of love.

This enormously involved story, written in prose, and interspersed with songs and eclogues in verse, is dedicated 'To My Dear Lady and Sister, the Countess of Pembroke':

'Here now have you (most dear, and most worthy to be the most dear Lady) this idle work of mine, which, I fear (like the spider's webbe) will be thought fitter to be swept away than worn to any other purpose.'

But here was no filigree web of words, but a huge tapestry woven to bewilder and to keep out the light. It is all ornament, spectacle and splendour, pageantry, pomp, and sumptuous profusion, frill, lace, gold and jewel, paradox, jingle, personification, descriptions of natural scenery and ethical reflections, battles, tournaments, sad shepherd's sheepish lyrics, all blurring beautifully and drowning at triumphal length.

He had written poetical theory, and now he tried his hand at poetical experiment, 'freely ranging within the Zodiack of his owne wit'.

The garlands hang their all too windy heads; the colours run and vanish; the cornucopia is full of holes; rhymes hang blowsy on the brow of the melting monument. How few the clear calm seconds in

164

that rich desert of stationary time: these lines, perhaps, or are they too 'dainty'?

> The messenger made speed, and found Argalus at a castle of his own, sitting in a parlour with the fair Parthenia, he reading in a book the stories of Hercules, she by him, as to hear him read; but while his eyes looked on the book she looked on his eyes, and sometimes staying him with some pretty question, not so much to be resolved of the doubt as to give him occasion to look upon her. A happy couple, he joying in her, she joying in herself, but in herself because she enjoyed him.

And the famous description of the water-spaniel. And the eminently malicious line, interpreted by some critics as a statement of chivalrous loyalty: 'She was a queen, and therefore beautiful.'

But it is only in the sonnet sequence, *Astrophel and Stella*, that he is to be seen as a great poet. It was published five years after his death, in 1591. Nash says of it: 'This tragic-comedy of love is performed by starlight.' The sonnets are addressed to Penelope Devereux, whose father wished Sidney to marry her. They begin with elegance and pretence, poems moving like courtiers dressed in the habit of love. They are *about* love, they are not *in* love; they *address* love, they do not speak *out* of it. The raptures are almost easily come by; the despair almost as easily relinquished. They are the most perfect exercises for a man about to be in love. And Penelope married, and Sidney had lost her, and the sonnets were no longer rehearsals for a poetic event but poetry itself, striding and burning:

> I might, unhappy word, (woe me) I might,
> And then would not, nor could not see my blisse:
> Tyll now, wrapt in a most infernal Night,
> I finde, how heavenly day (wretch) did I misse;
> Hart rent thy selfe, thou doost thy selfe but right.
>> No lovely Paris made thy Helen his,
>> No force, no fraude, rob'd thee of thy delight,
> No fortune of thy fortune Author is;
> But to my selfe, my selfe did give the blow,
> While too much wit forsooth so troubled me,
> That I respects for both our sakes must showe.

165

> And could I not by rysing morne for-see,
>> How faire a day was neere, (ô punisht eyes)
>> That I had beene more foolish, or more wise.

In these sonnets we see, held still in time for us, a whole progress of passion, physical and spiritual, coursing through rage and despair, self-pity, hope renewed, exultancy, moon-moved dreams, black fear, and blinding bright certainty of final loss.

There are several songs among the sonnets. In the eighth song, Stella gently kills his hope of possessing her.

> In a grove most rich of shade;
> Where birds wanton Musicke made;
> Maie then young his pide weeds shewing,
> New perfumes with flowrs fresh growing. . . .

In the storming of Zutphen in the Netherlands, October the second, 1586, Sir Philip Sidney was struck by a musket-ball in the thigh. On his agonized way back to the camp 'being thirsty with excess of bleeding, he called for a drink, which was presently brought him; but, as he was putting the bottle to his mouth, he saw a poor soldier carried along, who had eaten his last at the same feast, ghastly casting up his eyes at the bottle, which Sir Philip, perceiving, took it from his head before he drank, and delivered it to the poor man with these words, "Thy necessity is yet greater than mine." '

The operations upon his wound were long and painful. 'When they began to dress his wound, he, both by way of charge and advice, told them that while his strength was still entire, his body free from fever, and his mind able to endure, they might freely use their art, cut, and search to the bottom.'

They used their art, and he was taken away to Arnheim. There he suffered. He became a mere skeleton. The shoulder-bones broke through the skin.

'He one morning lifting up the clothes for change and ease of his body, smelt some extraordinary noisome savour about him, differing from oils and salves, as he conceived.' Mortification had set in.

Eight days after he was wounded, he sent for ministers of many nationalities, and they prayed with him.

He asked for music.

166

He dictated his will.

He wrote a long letter in Latin.

He bade goodbye to his brother.

Very near death, he said: 'I would not change my joy for the empire of the world.'

18
The Poet and his Critic

The plan for the series 'The Poet and his Critic', the brain-child of producer E. J. King-Bull, is described in the *Radio Times* of 1 February 1947:

A sequence of four programmes is devoted to each Poet and Critic. The first comprises a number of poems selected by the Critic, as an introduction. In the second the Critic expresses his personal attitude to poetry, and his appreciation of the Poet. In the third the Poet replies. The fourth programme, introduced also by the Critic, consists of further examples of the Poet's work, which they have chosen in collaboration.

Thomas was to be the second poet chosen, after Edith Sitwell. His 'critic' was first G. W. Stonier (*Letters* p. 601), but ultimately T. W. Earp, whom Thomas had known well for years. Thomas wrote to him in December 1946: 'Commander King-Bull frightens me ... I'm so glad you're willing to do those Critical Scripts' (*Letters* p. 609).

Earp's selection of Thomas's poetry was broadcast on 1 February 1947 with readers Reginald Beckwith and Valentine Dyall. Earp's talk was on 8 February 1947. Then bad weather struck Britain, and the programmes for the following two weeks had to be cancelled. Thomas became very ill, and his own commentary was left till last, after the second selection of poems on 1 March 1947. Thomas's say was finally recorded on 6 March 1947 for transmission on 8 March 1947. Thomas wrote to Earp: 'I found the greatest difficulty in writing my piece, and have become rather hysterical in my generalizations. My references to your critical remarks are warm-hearted and dull' (*Letters* p. 619). But King-Bull wrote to Thomas 11 March 1947:

169

Speaking for myself, I was much impressed when listening to you on Saturday evening, much more so than previously in the studio ... I hope you feel that on the whole substantial justice has been done. Earp and I have enjoyed ourselves.

Martin Armstrong made a short comment in *The Listener* (20 March 1947): 'Thomas Earp dealt with Dylan Thomas, and Dylan Thomas dealt with himself. Both speakers were exceptionally good on their theme.'

The fact that the BBC Written Archives does not contain a copy of Thomas's script is perhaps explained by Thomas's request to King-Bull to send it to Edith Sitwell to help with an essay she was writing on his poems (*Letters* p. 624). There is no evidence that he complied; but the script is missing, and the present text relies entirely on an untitled holograph manuscript in the Humanities Research Library, Texas, which, it is assumed, is what was originally submitted to the BBC.

The Poet and his Critic

It is difficult for a poet to talk about his own poetry, unless he has finished with it or it has finished with him. His own early work may seem to him remote from what he is trying to do now; he may re-read it, with uneasy enjoyment or distaste, as calmly, he thinks, as he would the work of a contemporary or a dead man; but every now and then a line or a phrase or a whole passage, not necessarily, by any means, the most effective or memorable, springs from the page and attacks him in its origin. A house where you once lived and where you were happy and sad, in love, in peace or at war, divided against yourself, humbly, royally, or pugnaciously alone, where so much had happened, within those chosen walls, you'd think the past would come bounding and crying out, may, when you visit it again, raise only doubt and ghostly curiosity. Why did I live there? and did I, really, at all? Then suddenly, on a stone of the house, you see a little meaningless mark scraped with a nail. And you remember the nail itself, and the day you scraped with it on the stone, and the time of the day, and the weather, and exactly how you felt when you did it, and why. That alone of the house makes memories move in you. For the rest: the house is for other people. Re-reading an early poem, the poet may see, perhaps in one rearing line or one clumsy word, the nail-mark of the past, all that is left to him alone of the original reason for the poem and for his need to regard it again. For the rest: the poem is for other people.

Once a poem is completed, it is no longer the poet's property; except in the fact, of course, that he may, over the years, collect enough royalties from it to buy a shelf on which to put it, and that he is the one person whom critics hold responsible when they attack it for being what it is instead of being something else. But, once completed, bundled into print, posterity, diary, or a drawer, it is, to the poet, another failure serenely, exultantly, or gravely over, according to its temper. A poem is ended; and *poetry* begins again. Poems are things done, though they erupt and bless with life; poetry is the one thing doing.

Consider an imaginary old poet gazing back, at his work upon words, through the brutish, ardent century, rewarded, perhaps, by the love of a few contemporaries and the homage of some young. He is envied because of his position, but the envy is directed not so much against reverence and reputation as against his position itself, which is upright. He has been graphed and charted, analysed, researched and doggedly misinterpreted by a skein, or yank, of scholars. His words have been translated into many languages, his meaning into many preconceptions. He is represented in anthologies-for-schools by a handful of lyrics he wishes forgotten, extolling, maybe, the virtues of the contemplative life (it was Yeats who objected to, I think, a thousand boy-scouts reciting, in unison, in the Albert Hall, 'The Lake Isle of Innisfree', a poem about a lonely man desiring more loneliness). He is surrounded by books he need never read again; there arrive daily new books of verse, which he need never read once. He is beyond the need for self-expression or for communication. He has declared war in his poetry, and made his peace. All his work is there for him, and for all, to see. The nail-marks have almost faded. He cares so much that he does not care at all. 'Ye mid burn the old bass-viol that I set such value by.' One hand turns, without haste, the nearly anonymous pages; and one foot is in the grave.

But consider a young poet. He has both feet in his poems. And when he comes to talk about his poems, he puts both his feet in his mouth. There is so little for him to look back upon; his past has been fully occupied founding a future which he has not yet reached. By those of his contemporaries who do not know him personally he is over or under appreciated, and in both cases probably for the wrong reasons; and those who know him personally find it hard to believe in his work at all the more they see him away from it. He believes that he has voluntarily to slave at his poems which must spring from the life that his work, so it seems, prevents him from fully experiencing. He also has to earn a living, outside his poetry, for now the consecrated garret

172

is full of respectable lodgers, and the borough council has offices in the old master's brown study. And the only young poets who really think they know what they are up to when they talk about their poetry and their position in society on this turning bomb, are those who have had their thinking done for them. For a poet, when he is young, cannot, surely, talk either surely or calmly about why he writes poetry and what it is about. The answer is in his always growing poetry; or it isn't.

What, in reply to my Critic, can I say about my own poems except that I do so agree with him, without one pig's bristling of rancour, without one incredulous arching of an eyebrow, when he discusses, though too briefly, my swaggering and belligerent faults, and that if the purpose of this reply were to aid and supplement his all too considerate adverse criticism I could, by quotation and with delight, morass him under sentimental turgidities, wet wads of near-cliché, tortuous solipsism, crippled rhythm, forced rhyme, obscurity, eccentricity, muddledom and woolage.

For my poems are early poems. To a young poet, all his work is early work. (And a poet can be called young until he finds himself being regularly invited on to committees to judge the work of young poets.) They do not seem to me 'early' when I am writing them; they never did. During the bitterly and joyfully complicated process of making them, through the sweat and rages and the to-hell-with-it despair that anything will ever come right again, through the fears, always there, that the fire is doused or the need is dished or the skill's died on me, after the burning glory-be entrance of the one right word to a praise of private trumpets, through endless outscratchings and stettings, triumphs so soon to totter and be slashed as their full fool-sound rings or their ludicrous associations rise and glare, during all that work on words and is it worth it, during all that worrying of the sources and forces of language and birth and death and it is always worth it, when I am engaged in this preposterous and glorious pursuit I am never aware of those faults that, alas, I see, luckily soon afterwards perhaps, or after a long time and two editions, sit dripping in the middle of my hard-worked hard-won verses like a row of malicious and illiterate mourners.

(Do not think, please, that I am trying, by blackening the eyes of my poetry first, to spoil the enjoyment of any other critic who might

173

wish to have a slap at it. To conduct one's own lightning is not to steal somebody else's thunder. And besides: I am not really hitting myself very hard, or even at all. Perhaps I do not yet know where to hit my poetry so that it hurts most; or if I did, perhaps I would defend that particular piece of vulnerable nonsense at all costs, or attempt to disguise the depth of its vulnerability by confessing to a hundred more weak spots, all shallower.)

It is one thing to talk honestly, and in public, about a poet when he is dead, and quite another when he is living, however rude, or candid, we may be; but oh what a different kettle it is of stranger fish than ever swam under Sir John Squire's floorboards – remember 'the thin gnat-like voices of the trout'? – when the poet is, or so you have grown accustomed to imagining, yourself whom you know, or should know, so devilishly unsacredly. You may address yourself as the little girl addressed Matthew Arnold in Max Beerbohm's drawing: 'Why, pray, oh, why, can you not always be wholly serious?'

It is difficult, as I said at the beginning, for a poet to talk about his own poetry; and especially is it difficult to a poet who, when he is not working, austerely alone, at his own poetry, in that loud silence, cannot take himself with the seriousness which he imagines, and mostly wrongly, to be the perpetual addiction and habiliment of other poets – dead, alive, half alive, in the Athenaeum, or in America.

When a poet is not working at his poetry, he is like everybody else, only more so. When he *is* working at his poetry, he is, at his highest level, trying to write from everybody to everybody.

If I had a philosophy, it would be stated in my poems, or be their driving law; it would be the progression of reason, within the chosen necessity of prosody, that keeps the reader's intellect working from stage to stage while the poetry itself works upon him. I cannot see a philosophical belief, nor a philosophy-in-the-making, as a basis of poetry. Philosophy, religion, *and* politics can be to modern poetry, I think, what narrative is: a thread or moving column to satisfy one habit of the reader's mind. The narrative adventure which progresses through a poem may be philosophical or political; but the final effect of the true poem on the reader has little to do with its philosophy or politics. It is the poetry remains. The religious or philosophical argument may achieve the work of narrative: it may lead-along one habit of the mind to expect, at the inevitable moment, the divine accident

174

of poetry which is the death of habit and the illumination of all the mind: it has prepared *one* way, however dark, towards poetry, which is everything: And everything happens in a blaze of light.

But *I* have no philosophy. I believe in universal turbulent acceptance, which is no more than to say I live.

And I believe in the Aztec Emperors who held council, yearly, to deliberate upon the movements of the sun, and to question its power; and to search into its meaning. And, yearly, they allowed the sun to continue on its wonted course.

19
Return Journey

The *Radio Times* announced for 15 June 1947 Home Service 7.00–7.30 p.m. 'Return Journey. A feature programme written and narrated by Dylan Thomas, and produced by P. H. Burton. In February of this year, the poet Dylan Thomas paid a visit to Swansea. In this programme he describes his search for the Swansea he knew as a boy and a young man.' Rehearsals and recording were in the Cardiff studios on 1–2 April 1947, for transmission in the London Home Service on 15 June 1947, in the Welsh Home Service on 20 June 1947, in Third Programme on 28 June 1947, in the General Overseas Service on 13 August 1947, with many further repeats in subsequent years. Thomas's fee for script and narrator's part was fifty guineas.

'Return Journey' was a series initiated by producer R. D. Smith, who accompanied Thomas during the three days in Swansea. The notebook he used (now at Texas) shows that Thomas approached the assignment with some deliberation, wanting to be especially precise about the bomb damage from the air raids of February 1941: 'Emlyn Road badly hit. Teilo Crescent was wiped out' etc. He apologized later to Vernon Watkins for not being able to see him on his last evening, as he 'had to go and see a master from the Swansea Grammar School to find out how much of the school was burned' (*Letters* p. 620). Cecil Price once asked him how he had managed to remember the names of all the shops destroyed in the bombing:

'It was quite easy,' he answered. 'I wrote to the Borough Estate Agent and he supplied me with the names.' I could think of nothing to say but, 'Why is it that no one ever credits a poet with common sense?' (Tedlock p. 20).

177

Vernon Watkins in the *Times Literary Supplement* (19 November 1954) called 'Return Journey' 'the most moving' of Thomas's broadcasts: 'He used a soft, quick, intimate voice, the exact tone of his natural conversation. This is the most intimate, the most strictly autobiographical of all the talks, and the most Welsh.' Douglas Cleverdon, in *The Growth of Milk Wood* (p. 15) called the script

> a model of its kind, written with a wry nostalgic humour and with evocative overtones that reverberate in the mind like the park-keeper's bell in Cwmdonkin Park. With his poet's insight and his practical experience of broadcasting techniques, Dylan knew exactly how to create a work of permanent value from the fluid medium of radio. I doubt whether there has ever been a better thirty-minute radio piece. As it was concerned with a Welsh subject, the programme was produced in Cardiff by P. H. Burton, with Dylan as narrator and as himself. It was altogether an admirable production, and had an enthusiastic response from listeners and critics.

Thomas referred to these responses in letters to his parents (*Letters* pp. 647, 653). An example of a reply to an admirer of the broadcast can be found in the *Letters* (p. 935).

The BBC has retained a recording of 'Return Journey', against which the typed script has been checked for the present edition.

Return Journey

NARRATOR: It was a cold white day in High Street, and nothing to stop the wind slicing up from the Docks, for where the squat and tall shops had shielded the town from the sea lay their blitzed flat graves marbled with snow and headstoned with fences. Dogs, delicate as cats on water, as though they had gloves on their paws, padded over the vanished buildings. Boys romped, calling high and clear, on top of a levelled chemist's and a shoe-shop, and a little girl, wearing a man's cap, threw a snowball in a chill deserted garden that had once been the Jug and Bottle of the Prince of Wales. The wind cut up the street with a soft sea-noise hanging on its arm, like a hooter in a muffler. I could see the swathed hill stepping up out of the town, which you never could see properly before, and the powdered fields of the roofs of Milton Terrace and Watkin Street and Fullers Row. Fish-frailed, netbagged, umbrella'd, pixie-capped, fur-shoed, blue-nosed, puce-lipped, blinkered like drayhorses, scarved, mittened, galoshed, wearing everything but the cat's blanket, crushes of shopping-women crunched in the little Lapland of the once grey drab street, blew and queued and yearned for hot tea, as I began my search through Swansea town cold and early on that wicked February morning.

I went into the hotel.

'Good morning.'

The hall-porter did not answer. I was just another snowman to him. He did not know that I was looking for someone after fourteen years, and he did not care. He stood and shuddered, staring through the glass of the hotel door at the snowflakes sailing down the sky like Siberian confetti. The bar was just opening, but already one customer puffed and shook at the counter with a full pint of half-frozen Tawe water in his wrapped-up hand. I said Good morning, and the barmaid, polishing the counter as vigorously as though it were a rare and valuable piece of Swansea china, said to her first customer:

BARMAID: Seen the film at the Elysium, Mr Griffiths, there's snow isn't it, did you come up on your bicycle, our pipes burst Monday.

NARRATOR: Pint of bitter, please.

BARMAID: Proper little lake in the kitchen, got to wear your Wellingtons when you boil a egg, one and four please...

CUSTOMER: The cold gets me just by here.

BARMAID: ... and eightpence change that's your liver Mr Griffiths, you've been on the cocoa again.

NARRATOR: I wonder whether you remember a friend of mine? He always used to come to this bar, some years ago. Every morning, about this time.

CUSTOMER: Just by here it gets me. I don't know what'd happen if I didn't wear a band.

BARMAID: What's his name?

NARRATOR: Young Thomas.

BARMAID: Lots of Thomases come here, it's a kind of home from home for Thomases isn't it, Mr Griffiths, what's he look like?

NARRATOR (*slowly*):   He'd be about seventeen or eighteen...

BARMAID: I was seventeen once.

NARRATOR: ... and about medium height. Above medium height for Wales, I mean, he's five foot six and a half. Thick blubber lips; snub nose; curly mousebrown hair; one front tooth broken after playing a game called Cats and Dogs in the Mermaid, Mumbles; speaks rather fancy; truculent; plausible; a bit of a shower-off; plus-fours and no breakfast, you know; used to have poems printed in the *Herald of Wales*; there was one about an open-air performance of *Electra* in Mrs Bertie Perkins's garden in Sketty; lived up the Uplands; a bombastic adolescent provincial bohemian with a thick-knotted artist's tie made out of his sister's scarf, she never knew where it had gone, and a cricket-shirt dyed bottle-green; a gabbing, ambitious, mock-tough, pretentious young man; and mole-y, too.

BARMAID: There's words, what d'you want to find *him* for, I wouldn't

180

touch him with a barge-pole, would you, Mr Griffiths? Mind, you can never tell. I remember a man came here with a monkey. Called for 'alf for himself and a pint for the monkey. And he wasn't Italian at all. Spoke Welsh like a preacher.

NARRATOR: The bar was filling up. Snowy business bellies pressed their watch-chains against the counter; black business bowlers, damp and white now as Christmas puddings in their cloths, bobbed in front of the misty mirrors. The voice of commerce rang sternly through the lounge.

FIRST VOICE: Cold enough for you?

SECOND VOICE: How's your pipes, Mr Lewis?

THIRD VOICE: Another winter like this'll put paid to me, Mr Evans.

FOURTH VOICE: I got the 'flu.

FIRST VOICE: Make it a double.

SECOND VOICE: Similar.

BARMAID: Okay, baby.

CUSTOMER (*confidentially*): I seem to remember a chap like you described. There couldn't be two like him, let's hope. He used to work as a reporter. Down the Three Lamps I used to see him. Lifting his ikkle elbow.

NARRATOR: What's the Three Lamps like now?

CUSTOMER: It isn't like anything. It isn't there. It's nothing mun. You remember Ben Evans's stores? It's right next door to that. Ben Evans isn't there either... (*Fade*)

NARRATOR: I went out of the hotel into the snow and walked down High Street, past the flat white wastes where all the shops had been. Eddershaw Furnishers, Curry's Bicycles, Donegal Clothing Company, Doctor Scholl's, Burton Tailors, W. H. Smith, Boots Cash Chemists, Leslie's Stores, Upson's Shoes, Prince of Wales, Tucker's Fish, Stead & Simpson – all the shops bombed and vanished. Past the hole in space where Hodges the Clothiers had been, down Castle Street, past the remembered, invisible shops, Price's Fifty Shilling, and Crouch the Jeweller's, Potter Gilmore Gowns, Evans Jeweller's, Master's Outfitters, Style and Mantle, Lennard's Boots, True Form, Kardomah, R. A. Jones's, Dunn's Tailor, David Evans, Gregory Confectioners, Bovega, Burton's, Lloyd's Bank, and nothing. And into Temple Street. There the Three Lamps had stood, old Mac magisterial in his corner. And there the Young Thomas whom I was searching

for used to stand at the counter on Friday paynights with Freddie
Farr, Half Hook, Bill Latham, Cliff Williams, Gareth Hughes, Eric
Hughes, Glyn Lowry, a man among men, his hat at a rakish angle,
in that snug, smug, select, Edwardian holy of best-bitter holies.

[BAR NOISES IN BACKGROUND]

OLD REPORTER: Remember when I took you down the mortuary for
the first time, Young Thomas? He'd never seen a corpse before, boys,
except old Ron on a Saturday night. 'If you want to be a proper
newspaperman,' I said, 'you got to be well known in the right circles.
You got to be persona grata in the mortuary, see.' He went pale
green.

FIRST YOUNG REPORTER: Look, he's blushing now.

OLD REPORTER: And when we got there, what d'you think? The
decorators were in at the mortuary, giving the old home a bit of a
re-do like. Up on ladders having a slap at the roof. Young Thomas
didn't see 'em, he had his pop eyes glued on the slab, and when
one of the painters up the ladder said 'Good morning, gents' in a
deep voice, he upped in the air and out of the place like a ferret.
Laugh!

BARMAID (*off*):   You've had enough, Mr Roberts. Now, *you* heard
what I said. Now, now, please don't let's have any...

[NOISE OF A GENTLE SCUFFLE]

SECOND YOUNG REPORTER (*casually*):   There goes Mr Roberts.

OLD REPORTER: Well, fair do's, they throw you out very genteel in
this pub.

FIRST YOUNG REPORTER: Ever seen Young Thomas covering a soccer
match down the Vetch and working it out in tries?

SECOND YOUNG REPORTER: And up the Mannesman Hall shouting
'Good footwork, sir,' and a couple of punch-drunk colliers galum-
phing about like jumbos.

FIRST YOUNG REPORTER: What you been reporting today, Young
Thomas?

SECOND YOUNG REPORTER: Two-typewriter Thomas, the ace news-
dick.

OLD REPORTER: Let's have a dekko at your note-book. 'Called at
British Legion: Nothing. Called at Hospital: One broken leg. Auction

at the Metropole. Ring Mr Beynon re Gymanfa Ganu. Lunch: Pint and pasty at the Singleton with Mrs Giles. Bazaar at Bethesda Chapel. Chimney on fire in Tontine Street. Walters Road Sunday School Outing. Rehearsal of the *Mikado* at Skewen' – all front page stuff. (*Fade*)

NARRATOR: The voices of fourteen years ago hung silent in the snow and ruin, and in the falling winter morning I walked on through the white centre where once a very young man I knew had mucked about as chirpy as a sparrow after the sips and titbits and small change of the town. Near the *Evening Post* building and the fragment of the Castle I stopped a man whose face I thought I recognized from a long time ago. I said: I wonder if you can tell me . . .

PASSER-BY: Yes?

NARRATOR: He peered out of his blanketing scarves and from under his snowballed balaclava like an Eskimo with a bad conscience. I said: If you can tell me whether you used to know a chap called Young Thomas. He worked on the *Post* and used to wear an overcoat sometimes with the check lining inside out so that you could play giant draughts on him. He wore a conscious woodbine, too . . .

PASSER-BY: What d'you mean, conscious woodbine?

NARRATOR: . . . and a perched pork pie with a peacock feather and he tried to slouch like a newshawk even when he was attending a meeting of the Gorseinon Buffalos.

PASSER-BY: Oh, *him*! He owes me half a crown. I haven't seen him since the old Kardomah days. He wasn't a reporter then, he'd just left the grammar school. Him and Charlie Fisher – Charlie's got whiskers now – and Tom Warner and Fred Janes, drinking coffee-dashes and arguing the toss.

NARRATOR: What about?

PASSER-BY: Music and poetry and painting and politics. Einstein and Epstein, Stravinsky and Greta Garbo, death and religion, Picasso and girls.

NARRATOR: And then?

PASSER-BY: Communism, symbolism, Bradman, Braque, the Watch Committee, free love, free beer, murder, Michelangelo, ping-pong, ambition, Sibelius, and girls.

NARRATOR: Is that all?

PASSER-BY: How Dan Jones was going to compose the most pro-

digious symphony, Fred Janes paint the most miraculously meticulous picture, Charlie Fisher catch the poshest trout, Vernon Watkins
and Young Thomas write the most boiling poems, how they would
ring the bells of London and paint it like a tart.

NARRATOR: And after that?

PASSER-BY: Oh the hissing of the butt-ends in the drains of the coffee-
dashes and the tinkle and the gibble-gabble of the morning young
lounge lizards as they talked about Augustus John, Emil Jannings,
Carnera, Dracula, Amy Johnson, trial marriage, pocket-money, the
Welsh sea, London stars, King Kong, anarchy, darts, T. S. Eliot, and
girls. Duw, it's cold!

NARRATOR: And he hurried on, into the dervish snow, without a
good morning or goodbye, swaddled in his winter woollens like a
man in the island of his deafness, and I felt that perhaps he had
never stopped at all to tell me of one more departed stage in the
progress of the boy I was pursuing. The Kardomah Cafe was razed
to the snow, the voices of the coffee-drinkers – poets, painters, and
musicians in their beginnings – lost in the willy nilly flying of the
years and the flakes.

MINISTER: *Ydych chi wedi colli rhywbeth – dan yr eira?* ... Oh, I see,
English. Lost anything – under the snow? A bookshop. Yes, I knew
it well. Ashes now, under the snow. A young man like you might
be, only younger – and different too, come to think of it – used to
rub shoulders with me by the shelves in the back corner on the
right – just by there it would be. You see, poetry and theology was
next door to each other. He was swimming out of his depth in a
flood of words, and I was toiling up high mountains of biblical
exegesis. I could see him down there in the flood, but he never
looked up to me on the mountain. Believed nothing, he did. My
pleasure was to find a translation of a new Germany commentary on
Mark and a second-hand copy of the collected sermons of Christmas
Evans. His pleasure was to read at me, like the bull of Basan, some
Babylonian lines from a man he called Ezra Pound. Tried to shock
me he did, but I was not shocked.

NARRATOR: Down College Street I walked then, past the remembered
invisible shops, Langley's, Castle Cigar Co; T. B. Brown's, Pullar's,
Aubrey Jeremiah, Goddard Jones, Richards, Hornes, Marles, Pleas-
ance and Harper, Star Supply, Sidney Heath, Wesley Chapel and

nothing. My search was leading me back, through pub and job and cafe, to the School. (*Fade*)

[SCHOOL BELL]

SCHOOLMASTER: Oh yes, yes, I remember him well, though I do not know if I would recognise him now: nobody grows any younger, or better, and boys grow into much the sort of men one would suppose, though sometimes the moustaches bewilder and one finds it hard to reconcile one's memory of a small none-too-clean urchin lying his way unsuccessfully out of his homework with a fierce and many-medalled sergeant-major with three children or a divorced chartered accountant; and it is hard to realise that some little tousled rebellious youth whose only claim to fame among his contemporaries was his undisputed right to the championship of the spitting contest is now perhaps one's own bank manager. Oh yes, I remember him well, the boy you are searching for: he looked like most boys, no better, brighter, or more respectful; he cribbed, mitched, spilt ink, rattled his desk and garbled his lessons with the worst of them; he could smudge, hedge, smirk, wriggle, wince, whimper, blarney, badger, blush, deceive, be devious, stammer, improvise, assume offended dignity or righteous indignation as though to the manner born; sullenly and reluctantly he drilled, for some small crime, under Sergeant Bird, so wittily nicknamed Oiseau, on Wednesday half-holidays, appeared regularly in detention classes, hid in the cloak-room during algebra, was, when a newcomer, thrown into the bushes of the Lower Playground by bigger boys, and threw new-comers into the bushes of the Lower Playground when *he* was a bigger boy; he scuffled at prayers, he interpolated, smugly, the time-honoured wrong irreverent words into the morning hymns, he helped to damage the headmaster's rhubarb, was thirty-third in trigonometry, and, as might be expected, edited the School Magazine. (*Fade*)

NARRATOR: The Hall is shattered, the echoing corridors charred where he scribbled and smudged and yawned in the long green days, waiting for the bell and the scamper into the Yard: the School on Mount Pleasant Hill has changed its face and its ways. Soon, they say, it may be no longer the School at all he knew and loved when he was a boy up to no good but the beat of his blood: the

185

names are havoc'd from the Hall and the carved initials burned from the broken wood. But the names remain. What names did he know of the dead? Who of the honoured dead did he know such a long time ago? The names of the dead in the living heart and head remain for ever. Of all the dead whom did he know?

[FUNERAL BELL]

VOICE: Evans, K. J.
  Haines, G. C.
  Roberts, I. L.
  Moxham, J.
  Thomas, H.
  Baines, W.
  Bazzard, F. H.
  Beer, L. J.
  Bucknell, R.
  Tywford, G.
  Vagg, E. A.
  Wright, G. (*Fade*)

NARRATOR: Then I tacked down the snowblind hill, a cat-o'-nine-gales whipping from the sea, and, white and eiderdowned in the smothering flurry, people padded past me up and down like prowling featherbeds. And I plodded through the ankle-high one cloud that foamed the town, into flat Gower Street, its buildings melted, and along long Helen's Road. Now my search was leading me back to the seashore.

[NOISE OF SEA, SOFTLY]

NARRATOR: Only two living creatures stood on the promenade, near the cenotaph, facing the tossed crystal sea: a man in a chewed muffler and a ratting cap, and an angry dog of a mixed make. The man diddered in the cold, beat his bare blue hands together, waited for some sign from sea or snow; the dog shouted at the weather, and fixed his bloodshot eyes on Mumbles Head. But when the man and I talked together, the dog piped down and fixed his eyes on me, blaming me for the snow. The man spoke towards the sea. Year in, year out, whatever the weather, once in the daytime, once in the dark, he always came to look at the sea. He knew all the dogs and boys and old men who came to see the sea, who ran or gambolled on the sand or stooped at the edges of the waves as though over a wild, wide, rolling ash-can. He knew the lovers who went to lie in the sandhills, the striding, masculine women who roared at their terriers like tiger-tamers, the loafing men whose work it was in the world to observe the great employment of the sea. He said:

PROMENADE-MAN: Oh yes, yes, I remember him well, but I didn't know what was his name. I don't know the names of none of the sandboys. They don't know mine. About fourteen or fifteen years old, you said, with a little red cap. And he used to play by Vivian's Stream. He used to dawdle in the arches, you said, and lark about on the railway-lines and holler at the old sea. He'd mooch about the dunes and watch the tankers and the tugs and the banana boats come out of the docks. He was going to run away to sea, he said. *I* know. On Saturday afternoon he'd go down to the sea when it was a long way out, and hear the foghorns, though he couldn't see the ships. And on Sunday nights, after chapel, he'd be swaggering with his pals along the prom, whistling after the girls.

GIRL (*Titter*): Does your mother know you're out? Go away now. Stop following us. (*Another girl titters*)

GIRL: Don't you say nothing, Hetty, you're only encouraging. No thank *you*, Mr Cheeky, with your cut-glass accent and your father's trilby! I don't want *no* walk on *no* sands. What d'you say? Ooh, listen to him, Het, he's swallowed a dictionary. No, I don't want to go with *no*body up *no* lane in the moonlight, see, and I'm not a baby-snatcher either. I seen you going to school along Terrace Road, Mr Glad-Eye, with your little satchel and wearing your red cap and all. You seen me wearing my ... no, you never. Hetty, mind your glasses! Hetty Harris, you're as bad as them. Oh, go away and do your homework, you. No, I'm not then. I'm nobody's homework, see. Cheek! Hetty Harris, don't you let him! Oooh, there's brazen! Well, just to the end of the prom, if you like. No further, mind.

PROMENADE-MAN: Oh yes, I knew him well. I've known him by the thousands.

NARRATOR: Even now, on the frozen foreshore, a high, far cry of boys, all like the boy I sought, slid on the glass of the streams and snowballed each other and the sky.

But I went on my way from the sea, up Brynmill Terrace and into

Glanbrydan Avenue where Bert Trick had kept a grocer's shop and, in the kitchen, threatened the annihilation of the ruling classes over sandwiches and jelly and blancmange. And I came to the shops and houses of the Uplands. Here and around here it was that the journey had begun of the one I was pursuing through his past.

[OLD PIANO CINEMA-MUSIC IN BACKGROUND]

FIRST VOICE: Here was once the flea-pit picture-house where he whooped for the scalping Indians with Jack Basset and banged for the rustlers' guns.

NARRATOR: Jackie Basset, killed.

THIRD VOICE: Here once was Mrs Ferguson's, who sold the best gobstoppers and penny packets full of surprises and a sweet kind of glue.

FIRST VOICE: In the fields behind Cwmdonkin Drive, the Murrays chased him and all cats.

SECOND VOICE: No fires now where the outlaws' fires burned and the paradisiacal potatoes roasted in the embers.

THIRD VOICE: In the Graig beneath Town Hill he was a lonely killer hunting the wolves (or rabbits) and the red Sioux tribe (or Mitchell brothers).

[FADE CINEMA-MUSIC INTO BACKGROUND OF CHILDREN'S VOICES RECITING, IN UNISON, THE NAMES OF THE COUNTIES OF WALES]

FIRST VOICE: In Mirador School he learned to read and count. Who made the worst raffia doilies? Who put water in Joyce's galoshes, every morning prompt as prompt? In the afternoons, when the children were good, they read aloud from Struwwelpeter. And when they were bad, they sat alone in the empty classroom, hearing, from above them, the distant, terrible, sad music of the late piano lesson.

[THE CHILDREN'S VOICES FADE. THE PIANO LESSON CONTINUES IN BACKGROUND]

NARRATOR: And I went up, through the white Grove, into Cwmdonkin Park, the snow still sailing and the childish, lonely, remembered music fingering on in the suddenly gentle wind. Dusk was folding the Park around, like another, darker snow. Soon the bell would ring for the closing of the gates, though the Park was empty. The park-keeper walked by the reservoir, where swans had glided, on his rounds. I walked by his side and asked him my questions, up the swathed drives past buried beds and loaded utterly still furred and birdless trees towards the last gate. He said:

PARK-KEEPER: Oh yes, yes, I knew him well. He used to climb the reservoir railings and pelt the old swans. Run like a billygoat over the grass you should keep off of. Cut branches off the trees. Carve words on the benches. Pull up moss in the rockery, go snip, snip through the dahlias. Fight in the bandstand. Climb the elms and moon up the top like a owl. Light fires in the bushes. Play on the green Bank. Oh yes, I knew him well. I think he was happy all the time. I've known him by the thousands.

NARRATOR: We had reached the last gate. Dusk drew around us and the town. I said: What has become of him now?

PARK-KEEPER: Dead.

NARRATOR: The Park-keeper said:

[THE PARK BELL RINGS]

PARK-KEEPER: Dead ... Dead ... Dead ... Dead ... Dead ... Dead.

20
A Dearth of Comic Writers

This conversation with Arthur Calder-Marshall, the presiding editor of the Light Programme series 'Books and Authors' at the time, was recorded on 10 February 1948 and broadcast on 14 February 1948. The producer was James Langham. Thomas's fee was seven guineas.

The programme was billed in the *Radio Times* as being about 'the dearth of comic books'; but the subject is really adult humorous writing, and Aneirin Talfan Davies's title for this piece in *Quite Early One Morning* is retained here as being more accurate. The present text is the BBC script in full.

A Dearth of Comic Writers

ARTHUR CALDER-MARSHALL: Now here in the studio today, we've got Dylan Thomas ... Well, Dylan Thomas, you're going to talk about the dearth of comic books. What are these comic books of which you think there's a dearth now?

DYLAN THOMAS: You don't want a string of laughterpieces of the past, an Old Guffaw's Almanac, a Recommended List of Laughs for the Inrisible Man; we can still laugh with the dead, but to laugh with living writers is, on the whole, a serious undertaking. And if anybody listening is reserving the writing of *his* comic book for a rainy day, then what does he think *this* is? – the dry spring of the world?

ARTHUR CALDER-MARSHALL: Agreed. But why? What's the reason for it?

DYLAN THOMAS: Well, there's one obvious reason. The condition of the world is such that most writers feel they cannot truthfully be 'comic' about it. (Was the world ever such that they could?) Perhaps they say: Can we single out the amiably comic eccentricity of individual beings, the ludicrous, the gauche, the maximless gawky, the dear and the daft and the droll, the runcible Booby, the Toby, the Pickwick, the barmy old Adam, when daily we are confronted, as social beings, by the dolt and the peeve and the minge and the bully, the maniac new Atom? I prefer the attitude of Pepys: '12th, Friday. Up, finding our beds good, but lousy; which made us merry.'

ARTHUR CALDER-MARSHALL: But bombs aren't as funny as bugs.

DYLAN THOMAS: Not in themselves. Comic writers can't expect society to be comic just for *them*. 'Do you serve women at this bar?'

192

'No,' says the barman, 'you've got to bring your own.' And society, to a comic writer, is always funny, even, or especially, on its death-bed. People walking into open lift-shafts, being wolfed by lions, missing the swung trapeze, are conventional subjects for a comic draughtsman; and the sight of society falling on its ear, and the prospect of civilisation itself going for a burton, offer writers possi-bilities of every kind of laugh. 'There is something in the house,' said the wife of a comic writer, in one of Algernon Blackwood's 'John Silence' stories, 'that prevents his feeling funny'. There's enough, God knows, going on in *our* house to drive Peacock's Prince Seithennyn from drink; but that doesn't prevent a writer from creating a great comic world of his own out of the tragic catastrophe of this. 'The best lack all conviction, while the worst are full of passionate intensity,' wrote Yeats. But grave, censorious, senatorial, soul-possessing Man, erect on his two spindles, is still a colossal joke. A man in love makes a practical cat laugh. A man in power makes Engels weep – with laughter.

ARTHUR CALDER-MARSHALL: A great comic world of his own; that's what you said wasn't it? Well, what about W. W. Jacobs?

DYLAN THOMAS: One of the trimmest, funniest, and most exact Edwardian writers, whose dialogue is as neat and sly and spare and taut as his mercenary and matrimonial plots. Here, in what I call a *minor* comic world, are the landlubber dreams of sailors-on-leave, the visions of a pocketfull of bradburies in snug saloons with buxom barmaids. Here are the intricate discomfitures of rival seamen; trucu-lent unpaid rolling-pinned landladies; free fills of baccy; beer on the sly and the nod and the slate. Here all married women are harridans, all widows are plump and comfy and have a little bit put by, all unmarried girls are arch and mysterious, all men without exception are knaves or fools, and very often both, and are solely occupied in strategies concerning money and women and the getting and losing of them.

ARTHUR CALDER-MARSHALL: That's Jacobs's dockside world; and of course there's the other comic world of the country, the Cauliflower Inn and Bob Pretty. I agree they are *minor* comic worlds. They are comic worlds in contrast to Pett Ridge and Barry Pain. But what would you say about Stephen Leacock?

DYLAN THOMAS: I read only his 'Sunshine Sketches of a Little Town',

193

for only in these did Leacock create a *home* for his imagination, a 'place' in which *his* people could be born and die, love, fall down, philosophize, have their hair cut, let their hair down, put their feet up.

ARTHUR CALDER-MARSHALL: Doesn't P.G. Wodehouse fit your definition of a comic world perfectly?

DYLAN THOMAS: Those chinless, dim and eyeglassed, asinine, bespatted Drones were borrowed, lock, stock and title, from memories of the *Pink 'Un* period and the *Smart Set*, from the ghostly, hansom past of the moneyed masher and the stage-door johnny. Some people like Jeeves, but include me out: I, for one, do not appreciate gentleman's gentleman's relish.

ARTHUR CALDER-MARSHALL: But why shouldn't a writer write about characters who existed – only in the past?

DYLAN THOMAS: A truly comic, invented world must live *at the same time* as the world we live in.

ARTHUR CALDER-MARSHALL: You're still dodging about in the Edwardian period. But what about this dearth of present day comic writers?

DYLAN THOMAS: What does it amount to? Funny columns in English newspapers, fence-sittings, Beachcombings, Shymakings; the laboured, witless whimsy and pompous facetiousness of that national institution – or poorhouse of ideas – which the *New Yorker* once called 'Paunch'.

ARTHUR CALDER-MARSHALL: Don't be so snooty! But what about books?

DYLAN THOMAS: What about them? All the best – or nearly all the best – modern comic books are written by Americans.

ARTHUR CALDER-MARSHALL: The *New Yorker* school?

DYLAN THOMAS: James Thurber, S.J. Perelman, Frank Sullivan, and Robert Benchley, all *have* written for that brilliant family magazine, but have nothing in common except their superiority to modern English comic journalists.

ARTHUR CALDER-MARSHALL: I'd say they had this in common. Ten years ago I thought them all very funny. Now I find them all much less funny.

DYLAN THOMAS: Maybe, but it's still impossible to compare the shy and baffled, introspective essays, fables, and fabulous reminiscences

194

of Thurber, his cowering terror before the mechanical gadgets, the militant neuroses, the ubiquitous women, the democratic pitfalls and big-business bogies of this modern Americanised Age, it's impossible to compare him, class him, school him, with the glib Groucho zaniness of S. J. Perelman, who writes like a Hollywood advertising copywriter after reading James Joyce, Amanda Ross, Kraft-Ebbing, Doctor Spooner, E. E. Cummings, and Sam Goldwyn's ace publicity stooge in a state of hypertension in a Turkish Bath managed by Man-Mountain Dean. But Thurber, Sullivan, Perelman, Benchley, all excellent comic writers, are all *essayists*; and I am concerned with comic, constructive writers of *stories*. I want, without boisterous backslapping, without the hail-fellow guffaw of the tweedy pipe-sucking tankard-quaffing professional literary comedian, without nudge and titter, without the reedy neigh of the reviewer, I want laughter in books, the sight, and smell, and *sound* of laughter. And almost the only sound I hear from stories now recalls, to me, the sound of the watch in Frances Cornford's poem:

> I thought it said in every tick;
> I am so sick, so sick, so sick;
> O death, come quick, come quick, come quick,
> Come quick, come quick, come quick, come quick.

ARTHUR CALDER-MARSHALL: That was Dylan Thomas bewailing the dearth of comic books ... It takes a serious poet to do that ... Charley Chaplin's ambition I believe is to play Hamlet.

21
The English Festival of Spoken Poetry

For a fee of twelve guineas James Langham of the Third Programme arranged for Thomas to do a journalistic piece on the annual amateur competition held in London for the recitation of poetry. The script was broadcast on 30 July 1948, and printed (except for the last two paragraphs) in *The Listener* (5 August 1948).

The English Festival of Spoken Poetry

There is, in many people, a need to share enthusiasm, which is often expressed in behaviour known, nicely, as 'showing off'; common to actors, poets, politicians, and other trapezists. Many people who read poems like some of them so much that they cannot keep their liking to themselves. They are not content with saying, 'Do you know de la Eliot's "Waste Stranger" or W. H. Housman's "A Dog Beneath the Gallows". Isn't it, or aren't they, lovely?' But they needs must say, 'Listen to this,' and reel the lovely stuff off aloud. Sometimes they like the noise their voices make. They find that the words of the poem they reel, familiar and pleasant, acquire a surprising pleasant strangeness when boomed, minced, Keened, crooned, Dyalled, or Wolfitted. Known words grow wings; print springs and shoots; the voice discovers the poet's ear; it's found that a poem on a page is only half a poem. And the speakers, realizing the inadequacy of their hitherto silent interpretation, sometimes set about learning the business of reading aloud; which is to say, they set about learning the poems which they know by heart, by head and tongue. They put that noise-on-paper, which is a poem, into their chests and throats, and let it out. They find that good poets are better than they (the readers) thought they were, for crying out loud. And then some of these readers, wanting to show others all that is missed by reading poetry dumb, look around for an audience. Families, like countries, take their prophets unkindly, but a verse-speaker in the home is dishonour to be hooted. Show me the family circle that sits in silence while a son or daughter mouths, with gawky zeal, a lyric aloud, and I will recite the whole of *Hudibras* to a week-end convention of Moose. These readers cannot rush into the

Third Programme at a moment's notice, past the sentinel guard of artists' rifles, disturb the uneven tenor of Tibetan operas and the phalanx of harpsichords. They can found verse-speaking societies in their home places, but who is there to listen except other verse-readers who are only waiting for them to stop? Where can people who like reading poems aloud very much do it? Do it, that is, to a discriminating, enthusiastic, and, on the whole, altruistic audience?

The Oxford Festival of Spoken Poetry was founded twenty years ago, and grew up around the love and care of the late Laurence Binyon. The festival took place in Oxford until the outbreak of the last never-to-be-repeated war. Now it is conducted in London, but its committee and their supporters hope soon to be able to return to Oxford. The Festival of Spoken Poetry is run by poets. Nearly all the judges are poets (poets: men who work hard at another job in order to be able to work hard at the job they really like when they're not working). The judges of the festival: cool (specially now), impersonal, knowledgeable, Nature, lofty uncompromising not-to-be-bribed-or-trifled-with ascetic remote creatures who (if only the competitors could know – and I speak for the masculine judges alone) sit there in their perspiring glory, thinking of cricket and ice and legs, their little hearts thumping among so many summery flowered dresses, bright smiles, untrammelled youth, high heels, endeavour, scent, and zeal.

It may perhaps be thought that I am frivolling about what is, really, a most sincere, conscientious, and extremely able festival. But it *is* a festival. It is not a cold competition. It runs for four days every year, and it is to be enjoyed. We all enjoy it, competitors, judges, carpers, audience and all. There were over three hundred people this year, from all over the country, who stood up and read Marlowe, Tennyson, Sydney Keyes, Pope, mostly because they love reading poems aloud, and here was the place and the time to read them with no strings or nonsense. This is no Phil the High-Falutin's Ball, but a festival of and for unfrumpish, unfreakish, sane people with voices. When a competitor is not reading, he or she is listening to the others read: and listening with a knowledgeable liking.

I'm not going to say that all the readers are first class. This is a festival and an amateur competition, not a professional day out for successful exhibitionists. Many of the competitors would wish to become full-time actors, readers, broadcasters; a few may be. Like everything that is any good, this festival is full of faults. I think that the readers should be allowed, if they want to, to have, in front of them, the text of the poems they are reading. I thought that when a *long* poem came up to be read, some of the competitors very dully over-slowed their reading because they had too much to remember and were, all too obviously, feeling for the next verse. I thought that some of the 'judgments' had to be made too hastily, so that a tepid, but finished, reading was likely to be valued higher than a true, warm but hesitant, occasionally blundering, one.

Many readings were plagued with the more obvious sicknesses of reading aloud: insistent sibilance, the (for want of a better phrase) 'Old Vic' voice: an affected inflecting that strangles rhythm and truncheons meaning. There was the 'dead voice': a way of speaking that pretends to emphasize the importance of flat understatement only because the ability to *give* isn't there. The smile, not the voice, beautiful: the supposition of an arch, nudging connivance between speaker and listener, the attitude of '*We* know, though the others don't.' There was, though rarely, the *acting* of the spoken word: the taught, but never taut, gesture to illustrate an unillustratable, except by inflexion, point or temper of a line; the starry-eyed horizon-searching; the mechanical handwork of simulated passion, like a soprano milking a goat.

But oh so rare. Nearly everyone, nearly *everyone*, enjoyed this festival, as it has been enjoyed for twenty years. No humbug. No Slade-fringed or tennis-party voice, no hairy crank with a jaegar lilt or a maypole accent, no henna'd and bangled New-lifing. And the standard of the reading was extremely high. Poems are written in lines, and if you shut your eyes, which was sometimes difficult to do, you could hear, with no jarring of brakes, where the lines stopped. You could *hear*.

And that leads me, finally, to say that the two readers, the first and second prize-winners, who you will hear in a moment, read on the platform of a good-sized theatre. They are not, now, going to adapt their voices to the microphone. They are going to speak as we heard them from the platform. The microphone's mucked up the music-hall. But never, I hope, the Oxford Festival of Spoken Poetry.

I will now ask Patricia Watson and Robert Sewell to speak the stanzas from Shelley's 'Adonais' which were set as the best piece for the night of the Finale.

22
Living in Wales

Through Roy Campbell, Thomas was invited to give a talk in the Scottish Region series 'Scottish Life and Letters', which turned out to be a personal piece on the unlikely subject of returning to live in Wales. The talk was recorded in London on 16 June 1949, and the discs were shipped to Aberdeen for transmission on 23 June 1949. Roy Campbell wrote a note to the Scottish producers Maurice Lindsey and George Bruce:

> Dylan Thomas's piece for you is first class rococo. He makes an exuberant attack on British Railways' buffet-cars and Oxford residents and paints a pretty dreary picture of Wales; the only country not attacked is fortunately Scotland. We shall record at 3 today, but wish to warn you that a solemn railway official might take treble umbrage. Please return discs here: I shall recommend it to Third.

The discs were damaged on return, and the talk was not rebroadcast.

Living in Wales

Before I came back to live in Wales, a very little time ago, I was travelling on a morning train from Oxford to London when, suddenly, the desire to live neither in Oxford nor in London, or to travel between them, came very near to knocking me down, which would not be difficult.

I was, at that moment, chillily perched on a stool, old from sleep, at the tumbler-circled counter in the bellying buffet-car, watching, over my black, lace-collared, but Liffeyless glass, the corpse-grey liver-sausage and dredgered tea, the putty rolls and washing-day lager, being wolfed and lapped by furtive, small, damp physicists and large ball-playing, booming boys with bulldog pipes and scarves as thick and many as a cabman's waistcoats.

There, all about me, chastely dropping, with gloved and mincing just-so fingers, saccharine tablets into their cups of stewed Thames-water, or poising their cigarette-holders like blowpipes, or daintily raising, the little finger crooked, a currant bun to the flashing snap of their long, strong teeth, tall and terrible women neighed: women inaccessible as goat crags, nowhere, on all this smacked and blossoming earth, at home except on lofty, cold bicycles with baskets at the front full of lettuce, library books, and starchless bread, aloofly scything along the High, the wind never raising their sensible skirts, and their knitted pastel stockings full of old hockey muscles.

There, all about me, long thin accents with yellow waistcoats and carefully windswept hair, one lock over the eye, bleated and fluted. In a drawl of corduroy at the tea-urn, vowels were plucked and trussed.

Tiny, dry, egghead dons, smelling of water-biscuit, with finickety lips and dolls' bowties like butterflies poisoned and pinned, solved the crossword puzzles behind their octagonal glasses and smirked their coffee up.

Slade-fringed, cowlike girls in, may be, hessian, put down the books they could not read and turned big, mooing eyes towards the passing landscape they could not paint.

One ox-broad, beardless boy, tattooed with his school colours, manfully drank up his gin and lemon, wishing it were all lemon.

And there I watched that dottle-tasting liquid history of scorched and shaken tea passing the lips and going the gastric rounds of gaunt and hairy horn-rimmed lecturers in French who tapped their Gaulloise on their Sartre and saw, with disdain, the pretty gasworks ripple by, ebullient Didcot come and go, red Reading fly by like a biscuit: they were bent on an existentialist spree.

And then and there, as I watched them all, desire raised its little fist.

I did not want to be in England, now that they were there.

I did not want to be in England, whether they were there or not.

I wanted to be in Wales.

Let me be fair, however much I dislike it. The men and women, and the others, in that carriage were not England. I do not point to one group of people, however repellent, and say, 'That, to me, is England. Help, let me out!' I distrust the man who says, 'Now *that* is England,' and shows me a tailwag of rich tweedy women babytalking to their poodles. That is no more England than a village cricket match is.

No, my desire not to be in England rose and crowned me at that very moment; and that is all.

For a long time, indeed, I had been tired of living among strangers in a dark and savage country whose customs and tribal rites I shall never understand, breathing an alien air, hearing, everywhere, the snobcalls, the prigchants, the mating cries, the tom-toms of a curious, and maybe cannibal, race. The reverence paid to the cultural witchdoctors sickened me, as did their ritual pomp, their odorous courts, and the periodic sacrifices of the young. I wanted to sit no longer, as I had sat for years, in that narrow-vowelled jungle, alone as it seemed, by my log fire – (a bright light keeps the beasts at bay) – rolling the word Wales round my tongue like a gobstopper of magical properties, ringing the word like a bell, making it rise and fall, whisper and thunder like the Welsh sea whose fish are great Liberals, fond of laver-bread and broth, and who always, on Sundays, attend their green and watery chapels.

Alone there, the wolves of Middlesex mewling outside my llanwigwam fire, I used to think, to keep me company, of the bits and pieces of sounds and pictures, tunes and colours, places and persons, that meant my home to me. The outpost Englishman, monkey-suited for dinner in the exotic bush, toasts Piccadilly in whiskey, or so I have read. I could not put on steeplehat and red flannel petticoat and drink to the bright lights of Llanstephan in light ale. All I could do was remember, and I am good at that.

I could remember, to keep me going through the long Saxon nights, the smell of the streets on Sunday, palpable as bombazine. The scooped hollow sound that Sunday made as I woke: religion in a black seashell. The melancholy endless mothballed avenues of Sunday in the sunken suburbs, where not a lawnmower stirs. The tinroofed chapel where I trebled 'Aberystwyth' and made calf eyes at the minto-sucking girls.

The primitive, dark promenade of hidden loves after chapel, the long, low Sunday whistle to make the girls turn round, and, always, mine had glasses. The rattle of the milkcart Monday morning, and the first tram hissing like a gander to the steelworks. The hunchback streets on Sunday morning, men with white mufflers and lean dogs waiting for a miracle outside the pub shut like a tomb, and the beetles passing them by with their noses and brollies in the air. The sound of the colliers' voices at night left on the air above the crippled street. 'Nos da, Will.' 'Nos da, Shoni.' 'Nos da, Evan.' 'Nos da.' 'Nos da.' And the stars coming out sweet as the smell of fish and chips. Anything, anything would do to remember to ward off the pinstriped wolves. Remember the shop at the corner, Mrs Evans the Pop, full of liquorice, bootlaces, lamp oil, pear-drops, and a smell that was comfier than roses. The front parlour, which nobody ever entered save the preacher on special occasions or sometimes the committee members of the Mothers' Union or the rare relative from England or another foreign country, and of course, the family mourners every now and then to sit on the edges of the unused chairs and hear the voice of the clock ticking their own lives away between the two china dogs.

But all this was easy stuff, like settles in the corners, hams on the hooks, hymns after stop-tap, tenors with leeks, the hwyl at Ebenezer, the cockles on the stalls, dressers, eisteddfodau, Welshcakes, slagheaps, funerals, and bethel-bells. What was harder to remember was what birds sounded like and said in Gower; what sort of a sound and a shape was Carmarthen Bay; how did the morning come in through the windows of Solva; what silence when night fell in the Aeron Valley.

I could not remember, try as I might, if I was a different man, if a man at all, when cockily bulking in Wales than when flinching in London from traffic and other writers or guiltily buttonholing the Soho night to unbosom my buckets of woes.

I knew, as I walked the City, the snarl of the grimestones of the bread-and-butter streets. Did the pavements of my home town bounce with a different cry?

I knew, oh I knew, what my face looked like in the cracked, advertisement-bitten looking-glass of the skies over Fleet and Wardour. Had I, awaking, the same face, then in the shaving-glass of the sky propped above the Welsh sea's sink?

I could not remember, try as I might, if the old, booted body that bore its grumbles and juices so scowlingly up Portland Place to do its morning rant was the same as that which, hoofed with seaweed, did a jig on the Llanina sands and barked at the far mackerel.

Lost and blown about in London town, a barrel-shaped leaf, am I still the same, I said to myself, as that safe and sound loller at the corners of Wales who, to my memory, was happy as a sandman.

How could I answer my silly questions unless I went back to Wales?

And now that I am back in Wales, am I the same person, sadly staring over the flat, sad, estuary sands, watching the herons walk like women poets, hearing the gab of gulls, alone and lost in a soft kangaroo pocket of the sad, salt West, who once, so very little time ago, trundled under the blaring lights, to the tunes of cabhorns, his beautiful barrow of raspberries?

The properties of my memory remain.

Still the rebuking chapel has a cold eye and a sweet voice. Sunday, still, wears spiderweb gloves, blows its nose in an umbrella, and smells of wet fur.

Market Day still clucks on the cobbles among the cockles and clogs, ducks, drakes, and gaiters, babyshawls, fishfrails, parchs and baskets.

Saturday night wears its cap on the side of its brilliantine, and is full of pints.

I know that I am home again because I feel just as I felt when I was not at home, only more so.

And still there are harps and whippets on the castled and pitheaded hills.

23
Edward Thomas

As part of the Welsh Home Service 'Arts Magazine', Thomas was
invited to make a selection of Edward Thomas's poetry, with comments.
'Enclosed the brief E. Thomas script and also the *Collected Poems*,' he
wrote to the producer Elwyn Evans on 13 July 1949. 'What time do
you need me on the night?' (*Letters* p. 939). The rehearsal was at
2.30 p.m. on 29 July 1949, in Cardiff, with transmission the same
evening.

In the present text, several of Edward Thomas's poems included in
the broadcast have been omitted; two of these, 'The Owl' and 'The
Child on the Cliffs', were included in 'Welsh Poetry' (script 5).

Edward Thomas

I do not know how much of a Welshman Edward Thomas was, and it does not matter. He was a poet, which means that he is a poet still, and always will be, whether in the future he is read or not, or whether no poems at all are read, or whether, because of the powerful insanity of rulers and the apathy or persecution of the innumerable ruled, there is nobody left to read them.

In his lifetime, he was known and loved by a very, loving few. Now, since his death, he is known and loved by very many, and yearly this is more so. There is in his poems an unassumingly profound sense of permanence. A war came, and ditched him, but his poems stay with no other wounds than those that caused them. Though that is not really true: it was the wish for wholeness made the poems, not the wounds of his melancholy.

The shy, passionate love he breathed into his compassionate and ennobling poems – poems, as Walter de la Mare says, that ennoble by simplification – lives now in a number of people. His love has multiplied. With time, the still, turning centre of his poems has broadened and deepened, though it still is as fresh as the dew, as inexplicably grievous as the dying of each day and the passing of seasons. He has grown, surely and simply and slowly, into our language, until we can hardly think that there was a time when he was not alive. It is as though we had always known his poems, and were only waiting for him to write them.

But I will not try to muddy his lucidity by portentous phrases, by chucking into a deep, pure pool old stones with labels. And even less is this a pool to play ducks and drakes on: a clever, skimming sentence raises no ridges of ripples there. It is best not to speak of Edward Thomas at all, but just to speak him. Here is his poem, 'The Owl'.

[Reads 'The Owl'.]

Edward Thomas knew and loved fields, woods and roads, mouse, wren, robin, the missel-thrush that loves juniper, the ghostly-white parsley-flower, hawthorn berry, hazel tuft, newmown hay, the cuckoo crying over the untouched dew, churchyards, farms and byres, children, wild geese, scarecrows, ferrets, horses in the sun.

He tried to know the inner meaning of grassblade and star, the unknown language of silence, the heartbreaking purpose of a pebble among millions and millions of pebbles, all making sense, but whose sense? He tried, not to answer, but to ask again, clearly, from his sad and lovely knowledge, the old, old question of 'Who are you?' to one's own self grown strangely evasive in the dusk deepening, and to God's world around to which one has never been properly introduced.

This poem is called 'The Sign-Post'.

[Reads 'The Sign-Post'.]

I said I did not know how Welsh he was, but we know from his poems that he loved the country of Wales. Walter de la Mare says of him, 'His voice was low and gentle, but musical, with a curious sweetness and hollowness when he sang his old Welsh songs to his children.' And here are three poems about children. The first: 'The Child In The Orchard'.

[Reads 'The Child In The Orchard'.]

And, next, the little poem called 'Snow'.

[Reads 'Snow'.]

And, last of these, 'The Child On The Cliffs'.

[Reads 'The Child On The Cliffs'.]

For those who have read de la Mare's introduction to Edward Thomas's *Collected Poems*, there can be little left to say about him. All of himself that is not in his poems is there, caught by a friend and another poet, in a few, clear, gay and grave pages. After those, there are only the poems.

And all that remains is to enjoy the poems, now. It has never really mattered what *poetry* is: we know what poems are, because it is their joy and purpose to move us to knowledge.

If you want a definition of poetry, say that it is the one particular thing in poems that moves you most: the texture, the images, the cadences. Say, 'Poetry is what makes me cry, what tingles my hair and scalp, what makes me want to do this, or that, or nothing.' And leave it at that. All that matters about poetry is the enjoyment of it, however tragic it may be. All that matters is the eternal movement behind it, the vast undercurrent of human grief, folly, pretension, exaltation and ignorance, however unlofty the intention of the poem. Confronted by any poet, you cannot do more than let him speak confidentially for himself, which is as it should be. I shall read, now, what is, to me, one of his loveliest poems, 'The Unknown Bird'.

Three lovely notes he whistled, too soft to be heard
If others sang; but others never sang
In the great beech-wood all that May and June.
No one saw him: I alone could hear him
Though many listened. Was it but four years
Ago? or five? He never came again.

Oftenest when I heard him I was alone,
Nor could I ever make another hear.
La-la-la! he called, seeming far-off –
As if a cock crowed past the edge of the world,
As if the bird or I were in a dream.
Yet that he travelled through the trees and sometimes
Neared me, was plain, though somehow distant still
He sounded. All the proof is – I told men
What I had heard.
I never knew a voice,
Man, beast, or bird, better than this. I told
The naturalists; but neither had they heard
Anything like the notes that did so haunt me,
I had them clear by heart and have them still.
Four years, or five, have made no difference. Then
As now that La-la-la! was bodiless sweet:
Sad more than joyful it was, if I must say

210

That it was one or other, but if sad
'Twas sad only with joy too, too far off
For me to taste it. But I cannot tell
If truly never anything but fair
The days were when he sang, as now they seem.
This surely I know, that I who listened then,
Happy sometimes, sometimes suffering
A heavy body and a heavy heart,
Now straightway, if I think of it, become
Light as that bird wandering beyond my shore.

Among all modern poets of this century, there is not one who is more of a confidential speaker than Edward Thomas. His poetry is talk lifted to the sky, and rooted in the earth. It is both glowingly loose-woven and gravely careful, colloquially free and yet taut and crafted with all the loving care of a man to whom poetry, whatever its meaning, was the waving wheat from which the bread of life is made. Again to quote de la Mare, 'his poetry must be read slowly, as naturally as if it were talk, and then it will surrender himself, his beautiful world.'

But who did ever talk like this but Edward Thomas? And who but he could speak, 'To-night'?

Harry, you know at night
The larks in Castle Alley
Sing from the attic's height
As if the electric light
Were the true sun above a summer valley:
Whistle, don't knock, to-night.

I shall come early, Kate:
And we in Castle Alley
Will sit close out of sight
Alone, and ask no light
Of lamp or sun above a summer valley:
To-night I can stay late.

And who but Edward Thomas could so simply say – 'Sowing'?

It was a perfect day
For sowing; just
As sweet and dry was the ground
As tobacco-dust.

I tasted deep the hour
Between the far
Owl's chuckling first soft cry
And the first star.

A long stretched hour it was;
Nothing undone
Remained; the early seeds
All safely sown.

And now, hark at the rain.
Windless and light,
Half a kiss, half a tear,
Saying good-night.

He was twenty five years old when, in Alun Lewis's words, 'a bullet stopped his song', and the very last words for him could well be these opening lines of John Clare, a poet with whom he felt in deep sympathy:

Love lives beyond
The tomb, the earth, which fades like dew!
I love the fond
The faithful, and the true.

And here, to end with, is Edward Thomas's poem, 'Lights Out'.

[Reads 'Lights Out'.]

24
On Reading One's Own Poems

From London on 24 September 1949 Thomas read a selection of his own poems, with commentary, for the Third Programme. Production was by Hugh Stewart; his fee was twenty guineas.

The title was supplied by Aneirin Talfan Davies for publication in *Quite Early One Morning.* The present text is the BBC script checked against the extant BBC recording of the programme; the texts of the poems themselves have been omitted.

On Reading One's Own Poems

To choose what I should read tonight, I looked through seventy odd poems of mine, and found that many *are* odd indeed and that some may be poems. And I decided not to choose those that strike me, still, as pretty peculiar, but to stick to a few of the ones that do move a little way towards the state and destination I imagine I intended to be theirs when, in small rooms in Wales, arrogantly and devotedly I began them.

For I like to think that the poems most narrowly odd are among those I wrote earliest, and that the later poems are wider and deeper – though time, if interested, may well prove me wrong, and find that the reverse is true, or that each statement is false.

I do not remember – that is the point – the first impulse that pumped and shoved most of the earlier poems along, and they are still too near to me, with their vehement beat-pounding black and green rhythms like those of a very young policeman exploding, for me to see the written evidence of it. My interpretation of them – if that is not too weighty a word just for reading them aloud and trying to give some idea of their sound and shape – could only be a parroting of the say that I once had.

'And all that a reader-aloud of his own poems can hope to do is to try to put across his own memory of the original impulses behind his poems, deepening, maybe, and if only for a moment, the inner meaning of the words on the printed pages.' How I wish I could agree whole-heartedly with that, let alone hope to achieve it! But, oh, the danger! For what a reader-aloud of his own poems so often does is to mawken or melodramatize them, making a single simple phrase break with the

214

tears or throb with the terrors from which he deludes himself the phrase has been born.

There is the other reader, of course, who manages, by studious flatness, semi-detachment, and an almost condescending undersaying of his poems, to give the impression that what he really means is: Great things, but my own.

That I belong to the very *dangerous* first group of readers will be only too clear.

The first poem is titled by its first line: 'There Was a Saviour'.

[Reads 'There Was a Saviour'.]

The next poem tells of a mother and her child who is about to be born. It is not a narrative, nor an argument, but a series of conflicting images which move through pity and violence to an unreconciled acceptance of suffering: the mother's *and* the child's. This poem has been called obscure. I refuse to believe that it is obscurer than pity, violence, or suffering. But being a poem, not a lifetime, it is more compressed:

[Reads 'If my head hurt a hair's foot'.]

Reading one's own poems aloud is letting the cat out of the bag. You may have always suspected bits of a poem to be overweighted, overviolent, or daft, and then, suddenly, with the poet's tongue around them, your suspicion is made certain. How he slows up a line to savour it, remembering what trouble it took, once upon a time, to make it just so, at the very moment, you may think, when the poem needs crispness and speed. Does the cat snarl or mew the better when its original owner – or father, even, the tom-poet – lets it out of the bag, than when another does, who never put it in?

Here is a poem called 'Poem in October'.

[Reads 'Poem in October'.]

The next poem I'll read is the only one I have written that is, directly, about the life and death of one particular human being I knew – and not about the very many lives and deaths whether seen, as in my first poems, in the tumultous world of my own being or, as in the later poems, in war, grief, and the great holes and corners of universal love.

215

[Reads 'After the funeral'. The script indicates he was to have read 'A Winter's Tale', but it is crossed out, with a note that 'A Refusal to Mourn' and 'In My Craft or Sullen Art' were to be inserted.]

25
Swansea and the Arts

Thomas wrote jocularly to John Davenport on 11 October 1949 that he had been 'broadcasting from Swansea with Dan Jones and the boys' (*Letters* pp. 719–20). The 'boys' were Vernon Watkins, Alfred Janes, and John Prichard. The broadcast – these were separate, scripted contributions rather than a discussion – was recorded in the Swansea studio, producer John Griffiths, on 6 October 1949, for transmission on 24 October 1949 in the Welsh Home Service. Thomas's fee was twelve guineas.

Only a small extract from this broadcast was published in *Quite Early One Morning*, under the title 'Wales and the Artist'. The present text prints all of Thomas's remarks.

Swansea and the Arts

ANNOUNCER: This is the Welsh Home Service. On this the occasion
of the Swansea Festival of Music – three writers, a composer and a
painter, all Swansea men, have come to the microphone to talk
about their art and about Swansea. They are Dylan Thomas, Vernon
Watkins, John Prichard, Daniel Jones and Alfred Janes. And here,
introducing the programme and his friends is Dylan Thomas.

DYLAN THOMAS: We speak from the Grove of Swansea. But if anyone
in the deep damp caverns of the rustic dead, in some Welsh tenebrous
regional, should have seen this programme announced in the Radio
Tombs, turned on his badger's set, tuned in on a long-forgotten
gravelength and caught that opening statement, let me hasten to
tell him that he, alas, would hardly recognise the Grove at all. Where
once, on the swain-littered grass, to the music of the jocund rebeck
and the cries of nymphs on the run, shepherds piped, elves pucked,
goats panned, dryads hama'd, milkmaids were merry, satyrs busy,
centaurs forward, now stands the studio of the B.B.C. Here notices,
cold as ice-cream, say, Silence, Please, where once you could not
hear a Phyllida drop for the noise of the Corydons. And here where
the microphones disapprove, like sneering aunts, amorous dianas
of the golden uplands stopped at the old pagan whistle. Everything
in the Grove has changed. Or nearly everything. I know where the
satyrs go by night, but that would be advertising.

Five of us, then, sit in this desecrated Grove, on chairs, not hillocks;
our little cloven feet are shoed; our shirtcuffs fray where flowery
bangles once budded; some of us wear glasses; and the mead is off.

218

Three writers, a painter, and a composer, have come together –
in a suburb of Swansea where maybe once a sweeter life haymade
in the old gold dogdays – to talk about (more or less) how they
regard the town of their birth or upbringing as a place in which to
do their work. (I except myself for the moment. Though Swansea
bore me, and though indeed I have bored Swansea in my time, I do
not now live in it. I am by nature a globe-trotter. I live in the next
county.)

Five artists – if you will excuse us – of Wales are all living and
working in Wales. Whatever our reasons for this – and some you
will hear – we do not say: 'Because we live and work in Wales, then
other artists of Wales who live and work in other places are less
honest, sensible, devoted, Celtic, etcetera, than we. Live where you
like', we say, 'if you can'.

But too many of the artists of Wales who go to live permanently
in, for example, London, begin almost at once to anglicise themselves
beyond recognition – (though this, of course, does not apply to
artists alone. I know in London a Welsh hairdresser who has striven
so vehemently to abolish his accent that he sounds like a man
speaking with the Elgin marbles in his mouth). They ape the narrow
'a'. They repudiate the Welsh language, whether they know it or
not. By the condescending telling of comic apocryphal tales about
Dai and Evan from the Valleys, they earn, in the company of cultural
lickspittles who condescend to them in their turn, sorry dinners and
rounds of flat drinks. They fall for the latest isms gullibly as pups for
rubber bones. They confirm, by their spaniel adulation and their
ignorance of the tradition that inevitably leads to the experiment,
the suspicions of unWelsh experimental artists that all the Welsh are
humbugs, especially Welsh artists. In exhibitions, concerts, cocktail
parties, there they are on the horn-rimmed edges, stifling their
natural ardour so that they may disparagingly drawl, and with
knowledgeable satiety, of the paintings, the music, the guests, their
host, corsetting their voices so that no lilt or inflection of Welsh
enthusiasm may exult or pop out. 'Ecktually,' they say, 'I was born
in Cwmbwrla, but Soho's better for my gouaches.' They set up, in
grey, whining London, a little mock Wales of their own, an exile
government of dispossessed intellectuals dispossessed not of their
country but of their intellects. And they return home, every long

now and then, like slummers, airily to treat and backslap their grooved old friends, to enquire, half-laughingly, the whereabouts of streets and buildings as though they did not know them in the deepest dark, to drag, with all the magnets of their snobbery, the christian names and numbers of wives of aged painters, the haunts of up-and-going poets, the intimate behaviour of the famous musicians whom they have not met, and to jingle in their pockets and mouths their foreign-made pennies, opinions, and intonations.

On the other hand, too many of the artists of Wales stay in Wales too long, giants in the dark behind the parish pump, pygmies in the nationless sun, enviously sniping at the artists of other countries rather than attempting to raise the standard of art of their own country by working fervently at their own words, paint, or music.

And too many of the artists of Wales spend too much time talking about the position of the artists of Wales.

There is only one position for an artist anywhere: and that is, upright.

First of all, then, Vernon Watkins, poet and present. I think him to be the most profound and greatly accomplished Welshman writing poems in English, and he is one of the few poets I know, intensely occupied with his craft, who happily makes a living in a way that has nothing to do with words. So many writers, because their own serious writing does not pay, live by writing about writing, lecturing about writing, reviewing other writers, scriptwriting, advertising, journalising, boiling pots for the chainstore publishers; Vernon Watkins writes nothing but poems. Very properly, he makes his living by other people's money: in a bank. He is proof against the dangers (so tempting to poets, such as myself, who are not qualified to extract their livelihoods other than by the use of language), the dangers of mellifluous periphrasis, otiose solipsism, the too-easy spin and flow of the paid word.

Vernon Watkins ...

[VERNON WATKINS SPEAKS.]

DYLAN THOMAS: Years ago, when he was a student at the Royal Academy of Arts, I shared rooms (and what rooms) with Alfred Janes, painter; and those ginger-bearded days seem full to me, now, of his apples carved in oil, his sulphurously glowing lemons, his infernal kippers. Waking up, one saw all around one the Welsh fires burning behind those fanatically diligent, minutely knife-cut, fossil-indented interlogical patterns of rind and scale, and felt like a fish on a red-hot flowery slab. After many Academy awards, and several paintings hung in London galleries, he returned to Swansea to work and experiment, which were synonymous. And a very strange world of enormous human (maybe) beings, in flowing Renaissance gowns and herringbone tweeds, acting peculiar, sometimes levitating, in geometrical alle(maybe)gories came into existence in number 90 High Street. The war took him away to Oldham and Egypt, and after the war he came home again, worked on landscapes real and imaginary, portraits, drawings, had an exhibition, in Swansea, of 40 paintings, and will soon have a one-man show in London. Why he lives in Swansea he'll tell you now.

[ALFRED JANES SPEAKS.]

DYLAN THOMAS: The first work of Daniel Jones I remember seeing was an historical novel called *Pembroke Castle*, written in exercise books at the age of eight. Though the influence of Sir Walter Scott was more than evident upon those immature pages, yet even then a discerning critic could see, in its vigorous, if chaotic, incidents, and its frequent, if impossible, dialogue, no sign at all that Daniel Jones would one day be a composer of music on a very great scale. Born in Pembroke, which no doubt influenced his early choice of historical subject, Daniel Jones moved to Swansea as soon as he could, and, by the time I met him, he had composed numerous songs and sonatas and much chamber music. He has never stopped writing music, with the possible exception of a time when, as an Intelligence Officer in the war, he was occupied, so far as I know, with translating Chinese: a language he must have picked up somewhere. This week, at the Swansea Festival, he is conducting the London Philharmonic Orchestra in a performance of his First Symphony. Daniel Jones ...

[DANIEL JONES SPEAKS.]

DYLAN THOMAS: John Prichard, writer, I can best introduce, perhaps, by saying that he is the only conspirator among us. He conspires with the leagues of silence against his own remarkably articulate

221

stories, with the dark gangs against his own peculiar, penetrating, lopsidedly smiling light. He lets his stories slip out, guiltily, like secrets. And what secrets they are! Full of the colourless colour and language of the stones of the streets round whose corners come all the ordinary men you ever met, drably radiant in their full, unrecognised eccentricity, misery, and exultation, full of the smell and feel of everyday dark talk, the raising of blinds on a thousand common, and therefore supremely extraordinary, windows in the known, unknown streets of the town he carefully and wryly opens. He will disagree, I know, with every word I have said. He has won an Atlantic Award, and has just finished a novel. He cannot disagree with that.

John Prichard . . .

[JOHN PRICHARD SPEAKS.]

DYLAN THOMAS: To end, may I say why *I* like Swansea so much, why I used to work so freely and happily in it, why I love coming back to it as often as I can, why I still live near to it? It's because it's the most *romantic* town I know. And I haven't time to say anything more than that.

ANNOUNCER: You have been listening to Dylan Thomas, Vernon Watkins, Alfred Janes, Daniel Jones and John Prichard giving their views on Swansea and the Arts.

26
Three Poems

'Poetry Programme', or, as it came to be called, 'Three Poems', was initiated and produced by Douglas Cleverdon for the Third Programme on 25 September 1950. Thomas's fee for script and reading was twenty guineas.

The present text is the transcription included in Douglas Cleverdon's presentation of 'In Country Heaven' in the Third Programme on 18 December 1966, checked against the recording of the talk itself. The texts of the three poems are omitted.

Three Poems

I'm going to read three poems. One, called 'In Country Sleep', appeared first in a magazine which raised its hands in despair of philistine apathy so beseechingly high and so often it has since lain down from fatigue, and later was published in a limited edition, ten copies of which are on vellum, available only to the rich who should be spending what is left of their time slimming for the eye of the needle. One of the two other poems, 'Over Sir John's Hill,' has been printed in a handsome and richly appointed palace of a quarterly erected in Rome. And the third poem is in manuscript, waiting for someone who prints strikingly few copies, at impossible prices, on fine soft Cashmere goat's hair.

These three poems will, one day, form separate parts of a long poem which is in preparation: that is to say, some of the long poem is written down on paper, some of it in a rough draft in the head, and the rest of it radiantly unworded in ambitious conjecture.

A miscellaneous writer, such as myself, who is prepared to sit in front of this cold utensil and talk, in public confidence, about his new long unwritten poem, deserves to be a successful man-of-letters. I used to think that once a writer became a man-of-letters, if only for half an hour, he was done for. And here am I now, at the very *moment* of such an odious, though respectable, peril. Perhaps, after this, I shall become transformed into establishment, all my old doubts and worries will be over, I need bother my head about nothing except birth, death, sex, money, politics, and religion, and, jowled and wigged, aloof as a bloodhound, I may summon my former literary delinquence before me and give it a long, periodic sentence.

What can I say about the plan of a long 'poem in preparation' – I

hope the quotation marks come stinging across this, to me, unbelievable lack of wires, like peeved bees – what can I say that can
interest anyone save, vaguely, myself, and of course my guardian
angel, a failed psychoanalyst in this life, who is even now prodnosing
in the air above me, casebook in claw, a little seedy and down-at-
winged-heel, in the guttural consulting-rooms of space? What can I
say about this long poem-to-be except that the plan of it is grand and
simple and that the grandeur will seem, to many, to be purple and
grandiose and the simplicity crude and sentimental? The poem is to
be called 'In Country Heaven.' The godhead, the author, the milky-
way farmer, the first cause, architect, lamplighter, quintessence, the
beginning Word, the anthropomorphic bawler-out and blackballer,
the stuff of all men, scapegoat, martyr, maker, woe-bearer – He, on
top of a hill in heaven, weeps whenever, outside that state of being
called his country, one of his worlds drops dead, vanishes screaming,
shrivels, explodes, murders itself. And, when he weeps, Light and His
tears glide down together, hand in hand. So, at the beginning of the
projected poem, he weeps, and Country Heaven is suddenly dark.
Bushes and owls blow out like sparks. And the countrymen of heaven
crouch all together under the hedges and, among themselves in the
tear-salt darkness, surmise which world, which star, which of their
late, turning homes, in the skies has gone for ever. And this time,
spreads the heavenly hedgerow rumour, it is the Earth. The Earth has
killed itself. It is black, petrified, wizened, poisoned, burst; insanity has
blown it rotten; and no creatures at all, joyful, despairing, cruel, kind,
dumb, afire, loving, dull, no creatures at all shortly and brutishly hunt
their days down like enemies on that corrupted face. And, one by one,
those heavenly hedgerow-men who once were of the Earth tell one
another, through the long night, Light and His tears falling, what they
remember, what they sense in the submerged wilderness and on the
exposed hair's breadth of the mind, what they feel trembling on the
nerves of a nerve, what they know in their Edenic hearts, of that self-
killed place. They remember places, fears, loves, exultation, misery,
animal joy, ignorance, and mysteries, all *we* know and don't know.
The poem is made of these tellings. And the poem becomes, at last, an
affirmation of the beautiful and terrible worth of the Earth. It grows
into a praise of what is and what could be on this lump in the skies.
It is a poem about happiness.

I do not expect that a first hearing of the three separate poems I am going to read can give any idea of how and where they will, eventually, take their places in that lofty, pretentious, down-to-earth-and-into-the-secrets, optimistic, ludicrous, knock-me-down moony scheme. I do not yet know myself their relevance to the whole, hypothetical structure. But I do know they belong to it.

The remembered tellings, which are the components of the poem, are not all told as though they are remembered; the poem will not be a series of poems in the past tense. The memory, in all tenses, can look towards the future, can caution and admonish. The rememberer may live himself back into active participation in the remembered scene, adventure, or spiritual condition.

The first poem is 'Over Sir John's Hill.' Sir John's Hill is a real hill overlooking an estuary in West Wales.

[Reads 'Over Sir John's Hill'.]

The next poem, 'In Country Sleep,' is divided into two parts.

[Reads 'In Country Sleep'.]

And here, lastly, is the first part of a poem – a poem within the poem-to-be – called 'In the White Giant's Thigh'. This, just written, will, no doubt, have many small details altered before it is printed, but the general feel and sound of it will remain the same even when I have cleared up some of its more obviously overlush, arch and exuberant, mauve gauche moments. This is the first part.

[Reads 'In the White Giant's Thigh' – actually, on the air, introduced merely with the words: 'Now, lastly, I'm going to read a poem which I've just written, "In the White Giant's Thigh".']

226

27
Poetic Licence

What Thomas called 'my Celtic huddle of poets' (*Letters* p. 773) took place 'after lunch' on 11 December 1950, the second in the series 'Poetic Licence', produced by Patrick Harvey. The first of these round-table discussions had involved C. Day Lewis, Henry Reed, Laurie Lee, Patric Dickinson, and Paul Dehn. Martin Armstrong's column in *The Listener* (21 December 1950) was devoted to the broadcast, which took place on the Home Service 13 December 1950:

> Last week the Home Service issued another 'Poetic Licence', the host this time being Dylan Thomas and the guests George Barker, Roy Campbell and W. R. Rodgers, and once again it was a highly interesting, if not completely successful experiment. From his opening words I gathered that Mr Thomas' aim was that the conversationalists should achieve real spontaneity; that, although at the outset they would unavoidably be aware of their huge eaves-dropping audience, they should, as they warmed up, forget it: whereas, I imagine, Paul Dehn, on the previous occasion, catered for the listener to the extent of urging his party not to talk all at the same time.
>
> I was interested to note last week how unerringly I could spot when I was being remembered and when forgotten by Mr Thomas and his crew. There were periods when I reached total nonentity, when every-body talked at once and my small room was filled with a cheerful animal noise from which only one or two human phrases emerged. It was wonderfully realistic, but was it desirable? If it had been a recording by Ludwig Koch of, say, feeding-time in the seal-pond, I would have enjoyed it unreservedly, but in the circumstances I kept trying, and failing, to catch what the poets were saying, and this a little dimmed my animal enjoyment. On the other hand, there were moments when the poets

suddenly remembered me, stared at me aghast and fell alarmingly silent, and I waited in a fever of sympathetic anxiety for them to get cracking again. Then, after a freezing pause, Mr Thomas or Mr Rodgers gallantly broke the ice and talk flowed free once more. Of the two programmes, the earlier one might, I think, be called an experiment in light conversation, the second an experiment in chatter – chatter that sparkled sometimes more, sometimes less, and every now and then threw out red, blue, and golden flares.

This free-for-all on the subject of 'Bad Poetry' is preserved only in a rather chaotic state, a transcription from a telediphone recording, which has received the editor's blue pencil in many places. The stenographer was often uncertain as to who was speaking; the producer went over the script adding names and corrections; but much remains conjectural. For these reasons the present text is an edited one, so that guesswork could be kept to a minimum.

Poetic Licence

DYLAN THOMAS: Just think of all the audience listening to us now, all those people – and it's no good pretending that we're not thinking of them at the moment – I daresay we'll forget them later on – but think of all of them listening, and saying to themselves, 'Bad Poetry! What a particularly proper subject for this huddle of Celts to talk about! Mr Barker, Mr Campbell' (I don't say they say 'Mr' to themselves; I wouldn't dare think what they say) 'Mr Rodgers and Mr Thomas, if *they* don't know what bad poetry is …! Why, they're experts, anybody knows that, and it's difficult to say which of them, through first-hand experience, knows most about it.' Some would plump for you, Roy, snoring in the foam, bugling and blasting to your militant tum-ti-tum, laying all about you with whips and scorpions cut to an exact metrical length. Or others would ask for you, George Barker, heaving, hot and guilty in an inexact bed of tumultuous and damp adjectives and exhibiting your elegies. Or you, Bertie, Bertie Rodgers, alliterative as an old hooded owl, hopkins-ing along, and playing with words so much you give 'em the hiccups. Or lots of them might, of course, might prefer me as being the expert on Bad Verse, me, Swansea's Rimbaud.

ROY CAMBELL: The thundering magician of the verb, from the backwoods.

DYLAN THOMAS: I know, and I won't forgive you for the 'Swansea's Rimbaud', because you called me that first, Roy, I remember.

W. R. RODGERS: Dylan's the man that can purple our passages for

229

us. He's so good at the imitation, but somebody was telling me the other day that the one time they didn't like Dylan was when he imitated himself.

GEORGE BARKER: How little they really can like him!

W. R. RODGERS: I think you're working at it very hard now, Dylan. But there is a theological belief that it's possible for people to lay up the treasury of merits and of goodness in heaven for other people. I think amongst us all we should be able to lay down and to salt down a 'golden treasury' of demerits in the underworld, just for the four of us.

GEORGE BARKER: And not so golden.

DYLAN THOMAS: Yes, a 'stuffed owl' from one Scotsman, from Durban, near Durban, Roy?

ROY CAMBELL: Aye, it was just outside.

DYLAN THOMAS: And one Irishman from London?

GEORGE BARKER: From Epping, yes.

W. R. RODGERS: You live in the forest.

DYLAN THOMAS: Oh, you're all Irish, I can't mix that one up.

W. R. RODGERS: The Black North.

DYLAN THOMAS: One from the Black North, and well, I'm entirely from Wales. Or I'm from Wales entirely! (*Laughter*) I think that we could have a little anthology of our own of really bad chosen pieces if we really tried. I'm not going to think of my own.

GEORGE BARKER: No, I'll think of those.

DYLAN THOMAS: What about your lines, Bertie? About the wind that 'with hag hands hugs the hooked hawk down'. And also, in the same poem 'Awake Awakes', you know, the wind that seeks sucks sacks; 'sack each, in each socket set tooth,/High over hoardings hurl, and all ways spill,/Hug the elbowing horde, hard under hill/Huddle hare and hound.'

GEORGE BARKER: You're bringing up your ...

230

DYLAN THOMAS: Oh, he had a feeling against 'h's' once.

ROY CAMPBELL: Well, you could say he is now Cockney, and that he's full of guts.

W. R. RODGERS: That was my grandslam days, but I hope those are over.

ROY CAMBELL: Is there a word for guts with an 'h' because he would have undoubtedly used it?

W. R. RODGERS: Hentrails.

DYLAN THOMAS: Hentrails. (*Laughter*) But the guts – that's noticeably lacking in those lovely four lines of Roy's. This isn't a mutual back-scratching society, by the way. (*Talking together*) Superb, let's have them all.

W. R. RODGERS: I always wanted to hear those lines.

ROY CAMPBELL: Oh, you mean about the horse?

> You praise the firm restraint with which they write,
> I'm with you there, of course,
> They use the snaffle and the curb alright
> But where's the bloody horse?

DYLAN THOMAS: But who were 'they'?

ROY CAMPBELL: Oh, those were some South African novelists. I'm not quite sure of the names now.

DYLAN THOMAS: Have they died by themselves first, or were those four lines the ones that flung them to death?

ROY CAMPBELL: With a little artificial respiration perhaps they . . .

W. R. RODGERS: But Roy's lines, they always stick in my mind. I always did associate them with a very good poet called 'Beach-comber', who has four excellent lines:

> Here lies the lighthousekeeper's horse,
> It wasn't ridden much, of course.
> How patiently it waited for

231

The lighthousekeeper's leave on shore.

DYLAN THOMAS: I still don't see why you call 'Beachcomber' a good poet.

W. R. RODGERS: Well, it seemed to me he was to the point, there, anyway. The point being that where *is* the bloody horse? This winged horse, as they used to call it, of poetry. Nobody seems to ride it nowadays.

DYLAN THOMAS: The wings get in the way when you try and ride it. It's not nearly as good as a motor-bike. (*Talking together*)

GEORGE BARKER: But what about this problem of the – everybody talks about it now – the flow of poetry. It comes thin, and seldom, and very restrained. It has got the curb, and it has got the snaffle alright, and the shape, but there isn't enough of it. The poets seem to be like lighthousekeepers, out on their own.

DYLAN THOMAS: The ivory tower?

GEORGE BARKER: Yes, especially if it's a lighthouse, 'cause at least that's solid.

DYLAN THOMAS: Yes, but do you really want a job?

GEORGE BARKER: Passionately, yes. A very well-paid job where I have to do almost nothing.

DYLAN THOMAS: But that's something to do with a spiv, not with a poet, isn't it?

GEORGE BARKER: Yes, it is. That's because poets are spivs. We want patrons each.

ROY CAMPBELL: There are always good jobs going for poets. I remember as a third-rate temporary assistant bogus clerk when I came out of the Army I filled more waste-paper baskets then than I've ever done with my poetry since.

DYLAN THOMAS: That I find hard to believe.

GEORGE BARKER: I need dustbins, not waste-paper baskets. (*Talking together*)

232

DYLAN THOMAS: Well, the most durable waste-paper baskets of the past are anthologies. Here's one you've got in front of you . . .

ROY CAMPBELL: I had to learn one at school when I was in Durban, and I still remember it with quiet feelings of vengeance.

> She said, 'We meet no angels now,'
> And soft light streamed upon her.
> And with white hands she touched a bow.
> She did it that great honour.
> What? Meet no angels, Pansy?

That's from—

W. R. RODGERS: Oh, most beautiful, just . . .

ROY CAMPBELL: Thomas Ash in the *Victorian Book of English Verse* by Quiller-Couch.

DYLAN THOMAS: Yes, it's sentimental, that's the trouble with it. What else is wrong with it, apart from the fact that it's just shocking bad verse.

GEORGE BARKER: No, when it gets that exaggerated it's not worth discussing.

DYLAN THOMAS: Apart from the last line, it isn't even funny.

W. R. RODGERS: But it is sentimental. I mean, you get lots of modern examples – and if I might quote one now, about a parachutist who is dropping, riddled with bullets. Now, these are the lines:

> The guns spell money's ultimate reason,
> In letters of lead on the spring hillside,
> But the boy lying dead under the olive trees
> Was too young and too silly to have been notable to
>   their important eye.
> He was a better target for a kiss.

DYLAN THOMAS: Should we ask who wrote that?

GEORGE BARKER: I think it'd be proper not to, don't you?

W. R. RODGERS: I think, in any case, if the boy was too silly and too unimportant, he might have been a better target for a tiff.

ROY CAMPBELL: Yes, or he could have been given something, like a season ticket for music hall, something that you'd give to somebody who really deserves it.

W. R. RODGERS: It seems to be, in a way, that there are, broadly, two kinds of bad verse: one just bad, dull; the other bad, funny, ludicrous.

DYLAN THOMAS: Would it be true to say about bad verse that it's bad just as people are bad? It's bad because it's pretending to be something that it isn't? It's a kind of snob of a poem; or it's lazy and vague and woolly and sloppy and wet? It's a sentimentalist of a poem, or it's long-winded, vaporous, without any humour, and it's swollen up with itself. It's a bore of a poem.

GEORGE BARKER: But the point is surely that bad poems are absolutely necessary. They're like excrement. It's very unhealthy for the whole body of the language not to produce them.

ROY CAMPBELL: Otherwise it would go ...

W. R. RODGERS: At this point, may I quote one of George's?

DYLAN THOMAS: You may. (*Laughter*)

W. R. RODGERS: He brought it up so nicely. And here we are – it's a fairly recent one:

> For half-a-dozen simple years
> We lived happily, so to speak,
> On twenty-seven shillings a week.
> And when worried and in tears
> My mercenary wife complained
> That we could not afford our marriage,
> 'It's twice as much,' I explained,
> 'As MacNeice pays for his garage.'

Again:

> I sat one morning on the can
> That served us for a lavatory,
> Composing some laudatory
> Verses on the state of man.

234

They have this virtue: they speak the truth. There's one slight exaggeration. I believe at that time MacNeice was only paying ten shillings a week for his garage.

GEORGE BARKER: I believe, as I said, that because bad verse does act as a kind of excrement, that it was a very proper occasion that one should use those images that are involved with this process.

ROY CAMPBELL: Yes, but one knows what to do with a bad verse. You don't publish it.

DYLAN THOMAS: But you're saying that bad verse is of use to good verse.

GEORGE BARKER: Well, yes, in that sense.

DYLAN THOMAS: You mean in that it manures the land?

GEORGE BARKER: No, by no means. No, but we should have got rid of the poison.

DYLAN THOMAS: But other people's bad verse doesn't get rid of your poison so that you can produce better verse.

GEORGE BARKER: No, but I don't think it's taken personally like that. It's a question of what happens to the language. It gets rid of the bad stuff in the language, like a cyst.

DYLAN THOMAS: It's good to have a whole volume of extremely bad verse in front of you so that you don't have to use those awful phrases any more, those clotted adjectives, those things that stick to the sides as they come out.

W. R. RODGERS: I think there's a thread of truth in what George says, in so far as this, that to get the physical is very important in poetry.

DYLAN THOMAS: Yes, if almost nothing else.

W. R. RODGERS: To get the physical image ... I can't ... (*Talking together*)

GEORGE BARKER: There's a beautiful example in Coleridge. It goes: 'Inoculation, heavenly maid, descend!'

W. R. RODGERS: He has a lovelier one: 'Urine, the sweet-flowing daughter of fright.'

ROY CAMPBELL: Yes, it is bad. But the point is there's no work been put in it, there's no imagination in it, which is what is wrong with a good deal, I think, of bad poetry.

W. R. RODGERS: Now, take this one, a Victorian one, two lines on the recovery of the Prince of Wales:

> Across the wires, the electric message came,
> He is not better, he is much the same.

GEORGE BARKER: I'm prepared to defend that. It says what it's got to say, quite briefly, there's not much agony to be gone through.

DYLAN THOMAS: Apart from the fact – apart from the fact that no one wants to hear it. Those lines of yours, George, you didn't excuse them wholly, but you excused them in part by saying that they were at least physical ... what did you say ... (*Talking together*) ...

W. R. RODGERS: I agree. Facts are never the truth. They're a quarter of the truth. The truth is something which a human being does with the facts.

DYLAN THOMAS: Exactly, yes. Is it whatever the human being does with the facts? Is it possible to do something with the facts which isn't true?

W. R. RODGERS: We see that being done every day. You've only to open a newspaper.

GEORGE BARKER: Yes, but that's not poetry.

W. R. RODGERS: But this is not poetry.

GEORGE BARKER: I defend that, technically, because in the writing of a long poem, I believe that there are some parts have got to go down. That is certainly one of the parts where it goes down.

DYLAN THOMAS: I think we all agree with that, that certain parts have got to have less intensity than others. They've got to carry the

236

argument along. They've got to be links. All I'm saying is they haven't got to go all that far down.

GEORGE BARKER: No, that's a point. But you're bound to make a really colossal error in the course of a thousand lines in rhyme. Roy would know that very much better than I do.

ROY CAMPBELL: Yes, I'm afraid I'm even more long-winded than you, George. In order to write one good line, that's to take a high jump, I have to take about twenty steps before I get going, and perhaps slip in the mud too.

W. R. RODGERS: Well, now, if I might take up and labour a point that I did make there, those two lines, 'Across the wires the electric message came' – now, one of the most difficult things to do without pathos, but well worth doing, is to bring in the new invention and a contemporary theme. Now 'the electric message' immediately makes us laugh, but it can be used very well in other ways. Roy here had four lines in a poem I like called 'The Zulu Girl', about a Zulu girl, who in the heat of the day throws down her hoe, and takes away her child to suckle it under a tree.

DYLAN THOMAS: A lovely poem.

GEORGE BARKER: Wonderful.

W. R. RODGERS: And he uses the word 'electric' – but how much better than the other.

ROY CAMPBELL: Oh, you mean this verse:

> She takes him to a ring of shadow,
> Pooled by thorn trees, purpled with the blood of ticks,
> While her sharp nails with soft electric clicks,
> Prowl through his hair.

DYLAN THOMAS: You wouldn't think Roy'd written that, would you? ... I still want to get back to this idea that you can, as long as you say 'physical facts' – no, I haven't confined it to physical facts, why should I? No, I know your attack, the attack of all of us, was really on abstract words. So that let the rubbish bins of the old anthologies for a moment, let them be full of the poems that talk about a

237

thing in terms of something else. And let our poems be about the something. Do you remember Ogden Nash said, 'One thing that literature would be greatly the better for,/Would be a more restricted employment by authors of simile and metaphor.'

GEORGE BARKER: Yes.

DYLAN THOMAS: Authors have always, be they Greeks, Romans, Teutons, or Celts, can't seem just to say anything is the thing it is, but have to go out of their way to say that it is like something else.

W. R. RODGERS: But, Dylan, the use of metaphor and simile is to shorten the number of words which one can tell a thing in. You never, for instance, use in poetry, you could never use the word 'dynamic'. You had to go about it – go around.

DYLAN THOMAS: Until you find there is a dynamo?

ROY CAMPBELL: Yes, but you have to produce the dynamo there, working.

DYLAN THOMAS: The dynamo can be the putting together of two quite undynamic words.

ROY CAMPBELL: Yes, you make an electric current with two words that you bring from opposite ends of the ...

DYLAN THOMAS: Yes, or in its context, the use of a very simple and static noun.

W. R. RODGERS: Quite by diversion – it's nothing to do with the subject – a story always comes into my head when poetry is mentioned. An acquaintance of mine, who had been a political prisoner once, was in the same cell as a very famous Irish gunman, a rather uneducated Irish gunman. In order to improve the pining hours, he read him Gray's 'Elegy'. And the gunman was entranced. In fact, when it came to the point at which, 'Let not ambition mock their useful toil,' the man rose up, says he: 'Who is this guy Ambition? I'll get him!'

DYLAN THOMAS: Yes, ambition gives me a horrible idea about our own ambitiousness. It's obviously our own ambition not to write bad verse.

GEORGE BARKER: I think it's disputable.

ROY CAMPBELL: But it's a very funny thing – we're so used to getting kicked in the pants, you know. If anyone told me that I sang out of tune, or played the piano badly, it would hurt me far worse than the usual thing that one is told by the critics. That's a very funny thing ...

DYLAN THOMAS: Can you play the piano?

ROY CAMPBELL: Well, not according to anyone but myself.

DYLAN THOMAS: Talking for myself alone, I'm perfectly capable of writing bad verse. What I want to do is become more and more conscious and knowledgeable about the bad verse I write, so that I don't at least publish it, and so that the verse I publish, however bad it may be, will at least have that badness out of it, the badness of which I know.

GEORGE BARKER: I think it's very much easier to judge other people's bad verse than to judge one's own, because the bad verse that one writes oneself is usually bad verse that one's put too much feeling in, or too little feeling in, and the business of feeling is so very personal.

DYLAN THOMAS: You don't think that one's own bad verse has that peculiar smell that other people's bad verse does?

GEORGE BARKER: It's like the dog returning to its own vomit; one brings up something worse.

DYLAN THOMAS: One can't smell oneself? A man who used to smell of violets, he came to somebody's dinner party, and before he came, the host told the other guests that the person who was just about to arrive thinks he smells of violets, and do all – do play him up. And when he came in, the lady sitting next to him said, 'What a delicious smell of violets,' and he blushed and looked down. He said, 'I know. It's me.'

W. R. RODGERS: Infinitely true, infinitely true ...

DYLAN THOMAS: It's quite possible the reek of the pit, of the platitude and the cliché in our own verse isn't ...

239

ROY CAMPBELL: I think it depends on a period of time. I mean, George very generously for some reason or other didn't give me – he showed me some things of mine, compared with which his were really first class verse.

GEORGE BARKER: I can write worse verse than you can.

ROY CAMPBELL: Oh, I believe that in order to jump high, you have to be able to sound deep.

GEORGE BARKER: I deeply believe that, and so if – I think really the worst verses you can get in English poets are among the greatest.

W. R. RODGERS: It's coming near the New Year now. If I were asked to make a resolution, I would say not that I shouldn't write bad verse, or good verse, but for myself and for my own sake, that my resolution would be that I shall write that a living dog would be better than a dead lion.

DYLAN THOMAS: You mean that bad verse is better than no verse at all? I agree with you there.

28
Persian Oil

In a letter of 7 December 1950 Thomas wrote: 'I'm about to go to Persia to write a filmscript for Anglo-Iranian Oil – some kind of technicolour documentary, though God knows what it will turn into' (*Letters* p. 775). No film was made, but the experience provided Thomas with a piece of radio, a contribution to 'Report to the People – Persian Oil', broadcast on 17 April 1951 on the Home Service. Thomas's fee was ten guineas.

The idea of Thomas doing a more substantial script on the same subject was dropped when Douglas Cleverdon wrote a memo 13 March 1951: 'I understand the Anglo-Iranian Oil Company has some kind of hold over what Dylan might say.' Clearly, however, the present script is far from tender towards his employer.

The extant BBC 'as broadcast' script has been checked against Thomas's holograph script (Texas) and a few emendations made.

Persian Oil

And there was nothing on that hot and hateful bone-dry blistering bank but some dates that nobody kept, and a few lizards who had nowhere else to go or, if they had, would not recognize it. And some jackals, I suppose, full of guilt and a vague sense of ill-being, howling at the Euphrates and waiting for man. Now there is a huge, tubed town, streamlined and reeking new: a kind of cinema organ of a town, with its petrified refinery pipes playing, all oily day, on the bank of the boiling river. In the very centre of the refinery stands a new Cat Cracker, worth eight million pounds and more; I would crack a lot of cats myself, for that money. The waste oil burns, night and day, at the top of thin chimneys: little flags of smelly fire. And round what is known as Stink Corner comes, in the right or wrong wind, the smell militant, the great barbed growling Niff with tail high and rampant breath.

At night, Abadan Refinery is beautiful: lost, violet souls float and crackle in a bubble and green-hot hubbub; puce, ectoplastic clouds go sultry over the boilers, and suddenly the sky's on fire like a dry blue bush. The clubs are packed: there are Burns suppers, Eisteddfodau, glycerine beer and beetroot vodka. Sad, homeless men are telling one another about what they were and did at home, and no one believes them. The night is nostalgic and sulphurous. The weight of longing, under the sky on fire, could press the town into the dhowed Gulf. In the main hotel of the bazaar, a bottle of beer costs ten times more at the bar than at the tables; at the bar you are served by a woman: a *real* woman. There is every frustration, except lack of work.

In the old Persia, the bazaars smell of carpets and incense and

242

poverty. Women with only their eyes showing through tattered, dirty, mud-trailing, thin, black sack-wraps, on splayed and rotting high-heeled shoes, slip-slop through the open-sewered streets. They do not wear their churdahs because they are patriotic and believe in the memory of Razah Shah; they wear them because they hide their poverty. Inside these wraps, they clutch their poverty to them; it is their only possession.

In Tehran, I went to a hospital one morning. In the children's wards I saw rows and rows of little Persian children suffering from starvation; their eyes were enormous, seeing everything and nothing, their bellies bloated, their matchstick arms hung round with blue, wrinkled flesh. One of them was crying, only one. I asked the English sister why. 'His mother went out every day,' she said, 'begging in the streets, and he was too weak to go with her and she was too weak to carry him. So she left him alone in her hovel. The hovel had a hole dug in the earth floor, where a fire always was; a heap of hot cinders, ready for cooking. The child fell into the fire, face down, and lay there all day burning until his mother came home at dusk. He'll get better, but he's lost one arm and all his toes.'

After that, I had lunch with a very rich man, who, of course, lived on the poor. He was charming and cultivated.

And then, on the train through the wonderful Zagros mountains, from Tehran to Abadan, oh the Lurish children rushing up out of the mud-hut villages, three-quarter naked, filthy, hungry, beautiful with smiles and great burning eyes and wild hair, begging for the smallest coins, pieces of bread, a sweet, anything! Philosophic buzzards wheeled above them.

In prosperous Abadan, everything is different. Everything. A community lives at the end of a pipe-line. People are there because oil is. Oil is first. Oil is all. People, exiled, come a long way afterwards in this dusty sun-fry.

On the blue, boiled water the dhows sail out of the Bible.

The elegant Arabs, as far above oil as eagles are, keep their ways and their dates.

The vast tribes move, with the heat of the sun, from their winter grounds to the high green palaces.

In the ruins of Persepolis, all is immemorial vanity.

Hyenas crack their abominable jokes all night.

Jackals are sorry for being jackals.
Engineers curse their dehydrated ale in the income-classed clubs.
The rich are rich. Oil's oily. And the poor are waiting.

29
The Festival Exhibition

In response to an invitation from Aneirin Talfan Davies, Thomas wrote 7 April 1951: 'I'd be delighted to do a Festival talk for the Welsh Service; and I think the Festival Exhibition on the South Bank – or the Festival Gardens and Funfair (what *is* the official title?) in Battersea – would be grand' (*Letters*, p. 793). Thomas went to London the second week in May, and recorded the talk in Cardiff on 5 June 1951, for broadcast in the 'Guest Speaker' slot after the nine o'clock news in the Welsh Home Service 19 June 1951. His fee was twenty guineas. It was repeated in the other Home Services in 'The World Today' – again after the nine o'clock news – on 14 August 1951.

Vernon Watkins in the *Times Literary Supplement* (19 November 1954) called it 'the most dazzling of all the talks'. Martin Armstrong reviewed it in *The Listener* (23 August 1951), calling it 'audible decoration':

> He arranges his torrent of words so as to produce musical and often amusing noise. Some of the noise he made about the Exhibition was highly amusing and some of it expressive, but I was occasionally chilled by the feeling that he was too continually determined to delight or amuse me. His fine careless raptures were too noticeably careful; the pentecostal outbursts were the least little bit too obviously superinduced.

The Festival Exhibition

The extent of the site of the Exhibition on the South Bank of the Thames in the heart of London is four and a half acres. There are twenty-two pavilions in the Exhibitions, and thirteen restaurants, cafés, bars, and buffets.

Some people visit the twenty-two pavilions first, then glazed and crippled, windless, rudderless, and a little out of their minds, teeter, weeping, to one of the thirteen restaurants, cafés, bars, and buffets to find it packed to the dazzlingly painted and, possibly, levitating doors.

Other people visit all thirteen restaurants, cafés, bars, and buffets before attacking the pavilions, and rarely get further than the Dome of Discovery, which they find confusing, full, as it is, of totem poles, real dogs in snow, locusts, stars, the sun, the moon, things bubbling, thunder and lightning machines, chemical and physical surprises. And some never return.

Most people who wish, at the beginning, anyway, to make sense of the Exhibition, follow the course indicated in the official Guide-book – a series of conflicting arrows which lead many visitors who cannot understand these things slap-splash into the Thames – and work their way dutifully right through the land of Britain, the glaciers of twenty thousand years ago, and the inferno of blown desert sand which is now Birmingham, out at last into the Pavilion of Health – where, perhaps, they stop for an envious moment at the sign that says Euthanasia – and on to the netted and capstaned, bollarded, buoyed, seashelled, pebbly beautiful seaside of summer childhood gone.

And other visitors begin, of course, at the end. They are the people without whom the Exhibition could not exist, nor the country it trombones and floats in, with its lions and unicorns made of ears of wheat, its birds that sing to the push of a button, its flaming water, and its raspberry fountains. They are the suspicious people over whose eyes no coloured Festival wool can be pulled, the great undiddleable; they are the women who 'will not queue on any account' and who smuggle in dyspeptic dogs; the strangely calculating men who think that the last pavilion must be first because it is number twenty-two; the people who believe they are somewhere else, and never find out they are not; sharp people who have been there before, who know the ropes, who chuckle to their country cousins: 'You get double your money's worth this way'; vaguely persecuted people, always losing their gloves, who know that the only way they could *ever* get around would be to begin at the end, which they do not want to; people of militant individuality who proclaim their right, as Englishmen, to look at the damnfool place however they willynilly will; people nervously affected by all such occasions, who want to know only, 'Where's the place?'; timid people who want to be as far from the Skylon as possible, because 'you never know'; foreigners, who have been directed this way by a school of irrepressible wits; glassy benighted men who are trying to remember they must see something of the Exhibition to remember before they go home and try to describe it to their families; young people, hand-in-love, who will giggle at whatever they see, at a goldfish in a pond, a model of the *Queen Elizabeth*, or a flint hammer; people too bored to yawn, long and rich as borzois, who, before they have seen it, have seen better shows in Copenhagen and San Francisco; eccentric people: men with their deerstalker caps tied with rope to their lapels, who carry dried nut sandwiches and little containers of yoghourt in hairy green knapsacks labelled 'glass with care'; fat, flustered women in as many layers of coats as an onion or a cab-driver, hunting in a fever through fifty fluffed pockets to find a lost packet of bird-seed they are going to give to the parrots who are not there; old scaly sneezing men, born of lizards in a snuff-bin, who read, wherever they go, from books in tiny print, and who never look up, even at the tureen-lid of the just-tethered dome or the shining Skylon, the skygoing nylon, the cylindrical leg-of-the-future jetting, almost, to the exhibition of stars; *real* eccentrics: people who have come to the South Bank to study the growth and development of Britain from the Iron Age till now. Here they will find no braying pageantry, no

247

taxidermal museum of Culture, no cold and echoing inhuman hygienic barracks of technical information, no shoddily cajoling Emporium of tasteless Empire wares, but something very odd indeed, magical and parochial: a parish-pump made of flying glass and thistledown gauze-thin steel, a rolypoly pudding full of luminous, melodious bells, wheels, coils, engines and organs, alembics and jorums in a palace in thunderland sizzling with scientific witches' brews, a place of trains, bones, planes, ships, sheep, shapes, snipe, mobiles, marbles, brass bands, and cheese, a place painted regardless, and by hand.

Perhaps you'll think I'm shovelling the colour on too thickly; that I am, as it were, speaking under the influence of strong pink. And what a lot of pink – rose, raspberry, strawberry, peach, flesh, blush, lobster, salmon, tally-ho – there is, plastered and doodled all over this four-acre gay and soon-to-be-gone Festival City in sprawling London. (London: to many of us who live in the country, the Capital punishment.) Perhaps you will go on a cool, dull day, sane as a biscuit, and find that the Exhibition does, indeed, tell the story 'of British contributions to world civilization in the arts of peace'; that, and nothing else. But I'm pleased to doubt it. Of *course* it is instructive; of *course* there is behind it an articulate and comprehensive plan; it can show you, unless you are an expert, more about, say, mineralogy or the ionosphere than you may want to know. It's bursting its buttons, in an orderly manner, with knowledge. But what everyone I know, and have observed, seems to like most in it is the gay, absurd, irrelevant, delighting imagination that flies and booms and spurts and trickles out of the whole bright boiling: the small stone oddity that squints at you round a sharp, daubed corner; the sexless abstract sculptures serenely and secretly existing out of time in old cold worlds of their own in places that appear, but only for one struck second, inappropriate; the linked terra-cotta man and woman fly-defying gravity and elegantly hurring up a w.c. wall; the sudden design of hands on another wall, as though the painter had said: 'Oh, to the daft devil with what I'm doing,' and just slap-slap-slapped all over the ochre his spread-out fingers and thumbs, ten blunt arrows, or as though large convict-birds, if there are any such, had waddled up the wall and webbed it as they went. You see people go along briskly down the wide white avenues towards the pavilion of their fancy – 'Our Humbert's dead keen on seeing the milk-separators' – and suddenly stop: another fancy swings or bubbles in front of their eyes. What is it they see? Indigo water waltzing to music. Row after row of rosy rolling balls spread on tall screens like the counting beads of Wellsian children fed on the Food of the Gods. Sheets of asbestos tied on to nowhere, by nothing, for nothing is anchored here, and at the clap of hands the whole gallimaufry could take off to Sousa and zoom up the flagged sky. Small childbook-painted mobiles along the bridges that, at a flick of wind, become windmills and thrum round at night like rainbows with arms. Or the steel-and-platinum figure – created by the Welsh engineer and architect, Richard Huws – of maybe a mer-woman standing, if that is the word for one who grows out of it, in arc-lit water; she weeps as she is wept on; first her glinting breast, then another plane of her, tips, slides, shoots, shelves, swings, and sidles out to take, from the lake of her birth, one ton of water at a time to Handel's *Water Music*, absorbs it, inhales it through dripping steel, then casts and cascades it off and out again. Or even the hundreds of little vivid steel chairs that look like hundreds of little vivid steel people sitting down.

In the pavilion called 'The Natural Scene', see the seals and eagles, the foxes and wild cats, of these still wild islands, and the natural history of owled and cuckooed, ottered, unlikely London. A great naked tree climbs in the middle of all, with prodigious butterflies and beetles on it. A blackbird lights up, and the aviary's full of his singing; a thrush, a curlew, a skylark.

And, in the 'Country', see all the sculpted and woven loaves, in the shape of sheaves of wheat, in curls, plaits, and whirls. And men are thatching the roofs of cottages; and – what could be more natural? – the men are made of straw. And what a pleasure of baskets! Trugs, creels, pottles and punnets, heppers, dorsers and mounds, wiskets and whiskets. And if these are not the proper words, they should be.

In 'The Lion and the Unicorn' is celebrated, under flights of birds, the British Character, that stubborn, stupid, seabound, lyrical, paradoxical dark farrago of uppishness, derring-do, and midsummer moonshine all fluting, snug, and copper-bottomed. Justice, for some reason, looms in the midst of the Hall, its two big wigs back to back, its black and scarlet robes falling below. The body of justice is shelves of law books. The black spaces beneath the white wigs look like the profiles of eagles. The white knight rides there too, too much a Don Quixote for my looking-glass land, and very potless and panless. A bravo-ing hand

249

pats his plaster back, and tells him good night. There is a machine for, I believe, grinding smoke. And a tea-set, I failed to see, of salmon bones. But, in all this authentically eccentric Exhibition, it is the Eccentrics' Corner that is the most insipid. Some of the dullest exhibits in the pavilion are relieved by surrounding extravagance; but the department devoted to the rhapsodic inspirations of extravagance is by far the dullest. Why was not the exquisite talent utilized of the warlock who, offering his services to the Festival authorities, assured them he would, to order, throw a rainbow over the Thames? I wish he would throw a rainbow over me as I walk through the grey days. 'Yes, we can tell it's him coming,' the envious neighbours would murmur, 'we recognize his rainbow.' And, on the balcony, there is a row of tiny theatres; in each, the stage is set for a Shakespearian play; and out of the theatres come the words of the players. If you're in luck, something may go wrong with the works and Hamlet rant from Dunsinane.

In 'Homes and Gardens', blink at the grievous furniture, ugly as sin and less comfy.

In the 'Transport Pavilion', goggle at the wizard diesels and the smashing, unpuffing streamlines and the miracle model railway for dwarf nabobs.

Then, if there are by this time no spots in front of your eyes, go to the Telecinema and see them astonishingly all around you: spots with scarlet tadpole tails, and spottedly sinuous tintacks dancing with dissolving zebra heads, and blobs and nubbins and rubbery squirls receding, to zig zag blasts of brass, down nasty polychrome corridors, a St Vitus's gala of abstract shapes and shades in a St Swithin's day of torrential dazzling darning needles. Sit still in the startling cinema and be kissed by a giraffe, who stretches his neck right out of the screen for you. Follow the deliberately coloured course of the Thames, the Royal River; the whispering water's more like water than water ever was; closer, closer, comes the slow kingfisher – blue water and suddenly it ripples all over you: that'll be the day when filmstars do the same.

Go to the South Bank first by day; the rest of your times, at night. Sit at a café table in the night of musical lights, by the radiant river, the glittering Skylon above you rearing to be off, the lit pavilions, white, black, and silver in sweeps of stone and feathery steel, transplendent round you as you sip and think:

This is the first time I have ever truly seen that London whose sweet Thames runs softly, that minstrel mermaid of a town, the water-streeted eight-million-headed village in a blaze. *This* is London, not the huge petty mis-shapen nightmare I used to know, as I humdrummed along its graceless streets through fog and smoke and past the anonymous unhappy bodies lively as wet brollies. This Festival is London. The arches of the bridges leap into light; the moon clocks glow; the river sings; the harmonious pavilions are happy. And this is what London should always be like, till St Paul's falls down and the sea slides over the Strand.

30
Edgar Lee Masters

The inception of this script was described by Douglas Cleverdon in *The Growth of Milk Wood* (pp. 18–19):

> Towards the end of 1950, knowing that he was particularly penniless, Laurence Gilliam and I took Dylan out and asked him what he would like to do for quick and easy money. Interestingly, he suggested a programme on Edgar Lee Master's *Spoon River Anthology*, the sequence of poems in which the dead of a town in the Middle West speak, from the graveyard, their honest epitaphs; possibly anticipating Rosie Probert speaking from the bedroom of her dust. He and I met again on 11th December to discuss the choice of poems for the programme, which had to be done quickly if the money was to be paid quickly.
>
> In spite of telegrams, the script of his commentary failed to arrive. As all routine bookings had been completed, my final (reply-paid) telegram warned him that we were facing disaster; his reply bade me 'Unface disaster script and self coming.' But neither script nor self appeared. The script was finally written in August 1952: and then only by making arrangements for him to be locked in the B.B.C. Reference Library all night.

Thomas submitted the script with the following letter (*Letters* pp. 833–4):

> Dear Douglas,
>   At long last – and with many apologies – 'Spoon River Anthology'.
>   You will see that I have chosen too many poems, probably, but I think it worth duplicating too many in the script for you to work on with the readers. The order need not be kept in the way I have indicated, but can – and should – be changed about, according to voice, mood etc. I'm

253

sorry I couldn't arrange the poems better – that is, make a real programme of them, alternating grim & (fairly) gay, etc – but I had only
that one afternoon in the library with the book. I didn't write much
then, only got engrossed in the poems until 6 o'clock.

I hope the introduction isn't too long and/or tendentious.

Will you drop me a line about this?

And, if it *is* possible to get a little money soon, could it be got, somehow,
straight to me, & not through my agents, d'you think? I'm in a hell of a
money mess, sued on all sides; trying to finish several things, including
'Llarreggub' & a long poem, but worried to death; ill with it.

> Ever,
> Dylan

I remember, when we last talked of this programme, your suggestion
that there shd be a few words by me between each poem. This, really,
isn't any good. After the introduction, the poems, I think, *must* come
one after the other, with only the pause when the Narrator says 'Joe
Smith'.

Thomas received a fee of twenty guineas for the script, but never
had the opportunity to record the talk. It was presented posthumously
in the Third Programme 23 January 1955 with Barbara Kelly and
Bernard Braden as readers.

Thomas's choice of poems to be read from the *Spoon River Anthology*
was as follows: Hod Putt, Amanda Barker, Constance Hately, Chase
Henry, Benjamin Pantier, Trainor the Druggist, Knowlt Hoheimer,
Frank Drummer, Hare Drummer, Julia Miller, Lois Spears, Deacon
Taylor, Nellie Clark, Doc Hill, Fiddler Jones, A. D. Blood, Nancy Knapp,
Petit the Poet, Carl Hamblin, Walter Simmons, Lucinda Matlock.

Edgar Lee Masters

The collection of short free-verse poems called *Spoon River Anthology* written by Edgar Lee Masters, a Chicago lawyer, was published in 1915 when he was forty-five years old; and it shocked the American public so profoundly that it sold a great number of copies. It became the first best seller of the 'poetic Renaissance' which began in the Middle West with Masters, Vachel Lindsay, Carl Sandburg and Harriet Monroe's oddly-named *Poetry: a Magazine of Verse*; and the memories of its sensational success have lasted so long that even today it is regarded, when it is regarded at all, with deep suspicion, though the reasons for the present suspicion are quite different from what they were when the book boomed out first to the hand-lifted horror of the giant parish press, the prairie pulpits, the thin, baffled, sour officials of taste in the literary periodicals, and the innumerable societies of militant gentility. Now, *Spoon River* is, I suppose, hardly read at all by the thousands of university students who 'take' poetry in such enormous doses. The poetry workshops attached to many universities and private colleges leave him, I should think, untaught and alone, except as a figure of minor historical interest, a cross, rhetorical, old Bohemian lawyer rambling and ranting away in the bad past about the conflict between materialism and idealism: a conflict considered so old-fashioned that many of those in the poetry workshops must imagine it to have been satisfactorily settled long ago.

(In poetry workshops, by the way, would-be poets are supposed to study the craft under some distinguished practitioner. Perhaps the original idea was to provide for apprentice poets what a master's studio once did for apprentice painters. But the master-painter used to paint

255

all the time, and his apprentices assisted him and were busy under his direction. A master-poet, if he exists, is supposed, in these literary warrens, to spend nearly all his time dealing with, and encouraging, the imitations, safe experiments, doodlings and batchings of his students, and to do his own stuff on the side. What a pity he does not have the apprentice poets to help him with the duller bits of his own work. There is a future in this, however ghastly.)

And the brash, antiseptic, forty-two-toothed, ardent, crewcut collegiates, grimly pursuing the art of poetry with net, notebook, poison bottle, pin and label, may be quite likely to dismiss Edgar Lee Masters altogether because, in his lifetime, he *was* so successful. I've noticed before, in the States, how very many students devotedly read and devour masses of modern poetry and insist, at the same time, that poetry devotedly read and devoured by such numbers of people can't be any good. Ezra Pound – for instance – can be appreciated by only a very few, say armies of culture-vultures every day as they drive through the *Cantos* with apparent ecstacy and understanding. Masters was too successful to be honest, I've heard it said: a rather touching remark, perhaps, to come from an enlightened representative of a people notoriously not averse to success in any way of life. But it was Masters' ironic honesty that made *Spoon River* so popular among its denigrators. Americans seem to enjoy being furious and indignant at being kicked in their most sensitive places – and what more sensitive a place than that great, dry backbone, the Middle West?

People bought and read *Spoon River,* when it first appeared, for many reasons, few of which had anything to do with the undoubted fact that it was poetry. Many people read it in order to deny that it was true; many, discovering that in essence it was, denied it even more loudly. One of the chief reactions to these angry, sardonic, moving poems seemed to be: '*Some* of the inhabitants of small towns in Illinois may indeed be narrow-minded and corrupt, fanatically joyless, respectable to the point of insanity, malevolent and malcontent, but not in the Illinois towns in which *we* live.' 'East is East and West is West, but the Middle West is terrible,' Louis Untermeyer once wrote, but he was a sophisticated cosmopolitan raconteur and man-of-smart-letters, and his opinion of the *Real America* could be taken as merely ignorant and facetious. (It is, I'm sure, significant that the most beautiful and exciting places in America are, without exception, all called untypical and un-

American.) Masters, however, was a proper Middle-Westerner; he knew what he was writing about; and his detestation of the bitter and crippling puritanism in which he struggled and simmered up was nothing less than treacherous. 'He knows us too well, the liar,' was a common attitude.

I am very fond, myself, of the writers who came out of the Middle West round about the beginning of the First World War. All the stale literary guidebook phrases aside – the 'honest ruggedness,' the 'pioneering vitality,' the 'earthy humour,' the 'undying folk tradition,' etc. – the hick-town radicals and iconoclasts, the sports journalists, the contributors to *Reedy's Mirror*, the drinking, noisy Chicago preachers and atheists and ballad singers and shabby professional men, did bring something rough and good into a language that was dying on its feet; and not its own feet, either.

There is Vachel Lindsay: the semireligious revivalist; re-creator of railroad songs and sagas; the chronicler of Johnny Appleseed, the Blackfeet, the Pawnees, John Brown, John L. Sullivan, P. T. Barnum; the first poet to love the moving-pictures and see what they might become; who wrote about Blanche Sweet and Lillian Gish; who tried to live on pamphlets, *Rhymes to be Traded for Bread*, which he hawked around the country; who became a popular platform act; who killed himself in 1931. And Sherwood Anderson, whose book of stories, *Winesburg, Ohio*, is so near in place and spirit to *Spoon River*, but whose remembered vision of youth in that rich, remote, constricting, Main-Streeted desert is so much more detailed and more gentle, in spite of its terrors. And Carl Sandburg, born of Swedish immigrant parents, who, when he began to write about the packinghouses and factories of Chicago, did not see them as ephemeral features of an industrial nightmare but as living and undeniable facts of concrete, steel, flesh, and blood, who knew that the material of legend and song and ballad can never die so long as there are men working together. And, most of all, Edgar Lee Masters, jaundiced missionary, stubborn tub-thumper with a snarl and a flourish, acute in the particulars of ironic portraiture and lavish with high-blown abstractions, verbose, grotesquely concise, a man with a temper he wouldn't sell for a fortune.

In this sequence of poems, the dead of the town of Spoon River speak, from the graveyard on the Hill, their honest epitaphs. Or, rather, they speak as honestly as they can, having, while on earth, been defeated by their honesty and therefore grown bitter, or by their dishonesty and therefore grown suspicious of the motives of all others. In life, they had failed to make their peace with the world; now, in death, they are trying to make their peace with God in whom they might not even believe.

'Here lies the body of' – and then the name the monumental mason insignificantly engraved. Masters stopped at 'Here lies,' and then engraved his fierce, wounded, compassionate version of the skewbald truth. He was never deluded into thinking that the truth is simple and one-sided, that values are clearly defined; he knew that the true motives of men about their business on earth are complex and muddled, that man moves in a mysterious way his blunders to perform, that the heart is not only a bloody pumping muscle but an old ball, too, of wet woolly fluff in the breast, a 'foul rag-and-bone shop,' in Yeats's phrase, a nest of errors, a terrible compulsion that lives by its hurt. And, what is more, he knew that people had poetry always, even if it wasn't always very good.

He wrote about the war between the sexes. The great gulf between men, that was created by the laws of men. The incompatibility of those who live their short lives together because of economic convenience, loneliness, the cavernous and ever-increasing distance from the first maternal grave, casual physical desire. Not that the reasons of economic convenience, or the assuaging of casual, though none the less urgent, lust are, in themselves, inconducive to a state of tranquility between two people lost; but who wants tranquility? Better burn than marry, if marriage puts the fire out.

He wrote about waste: how man wastes his vitality in the pursuit of cynical irrelevancies; and his aspirations through his allegiance to the bad laws, theologies, social institutions and discriminations, the injustices, greeds and fears, that have constantly and resentfully been reinforced by all those human beings of the past who also have suffered and died of them.

He wrote about the waste of man, but loudly, awkwardly, passionately revered the possibilities of greatness in what there was to waste.

31
Home Town – Swansea

9 April 1953 TV 8.15–8.45 'Home Town – Swansea. A programme in which viewers meet some of the interesting people who live in this old Welsh town.' Commentator, Wynford Vaughan Thomas; presented by David J. Thomas from Cardiff. Participants introduced by Dylan Thomas were Vernon Watkins, Alfred Janes, and Daniel Jones.

The first part of the present text is taken from Vernon Watkins' transcription of Dylan Thomas's manuscript at Texas, as published in *Texas Quarterly* (Winter 1961), where Watkins notes that the programme was 'devised by Dylan Thomas in conjunction with the producer'.

> In the actual production many details of this sketch were changed. The painting of Culver's Hole by Alfred Janes was found to be too long and narrow for the television screen, so another painting was substituted; and instead of reciting a part of my *Ballad of Culver's Hole*, I recited the opening of a poem about Swansea. The original plan to project the portraits of Daniel Jones, Dylan Thomas, and myself was kept; and immediately after the showing of each portrait the subject appeared and spoke impromptu or recited.

Dylan Thomas's own contribution and the ending come from the extant BBC script, and differ in a few details from the Texas manuscript.

Reginald Pound reviewed the programme in *The Listener* (16 April 1953):

> 'Home Town: Swansea' appeared to be the work of entirely competent hands. Introducing Dylan Thomas, the poet, was its chief pleasure for me, as doubtless for many others. He represented the surprise element

259

implicit in television at its best, the feeling that you never know who you are going to meet round the next corner.

Daniel Jones has written about this occasion in *My Friend Dylan Thomas* (pp. 79–81):

To turn from radio to television: by chance, I was present during Dylan's first performance in this medium; Fred Janes, John Prichard and I took part in it with him. It was the first time for all of us, and each hid from the others his secret apprehensions. To cushion ourselves against these we took even more than the usual amount of refreshment in one of the Cardiff pubs near the place of trial. The programme was not well planned by present-day standards; if the producer reads these words I hope he will forgive me for saying so. Instead of devising some sort of mingling of the participants, at least for part of the time, the producer had decided that each of us should do his own 'little piece'. Fred, John and I decided to prepare in advance only a vague outline of topics; apart from sticking to this, we thought it best to make our contributions extempore. This was not Dylan's plan. While the rest of us chatted and laughed nervously, Dylan covered the backs of several envelopes with his tiny handwriting. His eyes were glazed; he remained silent, but occasionally chuckled. All he would tell us was that his piece was about a certain Mrs Parsnip.

The testing time came. Fred, John and I acquitted ourselves without distinction but without shame. Dylan, as the star turn, was reserved for the last. Swinging his short legs, he sat on the studio table, his neck swelling, his face getting redder and redder in the hot lights as the camera 'zoomed in'. We all expected something amusing, and so it was. Unfortunately, the humour of the piece depended on manipulation of words, and, of course, they should have been properly memorized. All went well at first, but by the slipping of some ratchet of word-memory Dylan suddenly found himself at the beginning again, and, to our horror, we heard a repeat; then, at the same point, the same thing happened. I was reminded of something that may happen to reindeer when crossing a fjord; if the leader gets behind the tail of the herd, the animals will swim round and round in circles until they drown. The studio manager began to make frantic rotatory gestures, but instead of winding up, Dylan wound round. Towards the end of the third repeat, 'I had a landlady called Mrs Par . . .' Snip! Dylan's camera light went out, and the monitors showed an announcer who, wincing but with a forced smile, rounded off the programme.

This was the inauspicious beginning of a very short television career that was, it must be said, unsuccessful. I saw Dylan on television two or

260

three times later, but never with a feeling of comfort. What was wrong? If I closed my eyes, everything was fine. Perhaps, unlike children, Dylan was to be heard, not seen. If I opened my eyes, I was immediately struck by the intensity of the effort Dylan was making to project himself. This is the sort of technique that can be very successful in public, before an audience. But even a professional actor whom we have just seen performing splendidly before the camera may, when interviewed on television about his acting or himself, become embarrassingly inarticulate or uncomfortably artificial. The same tricks will not do in front of the treacherous television camera lens.

Dylan would, of course, have realized this if he could have seen himself, as he had so often heard himself from radio tapes. In any case, with experience, he might have learned how to handle the medium. But there was no time.

Home Town – Swansea

Paintings, framed and unframed – still lifes, portraits, landscapes, etc. –
on the walls. Canvases stacked against the walls. An easel. An old
upright piano. A few chairs. A rickety table, beer bottle and glasses on
it. A sofa. Alfred Janes is at work at the easel.

Wynford Vaughan Thomas comes into the studio and greets Janes,
who turns, brush in hand, from his canvas. Janes returns the greeting,
and then goes on working. We follow Vaughan Thomas as he goes
across to the paintings on the wall. As he moves, he talks about Janes
and his paintings, quite casually, saying, in effect: 'And now let's see
some of the work of Alfred Janes, the Swansea painter.' As he goes on
to talk about Janes and his work, we see, close, some of the paintings
on the wall: enough to give some idea of Janes' varying styles and
subject matter. Or perhaps, as we see the paintings, Janes' voice could
be heard briefly describing his methods and intentions as a painter.
We stop at a portrait of Vernon Watkins, and hear Vaughan Thomas's
voice saying (off) words to this effect: 'Oh, yes, I know this chap. This
is Vernon Watkins, the poet. How long did Janes make you sit for this,
Vernon?'

And the camera moves, from the portrait, to Watkins himself, who
is sitting on one of the chairs in the studio. Watkins replies (in his own
words) that it took quite a long time but he found it almost restful. He
says (maybe) that he found *he* could work, also, as Janes was painting
him; he could think of a poem that he was working on then; it was a
good time just to sit and think and let words move about in him.
Briefly, Watkins describes his own background and his way of writing
poetry. 'Perhaps I was thinking,' (he might say) 'of the beginning of

262

my poem called "The Ballad of Culver's Hole." I know the poem was in my mind just about that time. Culver's Hole is a cave in Gower, near S'sea, near where I live. Janes made a picture of it.' We hear the noise of sea waves. Camera now approaches the painting of Culver's Hole on the studio wall, until we see the painting close. And as the camera moves, so we hear Watkins' voice speaking a passage from his poem.

Now we see the studio again, Janes at his easel. We see, too, Watkins now sitting on a chair in the studio. Janes says: 'Have you seen that other portrait, of Dan Jones?' And the camera shows the portrait of Daniel Jones. And, as we look at it, Vaughan Thomas's voice is heard saying (off): 'Daniel Jones, the composer, of Swansea, Wales. What were *you* thinking about, Dan, when this was painted?' And the camera moves, from the portrait, to Jones himself, who is sitting on one of the chairs in the studio. (Or at the upright piano.) In this shot, we do not see Watkins.

And Jones replies: 'About Daniel Jones.'

He then goes on to say (very much in his own words) that he had been thinking about his music: of music on which he was working. He says that, about this time, he was working on his Second (?) Symphony. And, after a few argumentative words about his own music, he crosses to the piano (or is already at it) and plays.

Now we see the studio again, Janes at the easel. We see, too, Watkins sitting on the chair and Jones at the piano.

Janes says: 'Those portraits were painted in the last few years. But have you seen that other one, the one of Dylan Thomas? I painted that a long time ago.'

And the camera shows the portrait of Dylan Thomas.

And, as we look at it, we hear Dylan Thomas's voice saying, regretfully, 'Oh, yes, indeed, a long long time.'

And the camera moves, from the portrait, to Thomas, who is sitting on the sofa next to the rickety table with the bottle and glasses.

DYLAN THOMAS: It was a *terrible* long time ago, as is only too obvious. Before television – (I'm glad I'm not looking at television tonight, between a quarter-to-eight and a quarter-past-nine. There's faces you'll see, they tell me). Before the radio even, I shouldn't be surprised, when I see that dewy blubber-lipped frog-eyed mock-goblin from the Welsh bogs goggling at me out of the past. (I think that portrait must have been losing

263

weight; I can hardly recognize it now). Before the internal-combustion engine, before the invention of the wheel, oh what a long time ago, in the Golden Days. (*half-turning*) Do you remember them, Fred? The Golden Days, in London, when we were exiled bohemian boily boys. There were three of us then: you and me and Mervyn Levy, three very young monsters green and brimming from Swansea, stiff with lyrics and ambition and still-lives, all living together in one big, bare barmy beautiful room kept by a Mrs Parsnip, as far as I can remember, in Redcliffe Gardens. Two of us had beards, and I grew one, too, sparse and ginger and limp, like a depressed marmalade cat's; I don't know what happened to it; either it fell off, or was blown away, or it just grew in, I can't remember. Mervyn had a different beard every fortnight, and every one his own: spade-shaped, Assyrian, Captain Kettle, Victorian-celebrity, rabbi, Uncle Sam goatee, Southern Gentleman, goat; and once he grew only half a beard, oiled and curled and scented, on one side of his face; but nobody seemed to notice it in that neighbourhood, which was infuriating. Mrs Parsnip was always boiling cabbage downstairs, cabbage and lights and, maybe, mice; and one of us was painting mackerel mackerel all the time, day in day out, and the same mackerel too, until they used to get up and walk around the room just like real, live models; and the chimney huffed and puffed like a wolf; and I think there were tomcats lodging in the next room: perhaps they paid their rent in mice to Mrs Parsnip. Other odd lodgers were always coming and going: I remember an American woman with magenta hair and grey trousers – or perhaps it was the other way round – who drew nothing but grave-yards in a little leaking room off the stairs; and people in the room right above us, who were composing an opera, or so we believed, a rather unmusical opera heavily dependent on screams and the throwing of buckets and some kind of Eastern bagpipes; and a man we never saw who made, all night, a noise like a train full of owls going through a tunnel. These came and went, but we stayed on in our big room, surrounded by the stock props of the student life: candles in beerflagon candlesticks, half-finished paintings and tins of sardines, a nibbled volume of Dostoievski, a Picasso reproduction, a handful of pawn-tickets, and a guitar. Mervyn Levy was studying at the Royal College of Art, and just beginning other experiments; Janes was practising mackerel and ju-jitsu; and I was writing poems (of a kind) for immortality and the Poets' Corner of the *Sunday Referee*. What we cooked, I don't know, unless it was our next-room neighbours, miaows and all, but it tasted like the Ritz. There was no weather in those days, only light and dark, loud and soft, miserable and bouncing. We hadn't got any money at all, and to show you how young we were, even that was delightful: or is this middle-age talking, looking back through a ring o' roses?

Well, anyway, there we were. That's when that portrait of me, a frog in the springtime, was painted. And here I am nostalgically mourning those dead green salad days, and that very conventional period of anti-conventionality, just as we used to mourn, in this Parsnip's mousey-and-cabbagey palace, the town we had left behind us for ever and ever. For ever and for ever. And here we are, all back in the town again.

Here's to it!

And Thomas lifts his glass, as though in salutation.

Now we see the whole studio. Janes at his easel. Watkins in his chair. Jones at the piano. Thomas on the sofa. And they all have full glasses. And they all raise them.

32
The International Eisteddfod

Aneirin Talfan Davies in his notes to *Quite Early One Morning* (pp. 174–175) describes the circumstances in which this script was written:

> In July 1953 I took Thomas, with his wife Caitlin and little daughter Aeronwy, to spend a week at Llangollen, and to report his impressions in a radio talk.
>
> This trip with Thomas to the International Eisteddfod gave me an opportunity of studying his method of collecting material for these radio talks. The week was spent in apparently aimless meanderings through the crowded streets of the town, occasional half-hours in the Eisteddfod marquee, and many hours standing at the bars of the far from few pubs of the town. Now and then, while standing at the bar, Thomas would tear open an empty cigarette carton, take out a stub of pencil from his pocket, and behind the shelter of a friendly pint he would scribble a few words, sometimes just a single word, and deposit it in the depths of his capacious coat pocket. By the end of the week he had a harvest of these scribbled phrases. There was a moment of panic in the car on the way home when he thought that he had lost these notes. His jottings were afterwards copied out on to a sheet of paper, and then the task of writing began. He spent the whole of Sunday and most of Monday at this work, and arrived at the studio about an hour before the broadcast with his talk carefully written out in his boyish hand. I remember that it was about three minutes short, but there was no question of adding to it; and there was to be no hurried scribbling in the studio.

The talk was broadcast from Swansea 13 July 1953 in the Welsh Home Service. The fee was twenty guineas.

267

The International Eisteddfod

Llangollen. A town in a vale in rolling green North Wales on a windy July morning. The sun squints out and is puffed back again into the grey clouds blowing, full to the ragged rims with rain, across the Berwyn Hills. The white-horsed River Dee hisses and paws over the hills of its stones and under the greybeard bridge. Wind smacks the river and you, it's a cold, cracking morning; birds hang and rasp over the whipped river, against their will, as though frozen still, or are wind-chaffed and scattered towards the gusty trees. As you drift down Castle Street with your hair flying, or your hat or umbrella dancing to be off and take the sky, you see and hear all about you the decorous, soberly dressed and headgeared, silent and unsmiling inhabitants of the tame town. You could be in any Welsh town on any windy snip of a morning, with only the birds and the river fuming and the only brightness the numberless greens and high purples of the hills. Everything is very ordinary in Llangollen; everything is nicely dull, except the summer world of wind and feathers, leaves and water. There is, if you are deaf, blind, and dumb, with a heart like cold bread pudding, nothing to remark or surprise. But rub your eyes with your black gloves. Here, over the bridge, come three Javanese, winged, breastplated, helmeted, carrying gongs and steel bubbles. Kilted, spor-raned, tartan'd, daggered Scotsmen reel and strathspey up a side-street, piping hot. Burgundian girls, wearing, on their heads, bird-cages made of velvet, suddenly whisk on the pavement into a coloured dance. A Viking goes into a pub. In black felt feathered hats and short leather trousers, enormous Austrians, with thighs big as Welshmen's bodies, but much browner, yodel to fiddles and split the rain with their

268

smiles. Frilled, ribboned, sashed, fezzed, and white-turbaned, in baggy-blue sharavári and squashed red boots, Ukrainians with Manchester accents gopak up the hill. Everything is strange in Llangollen. You wish you had a scarlet hat, and bangles, and a little bagpipe to call your own, but it does not matter. The slapping bell-dancers, the shepherds and chamois-hunters, the fiddlers and fluters, the players on gongs and mandolins, guitars, harps, and trumpets, the beautiful flashing boys and girls of a score and more of singing countries, all the colours of the international rainbow, do not mind at all your mouse-brown moving among them: though you long, all the long Eisteddfod week, for a cloak like a blue sea or a bonfire to sweep and blaze in the wind, and a cap of bells, and a revelling waistcoat, and a great Alp-horn to blow all over Wales from the ruins of Dinas Brân.

Now follow your nose, and the noise of guitars, and the flying hues and flourish of those big singing-birds in their clogs and aprons and bonnets, veils, flowers, more flowers, and lace, past the wee Shoppes, through the babel of the bridge, by the very white policeman conducting from a rostrum, and up the tide of the hill, past popcorn and raspberryade, to the tented field. Green, packed banks run, swarming, down to the huge marquee there that groans and strains and sings in the sudden squalls like an airship crewed full of choirs. Music spills out of the microphones all over the humming field. Out of the wind-tugged tent it rises in one voice, and the crowd outside is hushed away into Spain. In a far corner of the field, young men and women begin to dance, for every reason in the world. Out skims the sun from a cloud-shoal. The spaniel ears of the little tents flap. Children collect the autographs of Dutch farmers. You hear a hive of summer hornets: it is the Burgundian vielle, a mandolin with a handle. Palestrina praises from Bologna to the choral picknickers. A Breton holiday sings in the wind, to clog-tramp and biniou.

Here they come, to this cup and echo of hills, people who love to make music, from France, Ireland, Norway, Italy, Switzerland, Spain, Java, and Wales: fine singers and faulty, nimble dancers and rusty, pipers to make the dead swirl or chanters with crows in their throats: all countries, shapes, ages, and colours, sword-dancers, court-dancers, cross-dancers, clog-dancers, dale-dancers, morris, ceilidhe, and high-land, bolero, flamenco, heel-and-toe. They love to make music move. What a rush of dancing to Llangollen's feet! And, oh, the hubbub of tongues and toes in the dark chapels where every morning there's such a shining noise as you'd think would drive the Sunday bogles out of their doldrums for ever and ever.

Inside the vast marquee that drags at its anchors, eight thousand people – and you – face a sea of flowers, begonias, magnolias, lupins, lobelias, grown for these dancing days in the gardens of the town. Banks and waves of plants and flowers flow to the stage where a company from Holland – eight married pairs of them, the oldest in their late fifties, the youngest twenty or so – are performing, in sombre black, a country dance called, 'Throw Your Wife Away'. This is followed, appropriately and a little later, by a dance called, 'You Can't Catch Me.' The movements of the humorous and simple dance are gay and sprightly. The men of the company dance like sad British railway-drivers in white clogs. Under their black, peaked caps, their faces are stern, weather-scored, and unrelenting. The quicker the music, the gloomier they clap and clog on the invisible cobbles of cold clean kitchens. The frenzied flute and fiddle whip them up into jet-black bliss as they frolic like undertakers. Long Dutch winter nights envelop them. Brueghel has painted them. They are sober as potatoes. Their lips move as they stamp and bow. Perhaps they are singing. Certainly, they are extremely happy.

And Austrians, then, to fiddles and guitar, sing a song of mowers in the Alpine meadows. Sworded Ukrainians – I mean, Ukrainians with swords – leap and kick above the planted sea. People from Tournas, in the Burgundy country, dance to accordion and cabrette, the Dance of the Vine – Dressers after Harvest. They plant the vines, put the leaves on the branches, hang up the grapes, pick the grapes, and press the wine. 'God gave us wine,' they sing as they dance, and the wine is poured into glasses and the dancers drink. (But the wine's not as real as the pussyfoot nudge and shudder down the aisles.)

All day, the music goes on. Bell-padded, baldricked, and braided, those other foreigners, the English, dance fiercely out of the past, and some have beards, spade, gold, white, and black, to dance and wag as well.

And a chorus of Spanish ladies are sonorous and beautiful in their nighties.

And little girls from Obernkirchen sing like pigtailed angels.

All day the song and dancing in this transformed valley, this green cup of countries in the country of Wales, goes on until the sun goes in. Then, in the ship of the tent, under the wind-filled sails, watchers and listeners grow slow and close into one cloud of shadow; they gaze, from their deep lulled dark, on to the lighted deck where the country dancers weave in shifting-coloured harvests of light. And then you climb down hill again, in a tired tide, and over the floodlit Dee to the town that won't sleep for a whole melodious week or, if it does at all, will hear all night in its sleep the hills fiddle and strum and the streets painted with tunes.

The bars are open as though they could not shut and Sunday never come down over the fluting town like a fog or a shutter. For every reason in the world, there's a wave of dancing in the main, loud street. A fiddle at a corner tells you to dance and you do in the moon though you can't dance a step for all the Ukrainians in Llangollen. Peace plays on a concertina in the vigorous, starry street, and nobody is surprised.

When you leave the last voices and measures of the sweet-throated, waltzing streets, the lilt and ripple of the Dee leaping, and the light of the night, to lie down, and the strewn town lies down to sleep in its hills and ring of echoes, you will remember that nobody was surprised at the turn the town took and the life it danced for one week of the long, little year. The town sang and danced, as though it were right and proper as the rainbow or the rare sun to celebrate the old bright turning earth and its bullied people. Are you surprised that people still can dance and sing in a world on its head? The only surprising thing about miracles, however small, is that they sometimes happen.

33
A Visit to America

Thomas had written 'A Visit to America' to use on his 1953 U.S. tour. His delivery of it at the Massachusetts Institute of Technology on 11 May 1953 was recorded. Aneirin Talfan Davies was keen to have Thomas do it for the Welsh Home Service, and managed to get a recording in Swansea 5 October 1953, the week before Thomas left Wales for the last visit to America. The broadcast was scheduled for a date which turned out to be the day of Thomas's funeral at Laugharne; so it was postponed until 30 March 1954. It was printed in *The Listener* 22 April 1954.

The present text is the BBC script checked against the M.I.T. recording.

A Visit to America

Across the United States of America, from New York to California and back, glazed, again, for many months of the year there streams and sings for its heady supper a dazed and prejudiced procession of European lecturers, scholars, sociologists, economists, writers, authorities on this and that and even, in theory, on the United States of America. And, breathlessly between addresses and receptions, in planes and trains and boiling hotel bedroom ovens, many of them attempt to keep journals and diaries. At first, confused and shocked by shameless profusion and almost shamed by generosity, unaccustomed to such importance as they are assumed, by their hosts, to possess, and up against the barrier of a common language, they write in their notebooks like demons, generalizing away, on character and culture and the American political scene. But, towards the middle of their middle-aged whisk through middle-western clubs and universities, the fury of the writing flags; their spirits are lowered by the spirit with which they are everywhere strongly greeted and which, in ever-increasing doses, they themselves lower; and they begin to mistrust themselves, and their apparent popularity – for they have found, too often, that an audience will receive a lantern-lecture on, say, ceramics, with the same uninhibited enthusiasm that it accorded the very week before to a paper on the Modern Turkish Novel. And, in their diaries, more and more do such entries appear as, 'No way of escape!' or 'Buffalo!' or 'I am beaten', until at last they cannot write a word. And, twittering all over, old before their time, with eyes like rissoles in the sand, they are helped up the gangway of the home-bound liner by kind bosom friends (of all kinds and bosoms) who boister them on the back, pick them up again, thrust bottles, sonnets, cigars, addresses into their pockets, have a farewell party in the cabin, pick them up again, and, snickering and yelping, are gone: to wait at the dockside for another boat from Europe and another batch of fresh, crisp green lecturers.

There they go, every spring, from New York to Los Angeles: exhibitionists, polemicists, histrionic publicists, theological rhetoricians, historical hoddy-doddies, balletomanes, ulterior decorators, max-factored actors, windbags, and bigwigs and humbugs, men in love with stamps, men in love with steaks, men after millionaires' widows, men with elephantiasis of the reputation (huge trunks and teeny minds), authorities on gas, bishops, best sellers, new spellers, editors looking for writers, writers looking for publishers, publishers looking for dollars, existentialists, serious physicists with nuclear missions, men from the B.B.C. who speak as though they had the Elgin Marbles in their mouths, potboiling philosophers, professional Irishmen (very lepri-corny), and, I am afraid, fat poets with slim volumes.

And see, too, in that linguaceous stream, the tall monocled men, smelling of saddle soap and club arm-chairs, their breath a nice blending of whisky and fox's blood, with big protruding upper-class tusks and county moustaches, presumably invented in England and sent abroad to advertise *Punch*, who to one's surprise one finds are here to lecture to women's clubs on some such unlikely subject as 'The History of Etching in the Shetland Islands.'

And the brassy-bossy men-women, with corrugated-iron perms, and hippo hides, who come, self-announced, as 'ordinary British housewives,' to talk to rich minked chunks of American matronhood about the iniquity of the English Health Service, the criminal sloth of the miners, the *visible* tail and horns of Mr Aneurin Bevan, and the fear of everyone in England to go out alone at night because of the organized legions of cosh boys against whom the police are powerless owing to the refusal of those in power to equip them with revolvers and to flog to ribbons every adolescent offender on any charge at all.

And there shiver and teeter also, meek and driven, their little eyes lost and rabbit-scared behind big glasses steamed over by the smoke of countless cocktail parties, those British authors unfortunate enough to have written, after years of unadventurous forgotten work, one bad novel which became enormously popular on both sides of the Atlantic. At home, when success first hit them, they were mildly delighted; a couple of literary luncheons went sugar-tipsy to their heads, like the washing sherry served before those luncheons; and perhaps, as the lovely money rolled lushly in, they began to dream in their moony writers' way, of being able to retire to the country, keep wasps (or was it bees?), and never write another lousy word. But in come the literary agent's triggermen and the publisher's armed narks: 'You must go to the States and make a Personal Appearance. Your novel is *killing* them over there, and we're not surprised either. You must go round the States lecturing to women.' And the inoffensive writers, who've never dared lecture anyone, let alone women – they are frightened of women, they do not understand women, they write about women as creatures that never existed, and the women lap it up – these novelists cry out: 'But what shall we lecture about?'

'The English Novel.'

'I don't read novels.'

'Great Women in Fiction.'

'I don't like fiction *or* women.'

But off they're wafted, first class, in the plush bowels of the *Queen Victoria* with a list of engagements long as a New York menu or a half-hour with a book by Charles Morgan, and soon they are losing their little cold-as-goldfish paws in the great general glutinous handshake of a clutch of enveloping hostesses.

It was Ernest Raymond, the author of *Tell England*, who once made a journey round the American women's clubs, being housed and entertained at each small town he stopped at by the richest and largest and furriest lady available. On one occasion he stopped at some little station, and was met, as usual, by an enormous motor-car full of a large hornrimmed business man, looking *exactly* like a large hornrimmed business man on the films – and his roly-poly pearly wife. Mr Raymond sat with her in the back of the car, and off they went, the husband driving. At once, she began to say how utterly delighted she and her husband and the committee were to have him at their Women's Literary and Social Guild, and to compliment him on his books. 'I don't think I've ever, in all my life, enjoyed a book so much as *Sorrel and Son*,' she said. 'What you don't know about human nature! I think Sorrel is one of the most beautiful characters ever portrayed.' Ernest Raymond let her talk on, while he stared, embarrassed, in front of him. All he could see were the three double chins that her husband wore at the back of his neck. On and on she gushed in praise of *Sorrel and Son* until he could stand it no longer. 'I quite agree with you,' he said. 'A beautiful book indeed. But I'm afraid I didn't write *Sorrel and Son*. It was written by an old friend of mine, Mr Warwick Deeping.'

And the large hornrimmed double-chinned husband at the wheel said without turning: 'Caught again, Emily.'

See the garrulous others, also, gabbing and garlanded from one nest of culture-vultures to another: people selling the English way of life and condemning the American way as they swig and guzzle through it; people resurrecting the theories of surrealism for the benefit of remote parochial female audiences who did not know it was dead, not having ever known it had ever been alive; people talking about Etruscan pots and pans to a bunch of dead pans and wealthy pots near Boston. And there, too, in the sticky thick of lecturers moving across the continent, go the foreign poets, catarrhal troubadours, lyrical one-night-standers, dollar-mad nightingales, remittance-bards from at home, myself among them booming with the worst.

Did we pass one another, en route, all unknowing, I wonder, one of us, spry-eyed, with clean, white lectures and a soul he could call his own, going buoyantly west to his remunerative doom in the great State University factories, another returning dog-eared as his clutch of poems and his carefully typed impromptu asides? I ache for us both. There one goes, unsullied as yet, in his Pullman pride, toying, oh boy, with a blunderbuss bourbon, being smoked by a large cigar, riding out to the wide open spaces of the faces of his waiting audience. He carries, besides his literary baggage, a new, dynamic razor, just on the market, bought in New York, which operates at the flick of a thumb, but cuts the thumb to the bone; a tin of new shaving-lather which is worked with the other, unbleeding, thumb and covers not only the face but the whole bath-room and, instantly freezing, makes an arctic, icicled cave from which it takes two sneering bell-boys to extract him; and, of course, a nylon shirt. This, he dearly believed from the advertisements, he could himself wash in his hotel, hang to dry overnight, and put on, without ironing, in the morning. (In my case, no ironing *was* needed, for, as someone cruelly pointed out in print, I looked, anyway, like an unmade bed.)

He is vigorously welcomed at the station by an earnest crew-cut platoon of giant collegiates, all chasing the butterfly culture with net,

277

note-book, poison-bottle, pin, and label, each with at least thirty-six terribly white teeth, and nursed away, as heavily gently as though he were an imbecile rich aunt with a short prospect of life, into a motor-car in which, for a mere fifty miles or so travelled at poet-breaking speed, he assures them of the correctness of their assumption that he is half-witted by stammering inconsequential answers in an over-British accent to their genial questions about what international conference Stephen Spender might be attending at the moment or the reactions of British poets to the work of a famous American whose name he did not know or catch. He is then taken to a small party of only a few hundred people all of whom hold the belief that what a visiting lecturer needs before he trips on to the platform is just enough martinis so that he can trip *off* the platform as well. And, clutching his explosive glass, he is soon contemptuously dismissing, in a flush of ignorance and fluency, the poetry of those androgynous literary ladies with three names who produce a kind of verbal ectoplasm to order as a waiter dishes up spaghetti – only to find that the fiercest of these, a wealthy huntress of small, seedy lions (such as himself), who stalks the middle-western bush with ears and rifle cocked, is his hostess for the evening. Of the lecture he remembers little but the applause and maybe two questions: 'Is it true that the young English intellectuals are *really* psychological?' or, 'I always carry Kierkegaard in my pocket. What do you carry?'

Late at night, in his room, he fills a page of his journal with a confused, but scathing, account of his first engagement; summarizes American advanced education in a paragraph that will be meaningless tomorrow, and falls to sleep where he is immediately chased through long, dark thickets by a Mrs Mabel Frankincense Mehaffey, with a tray of martinis and lyrics.

And there goes the other happy poet bedraggledly back to New York which struck him all of a sheepish never-sleeping heap at first but which seems to him now, after the ulcerous rigours of a lecturer's spring, a haven cosy as toast, cool as an icebox, and safe as skyscrapers.

34
Laugharne

'I nearly lost the opportunity of recording this talk,' Aneirin Talfan Davies wrote in a manuscript note. 'We had failed once (for what reason I cannot remember); then he started saying he was finding it difficult to complete. Caitlin Thomas rang me to say he would never finish it. I had a word with Dylan and in the end he came to Swansea to record. He tried every strategem to avoid recording. He could not finish it in time. He would record in America and send the tape by plane to Wales. But I remained adamant, and got him to the studio.'

This 5 October 1953 recording was used as part of a Welsh Home Service programme on 5 November 1953: 'Vintage Town. An impression of Laugharne in Carmarthenshire. J. C. Griffiths-Jones introduces some of the people who live there to Hywel Davies. Before an audience of fellow townsfolk at the memorial Hall in Laugharne.' Actually only four minutes of it was used, from 'Whatever the reason ...' to the end. The BBC retains the complete script and the sound recording.

In his notes to *Quite Early One Morning* Aneirin Talfan Davies recalls: 'At the end of the programme, in a short speech of thanks to the townspeople, I paid tribute to the great poet who lived among them. After I sat down Mrs Thomas turned to me to say that she had just received news by cable that her husband was lying unconscious in an American hospital.'

279

Laugharne

Off and on, up and down, high and dry, man and boy, I've been living now for fifteen years, or centuries, in this timeless, beautiful, barmy (both spellings) town, in this far, forgetful, important place of herons, cormorants (known here as billyduckers), castle, churchyard, gulls, ghosts, geese, feuds, scares, scandals, cherry-trees, mysteries, jackdaws in the chimneys, bats in the belfry, skeletons in the cupboards, pubs, mud, cockles, flatfish, curlews, rain, and human, often all too human, beings; and, though still very much a foreigner, I am hardly ever stoned in the streets any more, and can claim to be able to call several of the inhabitants, and a few of the herons, by their Christian names.

Now, some people live in Laugharne because they were born in Laugharne and saw no good reason to move; others migrated here, for a number of curious reasons, from places as distant and improbable as Tonypandy or even England, and have now been absorbed by the natives; some entered the town in the dark and immediately disappeared, and can sometimes be heard, on hushed black nights, making noises in ruined houses, or perhaps it is the white owls breathing close together, like ghosts in bed; others have almost certainly come here to escape the international police, or their wives; and there are those, too, who still do not know, and will never know, why they are here at all; you can see them, any day of the week, slowly, dopily, wandering up and down the streets like Welsh opium-eaters, half asleep in a heavy bewildered daze. And some, like myself, just came, one day, for the day, and never left; got off the bus, and forgot to get on again. Whatever the reason, if any, for our being here, in this timeless, mild, beguiling island of a town with its seven public-

280

houses, one chapel in action, one church, one factory, two billiard tables, one St Bernard (without brandy), one policeman, three rivers, a visiting sea, one Rolls-Royce selling fish and chips, one cannon (cast-iron), one chancellor (flesh and blood), one port-reeve, one Danny Raye, and a multitude of mixed birds, here we just are, and there is nowhere like it anywhere at all.

But when you say, in a nearby village or town, that you come from this unique, this waylaying, old, lost Laugharne, where some people start to retire before they start to work and where longish journeys, of a few hundred yards, are often undertaken only on bicycles, then, oh! the wary edging away, the whispers and whimpers, and nudges, the swift removal of portable objects!

'Let's get away while the going is good,' you hear.

'Laugharne's where they quarrel with boathooks.'

'All the women there's got web feet.'

'Mind out for the Evil Eye!'

'Never go there at the full moon!'

They are only envious. They envy Laugharne its minding of its own, strange, business; its sane disregard for haste; its generous acceptance of the follies of others, having so many, ripe and piping, of its own; its insular, featherbed air; its philosophy of 'It will all be the same in a hundred years' time.' They deplore its right to be, in their eyes, so wrong, and to enjoy it so much as well. And, through envy and indignation, they label and libel it a legendary lazy little black-magical bedlam by the sea. And is it? *Of course not,* I hope.

BBC Engagements Calendar

A diary of Dylan Thomas's recordings, broadcasts, and other engagements with the BBC.

Quotations are from the *Radio Times* unless otherwise indicated.

1933

28 JUNE 1933 (National) 10.55 'The Romantic Isle' (Dylan Thomas), read by Ian Sinclair Phail. 'This is an original and hitherto unpublished poem selected from the entries sent in by listeners for the B.B.C. Poetry Competition.'

1937

21 JANUARY 1937 BBC offers Thomas 15/– for the use of 'Especially when the October wind' in 'Poets in Conflict', a selection by George Barker for broadcasting on 6 February 1947. 'In fact it never materialized. Nor, presumably, did the fifteen bob' – 'The Dylan Thomas File' p. 2.

21 APRIL 1937 (West and Wales) 9.45–10 'Dylan Thomas will read some of his own poems.' He apparently also read W. H. Auden and John Crowe Ransom.

1938

13 JULY 1938 (Wales) 8.45–9 Keidrych Rhys talking on 'Modernism in Wales' included some of Thomas's poems. Thomas sent a postcard to Vernon Watkins: 'Are you listening-in tonight?' (*Letters* p. 313).

18 OCTOBER 1938 (National) 10.30–11.15 'The Modern Muse. A Recital of Contemporary Poetry by W. H. Auden, Louis MacNeice, Stephen Spender, C. Day Lewis, etc. Arranged by Michael Roberts and D. G. Bridson, including settings by Benjamin Britten and Norman Fulton. Compere, Michael

Roberts (*From the North*).' Thomas was in the Manchester BBC studio to read 'The hand that signed the paper.' His poem 'This bread I break' was sung by Frederick Seddon. Thomas's fee, 3 guineas for reading, 2 guineas for the use of the poem. A BBC recording of this programme exists.

1939

6 SEPTEMBER 1939 (Welsh Region) 'Modern Welsh Poets. A reading of his own poems by Dylan Thomas and some account of our modern school of poets by Keidrych Rhys.' The broadcast was cancelled because of the outbreak of war. After some negotiation, Thomas was allowed to keep £3.17.0 of the £5.15.6 fee.

1940

21 AUGUST 1940 Thomas submits script, 'Duque de Caxias', to producer Royston Morley; broadcast in Latin American Service 26 August 1940. Fee 12 guineas.

13 OCTOBER 1940 (Latin American Service) 'Cristobal Colon' – the script supplied by Thomas was re-written as 'not entirely suitable', and he received only 10 guineas of the 15 guineas contracted for.

24 NOVEMBER 1940 Thomas agrees to 12 guineas fee for writing a script, 'The March of the Czech Legion'. The script supplied to producer Royston Morley in January 1941 was found 'not suitable'.

1941

19 SEPTEMBER 1941 (Eastern) 'Civilian's War No. 19: Sailors' Home', produced by Francis Dillon. Thomas's first part in a radio drama; fee unknown. Rehearsal and broadcast at Monseignor Theatre 19 September 1941; repeated 20 September (American) 26 September (African) and 17 October (Pacific)).

1942

16 MAY 1942 Thomas records five of his own poems for 'Books and Authors', producer Gerald Bullett. Fee, 5 guineas. Broadcast 26 May 1942 (Overseas Service), introduced by Charles Claybrook: 'He was born in a Carmarthenshire village 28 years ago, the son of a schoolmaster and the

grandson of the village carrier. That means you have only to skip one generation to find his peasant roots' (BBC script).

10 NOVEMBER 1942 rehearsal scheduled for production of David Jones's *In Parenthesis* with Thomas taking part; fee, 8 guineas. 'At the last moment the transmission was cancelled, to provide space for Churchill's speech from the Mansion House ("blood, toil, tears and sweat")' – producer Douglas Cleverdon in *The Growth of Milk Wood* (p. 9).

29 NOVEMBER 1942 (Overseas) 'Britain to America – the British Tommy', producer Francis Dillon. Thomas took part; fee 8 guineas.

1943

7 JANUARY 1943 recording of 'Reminiscences of Childhood' (script 1) for transmission in Home Service 15 February 1943. Fee 7 guineas. Produced by Aneirin Talfan Davies.

5 FEBRUARY 1943 signed copyright release, fee 2 guineas, for use of 'Among those killed in the dawn raid' in the programme 'Themes for Poetry', poems by Welsh poets, selected by Keidrych Rhys, and presented by Stephen Potter; broadcast 8 February 1943 (Home Service).

31 JULY 1943 recorded 'A saint about to fall' for use in a talk by Desmond Hawkins on 'The Apocalyptic Poets'; transmitted 8 August 1943 (Eastern Service) in a series 'Calling All Students', produced by George Orwell, who described the series in 'Poetry and the Microphone' included in his *Collected Essays*:

About a year ago I and a number of others were engaged in broadcasting literary programmes to India, and among other things we broadcast a good deal of verse by contemporary and near-contemporary English writers – for example, Eliot, Herbert Read, Auden, Spender, Dylan Thomas, Henry Treece, Alex Comfort, Robert Bridges, Edmund Blunden, D. H. Lawrence. Whenever it was possible we had poems broadcast by the people who wrote them. Just why these particular programmes (a small and remote outflanking movement in the radio war) were instituted there is no need to explain here, but I should add that the fact that we were broadcasting to an Indian audience dictated our technique to some extent. The essential point was that our literary broadcasts were aimed at the Indian university students, a small and hostile audience, unapproachable by anything that could be described as British propaganda.

1944

14 DECEMBER 1944 recorded 'Quite Early One Morning' (script 2) for Aneirin Talfan Davies, in London; fee 10 guineas. Broadcast 31 August 1945 (Welsh Home Service).

1945

23 FEBRUARY 1945 recording session at BBC Carmarthen with Aneirin Talfan Davies: (1) as a reader for 'Porter to the Bards. Verse by Welsh Poets, introduced by Gwyn Jones.' Broadcast 27 February 1945 (Welsh Home Service); fee 7 guineas: (2) revised version of 'Reminiscences of Childhood' (script 3) recorded for broadcasting in the Children's Hour 21 March 1945; fee 5 guineas.

2 SEPTEMBER 1945 (Home Service) 'New Poems. The nineteenth in the series of new or recently published verse', produced by Patric Dickinson. Thomas read 'A Refusal to Mourn', 'This side of the truth', and 'Poem in October'; fee 5 guineas.

26 SEPTEMBER 1945 recorded 'Book of Verse' poems selected by Joyce Rowe (including Bridges, Southey, and Keats) for transmission 29 September 1945 (Eastern Service), produced by John Arlott. Fee 5 guineas. (*Note*: all 'Book of Verse' programmes were produced by John Arlott for transmission in the Eastern Service.)

10 OCTOBER 1945 recorded 'Book of Verse' poems selected by Clifford Bax (Kyd and Marlowe) for transmission 13 October 1945; fee 5 guineas.

24 OCTOBER 1945 contract for script on Augustus John for Indian Service 2 November 1945 – script not done.

31 OCTOBER 1945 recorded 'Book of Verse' poems selected by John Crow (Ben Jonson's 'On the Death of his Daughter') for transmission 3 November 1945; fee 5 guineas.

30 NOVEMBER 1945 contract for script on 'Nationalism in Poetry' for the Belgium Service for a fee of 7 guineas. (No evidence that the script was written.)

6 DECEMBER 1945 recorded 'Memories of Christmas' (script 4) in London for transmission 16 December 1945 (Welsh Home Service Children's Hour); fee 12 guineas.

14 DECEMBER 1945 (Home) 'Poetry Promenade 8 – A selection from the poetry of Dylan Thomas, chosen and read by the author', introduced by the producer, Patric Dickinson; fee 12 guineas. Thomas read 'In my craft or sullen art', 'If my head hurt a hair's foot', 'On the Marriage of a Virgin', 'Paper and Sticks,' 'Fern Hill', and 'Ceremony After a Fire Raid'.

1946

2 JANUARY 1946 recorded 'Welsh Poetry' (script 5) for transmission in 'Book of Verse' 5 January 1946. Fee for script and narration 20 guineas.

21 JANUARY 1946 recorded 'Book of Verse' poems for 'The English Poet Sees India' transmitted 25 January 1946; fee 5 guineas.

26 FEBRUARY 1946 recorded 'Book of Verse' (Thomas Dekker) for transmission 25 May 1946; fee 7 guineas.

4 MARCH 1946 recorded 'Book of Verse' (Abraham Cowley selected by G. V. Wedgwood) for transmission 9 March 1946; fee 7 guineas.

9 APRIL 1946 recorded 'Book of Verse' (Francis Thompson selected by Viola Meynell) for transmission 20 April 1946; fee 7 guineas.

12 APRIL 1946 recorded 'Book of Verse' (Charles M. Doughty selected by Eric Gillett) for transmission 27 April 1946; fee 7 guineas. Of this occasion, producer John Arlott wrote in *Adelphi* (February 1954):

In a programme on Doughty, he had to read a piece from *The Dawn in Britain* in which occurred a word whose meaning the producer, scriptwriter and reader all admitted they did not know, although it appeared to be the key word of an essential passage. Our sources of reference could not help and we pondered the problem at some length until Dylan said, comfortingly, 'Never mind, I'll say it with conviction'.

16 APRIL 1946 recorded 'Book of Verse' (Thomas Traherne selected by W. R. Childe) for transmission 4 May 1946; fee 7 guineas.

2 MAY 1946 (Light Programme) 'Rogues and Vagabonds' series: 'Captain Kidd', produced by R. D. Smith, written by J. Maclaren-Ross. Thomas took part; fee 10 guineas.

16 MAY 1946 (Light) 'Rogues and Vagabonds' – Thomas took part in 'Peacocks Can Be Poisonous. The story of Thomas Wainwright, artist, essayist, coffee-house crony of Charles Lamb and de Quincey, forger and poisoner', written by Terry Stanford. Thomas's fee 7 guineas.

16 MAY 1946 recorded contribution to 'The World Goes By' (script 6 'On Reading Poetry Aloud'), produced by Ian Cox, for transmission 19 May 1946; fee 5 guineas.

18 MAY 1946 recorded a role in 'Outer Suburb', 'This is London No. 9,' produced by R.D. Smith, for transmission 20 May 1946 (Africa); fee 7 guineas.

19 MAY 1946 (Home) 'Time for Verse. A Poetry Notebook edited by Patric Dickinson. Readers: Dylan Thomas and Felix Aylmer.' Thomas read Hardy; fee 7 guineas.

23 MAY 1946 (Light) 'Rogues and Vagabonds' – Thomas took part in 'The Stolen Duchess. How Adam Worth removed the Gainesborough,' written by Terry Stanford. Thomas's fee 7 guineas.

27 MAY 1946 'National Insurance Bill', producer R.D. Smith, was to have been recorded, but was cancelled. Thomas received 7 guineas fee and travel costs.

30 MAY 1946 recorded 'Book of Verse' (T.L. Beddoes, selected by Lawrence Whistler) for transmission 11 June 1946; fee 7 guineas.

31 MAY 1946 recorded 'Book of Verse' (W.H. Davies, compiler unknown) for transmission 31 August; fee 7 guineas.

4 JUNE 1946 script conference with James Stephens and producer Roy Campbell for a discussion in the 'Books and Writers' series about 'the poet's job' (script 7 'Poets on Poetry'); programme transmitted 18 June 1946 (Light). Thomas's fee was raised from 14 to 19 guineas.

6 JUNE 1946 (Light) 'Rogues and Vagabonds No. 6, The German Princess. The story of Mary Moders, whose life as an adventuress finished on the gallows at Tyburn,' written by Peter Jones and John Mackintosh, producer R.D. Smith. Thomas took part, fee 7 guineas.

19 JUNE 1946 recorded 'Wilfred Owen' (script 10) for 'Book of Verse' transmission 27 July 1946; fee for script and narration 20 guineas.

14 JULY 1946 (Home) 'Time for Verse. This week's number compiled by Dylan Thomas' (script 8 'Poems of Wonder'), produced by Patric Dickinson, who tried to get Thomas 20 guineas fee, but could only get 15 guineas.

15 JULY 1946 (Africa) 'This is London No. 13: The Londoner' (script 9), producer R.D. Smith. Thomas's fee for script 40 guineas, narrator 7 guineas.

16 JULY 1946 (Midland Region) read in programme on Byron, written by Edward Livesay. Fee 7 guineas.

18 JULY 1946 recorded 'Book of Verse' (W.B. Yeats selected by Vernon Watkins) for transmission 24 August 1946; fee 7 guineas.

I SEPTEMBER 1946 (Home) 'Time for Verse, edited by Patric Dickinson. This number is devoted to sea battles, and includes "The Battle of the Baltic" by Thomas Campbell; extracts from "The Nebara" by C. Day Lewis; and "The Ballad of the Revenge" by Tennyson.' Thomas's fee for reading 7 guineas.

3 SEPTEMBER 1946 recorded 'The Written Word: Biographers' (read Thomas Berwick), produced by John Arlott for transmission 21 October 1946 (Eastern Service); fee 10 guineas.

15 SEPTEMBER 1946 recorded 'Book of Verse' (Robert Graves selected by John Hampson) for transmission 28 September 1946; fee 10 guineas.

19 SEPTEMBER 1946 recorded 'Book of Verse' (Lascelles Abercrombie selected by Eric Gillett) for transmission 26 October 1946; fee 10 guineas.

22 SEPTEMBER 1946 'Margate–Past and Present' (script 11), produced at Maida Vale studios by Joel O'Brien, recording to be sent to New York in exchange. Thomas's fee for the script is unknown.

30 SEPTEMBER 1946 (Third) 'Comus' produced by Douglas Cleverdon. Thomas played the Second Brother; rehearsals 28–30 September 1946, fee 12 guineas.

8 OCTOBER 1946 (Home) 'In the Margin' produced by Roy Campbell. Thomas contributed 'How to Begin a Story' (script 12); fee 10 guineas.

11 OCTOBER 1946 recorded discussion with Edward Shanks in the series 'Freedom Forum' produced and chaired by A.E. McDonald (script 13 'What Has Happened to English Poetry?') for transmission in North American Service 16 and 19 October 1946, and African Service 22 October 1946. Thomas's fee 15 guineas.

15 OCTOBER 1946 recorded Edith Sitwell poems for 'The Poet and His Critic' produced by E.J. King Bull for transmission 26 October 1946 and 16 November 1946 (Third Programme); fee 10 guineas.

17 OCTOBER 1946 (Third) read a selection of Keats made by J. Middleton Murry, producer Roy Campbell; fee 10 guineas.

19–22 OCTOBER 1946 rehearsals for 'The Careerist', written and produced by Louis MacNeice, for transmission 22 and 23 October 1946 (Third). Thomas played The Chorus; fee 15 guineas.

25 OCTOBER 1946 (Third) 'Holiday Memory. Dylan Thomas recalls many experiences of a holiday by the sea in his childhood days' (script 14) produced by James Langham. Rebroadcast 13 November 1946 and 2 January 1947. Thomas's fee raised from 18 to 20 guineas.

29 OCTOBER 1946 (Light) 'Focus – On Joining Up', written by T. J. Waldron, producer R. D. Smith. Fee for taking part 7 guineas.

30 OCTOBER 1946 (Light) 'We Ran On German Petrol. An account of the cloak-and-dagger activities of Popski's Private Army,' written by Jack Hargreaves, producer Francis Dillon. Fee for taking part 7 guineas.

31 OCTOBER 1946 recorded 'Book of Verse', a programme of 'Modern Poetry' for transmission 2 November 1946 (but apparently not transmitted). Thomas received fee of 10 guineas.

14 NOVEMBER 1946 (Third) Thomas made a selection of Pope to be read by Mary O'Farrell (*Radio Times* only source for this item).

19 NOVEMBER 1946 (Third) David Jones's *In Parenthesis* produced by Douglas Cleverdon. Rehearsals 17–19 November 1946. Fee for taking part 20 guineas.

20 NOVEMBER 1946 recorded one of his poems for use in a discussion between L. A. G. Strong and Freda Newcombe on 'Narrative Verse' in the series 'Books and Verse' produced by Roy Campbell for transmission 22 November 1946 (Light). Fee 5 guineas.

28 NOVEMBER 1946 recorded a reading of Edith Sitwell's 'The Shadow of Cain' for the Third Programme 2 December 1946 'New Poems No. 3'. In fact, according to a letter (*Letters* p. 607), the recording was not used, and Thomas performed the poem live. Fee 10 guineas. Martin Armstrong in *The Listener* (12 December 1946) reported that Thomas's reading 'did full justice to the poem's fine qualities. Indeed, I have only one fault to find with it, not as a reading but as a broadcast, namely that here and there he suddenly dropped the pitch and intensity of his voice with the result that, though reception was good, I missed a word or two.'

28 NOVEMBER 1946 (Third) read Blake in a selection by James Stephens, produced by Roy Campbell. Fee 10 guineas.

30 NOVEMBER 1946 (Third) 'Living Writers – Walter de la Mare as a Prose Writer' (script 15). Fee 15 guineas for script and reading.

1 DECEMBER 1946 recorded 'Book of Verse' poems by Alun Lewis and Sidney Keyes selected by R. N. Curry for transmission 14 December 1946. Fee 10 guineas.

3 DECEMBER 1946 (Third) Louis MacNeice's 'Enemy of Cant'. Thomas played Aristophanes. Rehearsals 30 November–3 December 1946. Fee raised from 20 to 25 guineas.

5 DECEMBER 1946 recorded 'Book of Verse' – a selection of Thomas's own poems made by W. T. Delaney, for transmission 21 December 1946 (Eastern). Fee for reading 10 guineas.

6 DECEMBER 1946 re-recorded 'Holiday Memories' for BBC Archives; fee 5 guineas.

13 DECEMBER 1946 (Third) Louis MacNeice's 'The Heartless Giant' – Thomas played the part of a raven; fee 20 guineas. Rehearsals 11–13 December 1946.

22 DECEMBER 1946 (Home) 'Time for Verse No. 62', produced by Patric Dickinson. Thomas read selections from Lewis Carroll; fee 10 guineas.

27 DECEMBER 1946 (Home) 'Tonight's Talk' after the news was 'The Crumbs of One Man's Year' (script 16); fee for script and reading 20 guineas.

29 DECEMBER 1946 recording of 'Oxford-Princeton', produced by R. D. Smith for exchange with station WOR, New York. Fee 40 guineas for script, 12 guineas for participation. (Script not extant.)

1947

2 JANUARY 1947 recorded 'Book of Verse' – selections from *Richard III* made by B. Ivor Evans, for transmission 18 January 1947; fee 10 guineas.

8 JANUARY 1947 (Home) 'The Wednesday Story', produced by Roy Campbell, announced in the *Radio Times* as 'The Peaches', was changed at the last minute to 'A Visit to Grandpa's'. A BBC memo of 14 January 1947 noted: 'It seems to be in Thomas's more operatic manner. The Recording Engineer reports sourly that "there's no point in it," but our more subtle listeners may think better of it.'

9 JANUARY 1947 recorded 'Book of Verse' selections from *Titus Andronicus*

made by M. William Disher for transmission 8 February 1947; fee 10 guineas.

14–16 JANUARY 1947 Thomas went with Michael Ayrton to Gravesend researching a script on Hogarth for the General Overseas Service, but later backed out of the project (*Letters* p. 619).

24 JANUARY 1947 (West of England) 'Literature in the West – Sir Philip Sidney' (script 17), produced by Desmond Hawkins in Bristol. Fee for script and reading 12 guineas.

14 FEBRUARY 1947 Thomas was to have recorded his contributions to 'The Poet and His Critic', but it was postponed because of crippling weather and Thomas's illness. Note also a letter from Thomas's agent Jean LeRoy to the BBC 17 February 1947: 'Dylan Thomas has been smitten with 'flu and food poisoning and asks us to cancel his contract for 'The Hare' programme which was to have been recorded in Belfast, and for the readings from Llewellyn's *How Green Was My Valley*.' The latter was to have been ten installments for the 'Woman's Hour' with a fee of 5 guineas each; the former engagement was a Louis MacNeice production for which the fee would have been 20 guineas.

6 MARCH 1947 recorded his own poems and talk for 'The Poet and His Critic' (script 18), transmitted 8 March 1947 (Third). Fee for script and reading 20 guineas.

20 MARCH 1947 Vernon Watkins' 'The Ballad of the Mari Lwyd', produced by Patric Dickinson. Thomas's fee as one of the readers 10 guineas. Martin Armstrong in *The Listener* (18 September 1947) said of this programme: 'The variety of tone and intensity, from the *pianissimo* of Diana Morgan to the stentorian climaxes of Dylan Thomas, was graded and apportioned with a masterly judgment.'

23 MARCH 1947 recorded 'Book of Verse' selections from *Henry IV* made by R. N. Curry for transmission 26 April 1947; fee 10 guineas.

1–2 APRIL 1947 rehearsal and recording of 'Return Journey' (script 19), produced by P. H. Burton in Cardiff for transmission 15 June 1947 (Home). Fee for script and participation 50 guineas.

25 APRIL 1947 BBC trying to reach Thomas in Italy in regard to Schools Programme project (*Letters* p. 613). Further cable of 8 May 1947 received no response, and the project was dropped.

25 AUGUST 1947 recorded 'Poetry Magazine No. 1', produced by John Arlott for transmission 30 September 1947 (Eastern); fee 10 guineas.

26 AUGUST 1947 recorded 'Poetry Magazine No. 3', produced by John Arlott for transmission 14 October (Eastern); fee 10 guineas.

29 SEPTEMBER 1947 a new production of 'Comus' produced for the Third Programme by Douglas Cleverdon. Thomas played the Elder Brother; fee 12 guineas.

9 OCTOBER 1947 (Home) 'The Memoirs of the Dog Berganza', extracted from Cervantes' 'The Dog's Colloquy', produced by Roy Campbell as one of the broadcasts for Cervantes anniversary week. Thomas and John Chandos played the two dogs; fee 12 guineas. Martin Armstrong criticised the production in *The Listener* (16 October 1947):

Dylan Thomas by his violent variations of tone and tempo produced and transmitted to the listener a sense of strain which became physically exhausting. Not only that: tone and tempo were not used to reinforce the sense of the spoken word, but independently of it, producing the same sort of effect as if film and sound-track were not syncronised. At his best Dylan Thomas is a fine performer, but here there seemed to be a lack of control and a need for much more rehearsal.

19 OCTOBER 1947 (Third) 'Paradise Lost' Book I, produced by Douglas Cleverdon. Thomas apparently replaced Paul Schofield in the part of Satan at the last minute; fee 15 guineas.

26 OCTOBER 1947 (Third) 'Paradise Lost' Book II; fee 15 guineas.
Opinions were divided on the success of the 'Paradise Lost' broadcast, witness Martin Armstrong's discussion in *The Listener* (30 October 1947):

The Spoken Word: Matter and Manner

I have seldom approached a broadcast with less misgiving than when I switched on 'Paradise Lost'. The B.B.C. has at its beck and call so many excellent readers of poetry that I felt fairly certain that Milton's highly formal verse would receive due respect. My only doubt was whether partition of the verse among various voices (which I guessed would be the method employed) would break up too severely the essential unity of the poem. But, so far at least, this production seems to me a disastrous failure and I have no doubt of the reason. In Milton's poetry there is remarkably little stimulus for the mind's eye. He doesn't compel us to visualise. But he is a past master of the aural: he compels us to feel by hearing. His skilful use of consonants, vowels and rhythm evokes the appropriate impressions and emotions and he can produce, purely by verbal magic, any intensity of sound from pianissimo to fortissimo. Take such a line as 'Thrones and imperial Powers, offspring of Heav'n': it booms and resounds however softly you read it and if you impose your own boom on Milton's the noise becomes unbearable. For this reason Milton must be read soberly and quietly and with a meticulous attention to rhythm and the values of consonant and vowel. Abraham Sofaer as the narrator carefully observes the structure of the verse. His reading is rhythmical and balanced; but Milton's employment of emotive tone – his exploitation of the vowels and the consonants – eludes him, and so his reading, though it gives us the design of the sound-picture, denies us the colour. But the real trouble began (as it generally does) with Satan. He was resolved to outboom Milton, and he did. In the most literal sense of the expression, there was the Hell of a row. It swamped Milton, it swamped 'Paradise Lost', it occasionally swamped even the sense, for the louder Dylan Thomas shouts the more his articulation deteriorates, until one fails to hear the words for the noise. At present, then, I look forward to the remaining broadcasts of 'Paradise Lost' with misgiving, if not with terror, but perhaps we shall breathe a more peaceful air in the Garden of Eden.

2 NOVEMBER 1947 (Third) 'Paradise Lost' Book III; fee 15 guineas.

9 NOVEMBER 1947 (Third) 'Paradise Lost' Book IV; fee 15 guineas.

16 NOVEMBER 1947 (Third) 'Paradise Lost' Book V; fee 15 guineas.

20 NOVEMBER 1947 recorded 'Book of Verse – Modern Poetry Magazine', produced by John Arlott, for transmission 25 November 1947 (Eastern); fee 10 guineas.

23 NOVEMBER 1947 (Third) 'Paradise Lost' Book VI; fee 15 guineas.

25 NOVEMBER 1947 recorded 'Book of Verse – Modern Poetry Magazine' script by C. Day Lewis, for transmission 2 December 1947; fee 10 guineas.

27 NOVEMBER 1947 recorded 'Book of Verse – Modern Poetry Magazine' script by G. W. Stonier, for transmission 16 December 1947; fee 10 guineas.

7 DECEMBER 1947 (Third) 'Paradise Lost' Book IX; fee 15 guineas.

14 DECEMBER 1947 (Third) 'Paradise Lost' Book X; fee 15 guineas.

17 DECEMBER 1947 recorded 'Book of Verse – Modern Poetry Magazine' for transmission 23 December 1947; fee 10 guineas.

18 DECEMBER 1947 recorded the first three installments of W. H. Davies 'The Autobiography of a Super-Tramp', produced by Roy Campbell for transmission in the Home Service weekly from 28 December 1947 to 4 April 1948. Thomas's fee for each installment, 8 guineas. In *The Listener* (15 January 1948) Martin Armstrong recommended these episodes: 'good stuff and good reading!'

1948

5 JANUARY 1948 recorded second batch of three installments of 'Autobiography of a Super-Tramp'.

8 JANUARY 1948 recorded third batch of 'Autobiography of a Super-Tramp'.

29 JANUARY 1948 recorded 'Book of Verse', an anthology edited by producer John Arlott for transmission 16 February 1948; fee 10 guineas. Poems of Blake, Herrick, Wordsworth, Milton, and Coventry Patmore. Arlott wrote in *Adelphi* (February 1954):

The weight he gave to each word, idea and line in his reading demanded strength of thought and structure in a poem and once, exclaiming against the arrogance of a piece by Coventry Patmore, he said, 'Please don't ask me to read it: I hate it too much.'

8 FEBRUARY 1948 (Home) 'Country Magazine: The Windrush Valley. Introduced by Dylan Thomas. From The Fleece, Witney,' edited and produced by David Thomson. Thomas received a fee of 18 guineas, and 15/– taxi fare from his nearby home, the Manor House, Witney.

10 FEBRUARY 1948 recorded discussion with Arthur Calder-Marshall 'about the dearth of comic books' (script 20 'A Dearth of Comic Writers') for transmission 14 February 1948 (Light) 'Books and Authors' series, produced by James Langham. Fee 7 guineas.

12 FEBRUARY 1948 recorded 'Book of Verse', anthology by John Arlott for transmission 15 March 1948; fee 10 guineas. Poems read: Lewis Carroll and Edward Lear. Arlott wrote in *Adelphi* (February 1954):

He was receptive to every reaction poetry or verse could prompt. As the elder oyster and the young oysters in *The Walrus and the Carpenter*, or the dissident crew and, subsequently, the dramatic 'boo' – and final, lingering 'jum' in *The Hunting of the Snark*, he was gloriously and authentically funny.

18 FEBRUARY 1948 recorded episodes 9 and 10 of 'Autobiography of a Super-Tramp'.

19 FEBRUARY 1948 recorded 'Book of Verse' anthology by John Arlott for transmission 1 March 1948; fee 10 guineas. Poems read included Donne, Herbert, Vaughan, Crashaw.

27 FEBRUARY 1948 recorded episodes 11 and 12 of 'Autobiography of a Super-Tramp'.

18 MARCH 1948 recorded episodes 13 and 14 of 'Autobiography of a Super-Tramp'.

4 APRIL 1948 (Home) W. H. Davies's 'The Autobiography of a Super-Tramp', produced by Roy Campbell; the last episode read live by Thomas; fee 8 guineas.

9 MAY 1948 (Home) 'Time for Verse. This week's programme is compiled by Vernon Watkins on the subject of old age. It includes poems by William Shakespeare, A. E. Housman, W. B. Yeats, Jonathan Swift, John Donne, Thomas Hardy, Dylan Thomas. Readers: V. C. Clinton-Badderley and Dylan Thomas.' Produced by Patric Dickinson. Thomas's fee 10 guineas. He wrote to Watkins 17 April 1948: *'Of course*, please use my Man Aged A Hundred in your Old Age programme, and I'm glad and proud you want it, and that I shall definitely be one of the readers in the programme. I'll love that' (*Letters* p. 669).

27 MAY 1948 recorded 'Book of Verse', an anthology by John Arlott for transmission 13 July 1948; fee 10 guineas.

13 JUNE 1948 (Home) 'Country Magazine: Isle of Thanet. Introduced by Dylan Thomas. Edited and produced by David Thomson. From The Bell Inn, St. Nicholas at Wade.' Rehearsals 10–13 June 1948; fee 18 guineas.

19 JULY 1948 (Third) 'Two Wicked Sisters', written and produced by Louis MacNeice. Thomas played First Astronomer; fee 18 guineas.

24 JULY 1948 (Third) reading of Thomas Gray's 'The Bard', produced by James MacFarlan; fee 15 guineas.

30 JULY 1948 (Third) 'The English Festival of Spoken Poetry' (script 21), produced by James Langham; fee 12 guineas.

30 JULY 1948 recorded 'at last minute' a small contribution to 'Looking at Britain No. 18: Radnorshire', produced by R. D. Smith for transmission 10 August 1948 (Overseas); fee 6 guineas. 'Best payment I've received,'

Thomas wrote to his agent Jean LeRoy on 6 August 1948, '2 short lines of verse spoken without rehearsal! More jobs like that' (*Letters* p. 682).

1–2 SEPTEMBER 1948 recorded 'Book of Verse'; fee 10 guineas for each day; transmission date not known.

17 SEPTEMBER 1948 (Light) 'Focus – On Boxing', written by Walter Rault, producer R. D. Smith; fee 12 guineas for taking part.

22 SEPTEMBER 1948 (Third) 'The Life of Sub-human', written by Laurence Kitchin, producer Louis MacNeice; fee 15 guineas for taking part.

28 SEPTEMBER 1948 (Third) 'Dr Edith Sitwell talks about her later work. Poems read by Dylan Thomas', produced by E. J. King Bull; fee 12 guineas.

29 SEPTEMBER 1948 recorded 'Book of Verse'; no further information.

6 OCTOBER 1948 recorded 'Book of Verse'; no further information.

11 NOVEMBER 1948 (Third) 'In Parenthesis', produced by Douglas Cleverdon. A live repeat. Thomas played Private Dai Evans. Rehearsals 8–11 November 1948; fee 25 guineas.

12 NOVEMBER 1948 recorded 'Extraordinary Little Cough' for transmission 15 November 1948 (Third); fee increased from 8 to 12 guineas.

1–2 DECEMBER 1948 rehearsal and recording of 'Trimalchio's Feast' written and produced by Louis MacNeice for transmission 22 December 1948 (Third). Thomas played Agamemnon, a Professor of Rhetoric; fee 20 guineas.

1949

14 JANUARY 1949 (Third) 'The Background of Modern Poetry' – Thomas read some of his poems; fee 10 guineas.

18 MARCH 1949 accepted BBC offer to adapt *Peer Gynt* for radio, a project never finished.

28 MAY 1949 unable to complete adaptation of Wycherley's *Plain Dealer* (*Letters* p. 708).

16 JUNE 1949 recorded 'Living in Wales' (script 22), produced by Roy Campbell in London for transmission from BBC Scotland in 'Scottish Life and Letters' series 23 June 1949; fee 15 guineas.

29 JULY 1949 (Welsh) 'Arts Magazine' – Thomas contributed a piece on Edward Thomas (script 23), producer Elwyn Evans; fee 15 guineas for script and reading.

24 SEPTEMBER 1949 (Third) read poems (script 24 'On Reading One's Own Poems'), producer Hugh Stewart; fee 20 guineas.

6 OCTOBER 1949 recorded discussion at BBC Swansea with Vernon Watkins, John Prichard, Alfred Janes, and Daniel Jones, producer John Griffiths, for transmission 24 October 1949 (Welsh) as 'Swansea and the Arts' (script 25); fee 12 guineas.

14 DECEMBER 1949 recorded 'The Dark Tower – A Parable Play', written and produced by Louis MacNeice. Thomas played a Raven; fee 20 guineas. Transmitted 30 January 1950 (Home Service).

21 DECEMBER 1949 telegram to Elwin Evans BBC Cardiff – Thomas unable to be interviewed by Glyn Jones for the series 'How I Write' because of broken ribs; contract cancelled.

1950

23 JULY 1950 (Home) 'New Judgment on Edgar Allan Poe', script by John Harries; Thomas's fee 10 guineas for reading.

15 AUGUST 1950 (Third) read John Donne selection made by R.D. Smith, the producer; fee 10 guineas.

25 SEPTEMBER 1950 read 'Over Sir John's Hill', 'In Country Sleep', and 'In the White Giant's Thigh', with commentary (script 26 'Three Poems'), producer Douglas Cleverdon; fee 20 guineas.

22 NOVEMBER 1950 recorded 'Book of Verse' for John Arlott, for transmission 24 November 1950 (Eastern); fee 10 guineas.

22 NOVEMBER 1950 (Third) 'Poems for Liberty', selected by R.D. Smith; Thomas's fee 8 guineas for reading.

1 DECEMBER 1950 recorded 'Book of Verse' for John Arlott, for transmission 26 December 1950 (Eastern); fee 10 guineas.

11 DECEMBER 1950 recorded discussion with Roy Campbell, George Barker, and W.R. Rodgers in the series 'Poetic Licence' (script 27), produced by Patrick Harvey for transmission 13 December 1950 (Home); fee 20 guineas.

1951

7 JANUARY 1951 recorded D. H. Lawrence 'Birds, Beasts and Flowers', selected by R. D. Smith; fee 8 guineas for reading.

14 FEBRUARY 1951 (Home) 'new broadcast of "Return to Swansea"' – Thomas received 50 guineas fee, which 'includes Thomas's appearance at the microphone' (BBC memo).

MARCH 1951 contemplating collaboration with Ted Kavanaugh on comedy series 'Quid's Inn', which does not materialize (*Letters* pp. 789–90).

17 APRIL 1951 (Home) 'Report to the People No. 4 – Persian Oil', script by Aidan Philip and R. D. Smith. Thomas read a small contribution (script 28 'Persian Oil'); fee 10 guineas.

5 JUNE 1951 recorded 'Festival Exhibition' (script 29) in Cardiff for Aneirin Talfan Davies; transmission in the 'Guest Speaker' series 19 June 1951 (Welsh), repeated 14 August (Home Service); fee 20 guineas.

1 NOVEMBER 1951 recorded for transmission 10 November 1951 (Light) 'Say the Word visits Cambridge. Half an hour of fun, and a game with words – how to use them, how not to use them ... the word expert, Dylan Thomas. Quizmaster, Fielden Hughes.' Fee 20 guineas.

17 NOVEMBER 1951 recorded a segment of 'Wits About You' for transmission 16 December 1951 (Home).

18 NOVEMBER 1951 (Home) 'Portrait of Athens', written and produced by Louis MacNeice. Thomas played Male Chorus; fee 20 guineas.

21 NOVEMBER 1951 (Third) 'Retreat from Moscow', by Honor Tracy, producer Douglas Cleverdon; fee 25 guineas.

31 DECEMBER 1951 (Third) 'The Golden Ass', written and produced by Louis MacNeice. Thomas played Philebus, a priest; fee 25 guineas.

1952

16–18 JULY 1952 recorded his own selection from the poetry of Theodore Roethke and Robert Lowell, producer Peter Duval Smith. Some of these were unsatisfactory, and were re-recorded 1 August 1952. Transmission was on Third Programme 8 October 1952 Roethke's 'The Lost Son', 'The Long Alley', and 'The Shape of the Fire'; on 14 October 1952 Lowell's 'The Quaker Graveyard in Nantucket', 'The Ghost', and 'Falling Asleep over the Aeneid'.

19 AUGUST 1952 submits to Douglas Cleverdon a script on *Spoon River Anthology* (script 30 'Edgar Lee Masters'); fee 20 guineas for script.

16 OCTOBER 1952 recorded 'Prologue' for 'New Soundings', but had bad cold. Re-recorded it 24 October 1952 for transmission 26 October 1952 (Third) 'New Soundings No. 8. A monthly miscellany of new poetry and prose edited and introduced by John Lehmann,' producer Gilbert Phelps. Thomas's fee 8 guineas.

24 NOVEMBER 1952 recorded 'A Visit to Grandpa's' for transmission 3 November 1952 (Home Service Schools Programme); fee 8 guineas.

1953

14 JANUARY 1953 (Welsh) 'Three Ballads by Vernon Watkins, introduced by the author and read by Dylan Thomas,' produced by Aneirin Talfan Davies from Swansea; fee 15 guineas.

2–3 FEBRUARY 1953 preliminary discussion in Swansea of the proposed 'Anthologies'. There was 'a vain attempt to read owing to Dylan's voice breaking down' (Aneirin Talfan Davies personal communication).

9–10 FEBRUARY 1953 recorded the four 'Anthologies' for transmission in Welsh Home Service for four weeks beginning 1 March 1953; fee 25 guineas for each programme. Aneirin Talfan Davies wrote in 'The Golden Echo' *Dock Leaves* (Spring 1954):

For the first anthology, to be broadcast on St. David's Day, I had asked him to confine his choice to poems by Welsh authors, but for the remaining three he was given complete freedom. These three anthologies, therefore, gain in significance, and his choice throws a revealing light on his personality.

Dylan Thomas spent days and days in my office during the compiling of these anthologies. I had carted down all the books of poems and anthologies from my home to the office, and Dylan supplemented them with a bundle of new anthologies which he had brought back with him from America; these again were added to, in emergency, by telephone calls to the Swansea bank where Vernon Watkins worked by day; there was something intriguing in being able to phone a bank for a book other than a pass-book!

The process of anthologising was a long but not, for me at least, a tiring business. I would now and then throw out a suggestion, but he would make it quite clear, in his delightfully quiet, humble way that he would read no poems that he did not believe in – that is, of course, as

299

poems. Once, however, I suggested that he should read D. H. Lawrence's *Ship of Death*, a poem which had captured my imagination when I had read it many years ago, and which I still occasionally take down from my shelf to read. Dylan immediately said, "Yes, I'll read that. That *must* go in." And in it went. I have never heard a poem so lovingly read; that warm, rich, dark, soothing voice wrapping itself around each word and phrase, bringing them to life and making them stand and dance a moving pattern of sense and sound, which brought one as near as possible to the ecstacy of the creative act.

> Oh build your ship of death, oh build it in time
> and build it lovingly, and put it between the hands of
> your soul.

And this was one of the most wonderful things about Dylan Thomas's reading of poetry, it conformed so closely, it seemed to me, with the rhythm of creation. His sensitivity seemed to be such that it was possible for him to ally himself, as it were, with the poet in the very act of creating the poem. So that a reading of his became something more than an 'interpretation' – it became a revelation, a revealing. And if this was true of his reading of other poets' poems it was doubly true of his reading of his own.

Taking a hint from his own self-depreciating assessment of himself as a man with the gift of the gab, many have fallen to the heresy of equating his reading with ecstatic ranting *a la* the *hwyl* of the Welsh preacher. Close attention to the readings, which are now recorded for posterity, will reveal the exact opposite. His technical skill in reading the most amazing variety of poetry was astounding. I remember during the compiling of these anthologies that we were standing in the studio one day, ready to record the first selection of poems. I had a copy of Gerard Manley Hopkins's poems in my hand, and suddenly I turned to Dylan and asked him whether he would like to read *The Leaden Echo and The Golden Echo*. I had not intended that he should read it then, but merely that we should make a mental note of it for future reference. He took hold of my book, drew his finger rapidly down the page and in a second said: 'Yes, I'll do it now.' He proceeded to record this lovely but extremely intricate poem, and did it without a fluff or blemish. This leads one to believe that he must have spent a great deal of time in the company of Hopkins, which of course is evident from a careful study of his own work.

It is true that he possessed a voice of amazing richness and power, and it is true also that he loved to use it in all its glorious resonance; but he never used it for empty mouthing. But when it was used with all the stops out, O how it thundered like a cathedral organ filling all the holes and corners of the universe of man. I shall never forget, for instance, his reading of Edith Sitwell's *Still Falls the Rain*, and that sudden leap of the voice, an ecstatic shout, as he came to Marlowe's lines which are used in the poem:

> Then – O Ile leape up to my God: who pulles me doune –
> See, see where Christ's blood streames in the firmament!

One of his finest recordings is the one of his own poem, *Ceremony After a Fire Raid*. Who among those who listened to that reading will ever forget that magnificent last section of the poem, with the voice rolling on to the tremendous liturgical climax?

> Over the sun's hovel and the slum of fire
> And the golden pavements laid in requiems,
> Into the bread in a wheatfield of flames.
> Into the wine burning like brandy,
> The masses of the sea
> The masses of the sea under
> The masses of the infant-bearing sea
> Erupt, fountain, and enter to utter for ever
> Glory glory glory
> The sundering ultimate kingdom of genesis' thunder.

In listening to Dylan Thomas's reading of his own poems it becomes clear that his voice must have had a great influence on his work as a poet. Any future assessment of his verse, and indeed his prose, will have to take into account his voice, and also the fact that there was ready at hand the perfect instrument for its employment, radio.

He himself offered the opinion that reading aloud does bring you closer to the poet, and his work on the radio certainly contributed something towards that greater simplification and clarity which is found in his later poems. We must not make too much of the point, but it is worth remembering.

ANTHOLOGY NO. 1. Broadcast on 1 March 1953.
The Collier, Vernon Watkins.
Gwalia Deserta, Idris Davies.
Child Lovers, W. H. Davies.
Sacco writes to his son, Alun Lewis.
The child on the cliffs, Edward Thomas.
Strange meeting, Wilfred Owen.
Ceremony after a fire raid, Dylan Thomas.

ANTHOLOGY No. 2. Broadcast on 8 March 1953.
Lapis Lazuli, W. B. Yeats.
For Ann Gregory, W. B. Yeats.
John Kinsella's Lament for Mrs. Mary Moore, W. B. Yeats.
End of another home holiday, D. H. Lawrence.
To Lizbie Brown, Thomas Hardy.
O Boys! O Boys!, Oliver St. John Gogarty.
As I walked out one evening.

ANTHOLOGY No. 3. Broadcast on 1 March 1953.
Journey of the Magi, T. S. Eliot.
A dialogue of Self and Soul, W. B. Yeats.
Lent, W. R. Rodgers.
There was a Saviour, Dylan Thomas.
Stills Falls the Rain, Edith Sitwell.
The Golden Echo, Gerard Manley Hopkins.
Carol, John Short.

ANTHOLOGY No. 4. Broadcast 22 March 1953.
September 1st, 1939, W. H. Auden.
Oedipus at Colonus, W. B. Yeats.
Ship of Death, D. H. Lawrence.
To my Son, John Betjeman.
Sonnet to my Mother, George Barker.
Prayer Before Birth, Louis MacNeice.

Recordings made at the same time but not broadcast.

In Memory of Ann Jones, Dylan Thomas.
After a Journey, Thomas Hardy.
The Burning of the Leaves, Laurence Binyon.
In Death Divided, Thomas Hardy.
Passing the Graveyard, Andrew Young.
Sob Heavy World, W. H. Auden.
A Welsh Incident, Robert Graves.

13 MARCH 1953 re-recorded 'Reminiscences of Childhood' for Aneirin Talfan Davies in Swansea, for transmission 6 May 1953 (Welsh Home Service).

2 APRIL 1953 re-recorded 'Quite Early One Morning' and 'Holiday Memory' for Aneirin Talfan Davies in Swansea; fee 20 guineas for each. The talks were transmitted in the Welsh Home Service on 17 June 1953 and 26 December 1954 respectively.

9 APRIL 1953 TV 8.15–8.45 'Home Town – Swansea', produced by David J. Thomas (script 31). Thomas took part with Alfred Janes, Daniel Jones, and Vernon Watkins.

13 APRIL 1953 recorded 65 lines of Wordsworth's 'Prelude' for 'The Worthiness of Wales', produced by Aneirin Talfan Davies, for transmission 3 June 1953 (Welsh); fee 8 guineas.

13 APRIL 1953 recorded poems for 'Barbarous Hexameters', written and narrated by Daniel Jones, produced by Aneirin Talfan Davies. 'A study in the growth of the hexameter in English poetry, with special attention to the peculiar contribution of Richard Stanyhurst, author of the first lengthy poem in English hexameters, published in 1582.' Transmission in the Welsh Home Service 20 October 1953; fee 8 guineas. Daniel Jones wrote of this broadcast in *My Friend Dylan Thomas* (pp. 78–9):

> I put forward to Dylan my theory that while hexameters may work after a fashion in some foreign languages, for example in Goethe's *Hermann und Dorothea*, they seem always to drive poets writing in English mad, in the direction either of the absurdly prosaic or of the crazily fantastic. To prove my point, I showed him Longfellow's *Evangeline* and *Miles Standish*, Kingsley's *Andromeda* and Clough's *The Bothie of Tober-na-Vuolich*. Dylan urged me to write a half-hour script on the subject and persuaded Aneirin to fall in with the idea. I called the script 'Barbarous Hexameters' (a quotation from Tennyson), and arranged it so that I had to read all the link passages, which by the way, included an account of the sinister life of Stanyhurst himself, while Dylan was given the quotations. My part, of course, was easy: I had merely to keep a straight face and read in a matter-of-fact voice. Dylan's part in reading the quotations, on the other hand, demanded the greatest virtuosity. He was in excellent form, and we recorded straight away without a re-take. Two examples will show the kind of thing Dylan had to face in this performance:
>
> JONES: When Stanyhurst wants to achieve an onomatopoeic effect, his favourite trick is to hyphenate two words.
> THOMAS: Flush-flash clush-clash ruffe-raffe muff-maff crack-rack tag-rag, wig-wag rip-rap kym-kam rif-raf swish-swash thwick-thwack robble-hobble.
>
> Stanyhurst's storm scene:
>
> THOMAS: These flaws theyre cabbans with stur snar jarrye doe ransack,
> Like bandog grinning, with gnash tusk greedelye snarring,

Like wrastling meete winds with blaste contrarius huzing,
Where curs barck bawling, with yolp yalpe snarrye rebounding,
A sea-belch grounting on rough rocks rapfully frapping.

Dylan read all this magnificently, and, as I said, all went well. The chief danger, of course, was that we would spoil the recording by laughing out aloud; the script had to be 'put over' in a strictly straight-faced manner, of course. The danger was at its greatest when Dylan pronounced the words 'Miles Standish' in the following quotation; at that point he suddenly turned to me and, standing stiffly to attention, saluted smartly, just as if I were Priscilla the Puritan maid herself:

So I have come to you now, with an offer and proffer of marriage
Made by a good man and true, Miles Standish the Captain of Plymouth!

I still, of course, have the script of 'Barbarous Hexameters', and the recording was duly broadcast, but when I asked about the tape itself I was told that it was lost. This seems a pity for two reasons: it was the only broadcast made by Dylan and myself for which I wrote the script, and, in any case, I think it was funny.

15 APRIL 1953 recorded speeches for insertion in Douglas Cleverdon's production of David Jones's 'The Anathemata' for transmission 5 May 1953 (Third); fee 15 guineas.

13 JULY 1953 (Welsh) 'International Eisteddfod' (script 32), produced by Aneirin Talfan Davies; fee 20 guineas.

10 AUGUST 1953 TV 'Speaking Personally' – Dylan Thomas telling 'one of his unusual stories', from the Dean's Library, St. Asaph. In *The Listener* 20 August 1953, Reginald Pound said; 'Dylan Thomas' "Speaking Personally" fell only just short of being a television *tour de force.*' The script was published in *The Listener* (17 September 1953) with the title 'A Story' (known also as 'The Outing'). It was rebroadcast on radio 22 December 1953 (General Overseas Service).

28 SEPTEMBER 1953 recorded 'A Visit to America' for Aneirin Talfan Davies (script 33); fee 20 guineas.

5 OCTOBER 1953 re-recorded 'A Visit to America', broadcast posthumously 30 March 1954 (Welsh Home Service).

5 OCTOBER 1953 recorded 'Laugharne' (script 34) for Aneirin Talfan Davies; fee 5 guineas. Broadcast in part 5 November 1953 (Welsh).

OCTOBER 1953 script of *Under Milk Wood* delivered to BBC; broadcast posthumously 25 January 1954, producer Douglas Cleverdon.

Works Cited

John Arlott 'Dylan Thomas and Radio' *Adelphi* (First Quarter 1954) pp. 121–4.

Martin Armstrong 'The Spoken Word' – regular column in *The Listener*.

Richard Burton 'Genius Agonistes' *Book Week* (*The Washington Post* etc) 24 October 1965 pp. 1, 43.

Roy Campbell 'Memories of Dylan Thomas at the B.B.C.' *Poetry* (November 1955) pp. 111–14.

Douglas Cleverdon *The Growth of Milk Wood* (London: J. M. Dent 1969).

Aneirin Talfan Davies ed. *Quite Early One Morning* (London: J. M. Dent 1954).

'The Golden Echo' *Dock Leaves* (Spring 1954) pp. 10–17.

Letter to *Times Literary Supplement* (17 December 1954) p. 821.

Paul Ferris ed. *The Collected Letters of Dylan Thomas* (London: J. M. Dent 1985).

Dylan Thomas (Harmondsworth: Penguin Books 1978).

Constantine FitzGibbon *The Life of Dylan Thomas* (London: J. M. Dent; Boston: Little, Brown 1965).

Daniel Jones *My Friend Dylan Thomas* (London: J. M. Dent 1977).

L. C. Lloyd 'On the Air' *The Spectator* (20 June 1947) p. 717.

Louis MacNeice 'I Remember Dylan Thomas' *Ingot* (December 1954) pp. 28–30.

George Orwell 'Poetry and the Microphone' *The New Saxon Pamphlets* No. 3 (1944); also in *Collected Essays*.

Reginald Pound 'Television' *The Listener* (16 April 1953) p. 654.

Alan Rees 'The Dylan Thomas File' BBC script, 26 August 1973.

Edward Sackville-West 'Radio Notes' *New Statesman and Nation* (2 November 1946).

Wynford Vaughan Thomas 'Dylan Thomas' BBC script, 5 December 1953.

Bert Trick 'The Young Dylan Thomas' *Texas Quarterly* (Summer 1966) pp. 36–49.

Vernon Watkins note to 'A Painter's Studio' *Texas Quarterly* (Winter 1961) p. 54.

Anonymous review of *Quite Early One Morning*, *Times Literary Supplement* (19 November 1954) p. 731.